Tacit Racism

Compliments of
the College of Arts and Sciences
SIUE
July 2021

Tacit Racism

ANNE WARFIELD RAWLS
& WAVERLY DUCK

THE UNIVERSITY OF CHICAGO PRESS   CHICAGO AND LONDON

The University of Chicago Press, Chicago 60637
The University of Chicago Press, Ltd., London
© 2020 by The University of Chicago
All rights reserved. No part of this book may be used or reproduced in any manner whatsoever without written permission, except in the case of brief quotations in critical articles and reviews. For more information, contact the University of Chicago Press, 1427 E. 60th St., Chicago, IL 60637.
Published 2020
Printed in the United States of America

29 28 27 26 25 24 23 22 21 20   1 2 3 4 5

ISBN-13: 978-0-226-70355-8 (cloth)
ISBN-13: 978-0-226-70369-5 (paper)
ISBN-13: 978-0-226-70372-5 (e-book)
DOI: https://doi.org/10.7208/chicago/9780226703725.001.0001

Library of Congress Cataloging-in-Publication Data

Names: Rawls, Anne Warfield, 1950– author. | Duck, Waverly, author.
Title: Tacit racism / Anne Warfield Rawls and Waverly Duck.
Description: Chicago ; London : The University of Chicago Press, 2020. |
    Includes bibliographical references and index.
Identifiers: LCCN 2019057904 | ISBN 9780226703558 (cloth) |
    ISBN 9780226703695 (paperback) | ISBN 9780226703725 (ebook)
Subjects: LCSH: Racism—United States. | Social interaction—United States. |
    United States—Race relations.
Classification: LCC E184.A1 R36 2020 | DDC 305.800973—dc23
LC record available at https://lccn.loc.gov/2019057904

♾ This paper meets the requirements of ANSI/NISO Z39.48-1992 (Permanence of Paper).

I want justice, oceans of it. I want fairness, rivers of it. That's all I want. That's all I want.
—Elijah Cummings[1]

I have been gravely disappointed with the white moderate. I have almost reached the regrettable conclusion that the Negro's great stumbling block in his stride toward freedom is not the . . . Ku Klux Klanner, but the white moderate, who is more devoted to "order" than to justice. . . . Shallow understanding from people of good will is more frustrating than absolute misunderstanding from people of ill will.
—Martin Luther King Jr.

Contents

INTRODUCTION Racism Is a Clear and Present Danger 1

CHAPTER 1. "White People Are Nosey" and "Black People Are Rude": Black and White Greetings and Introductory Talk 33

CHAPTER 2. "Fractured Reflections" of High-Status Black Men's Presentations of Self: Non-Recognition of Identity as a Tacit Form of Institutional Racism 57

CHAPTER 3. Clashing Conceptions of Honesty: Black American "Honesty" in the White Workplace 81

CHAPTER 4. "A Man Is One Who Is Responsible for Others": Achieving Black Masculinity in the Face of Institutionalized Stigma and Racism 105

CHAPTER 5. The White Self-Interested "Strong Man" Ideal vs. the Black Practice of "Submissive Civility": In a Black/White Police Encounter 129
with Jason Turowetz

CHAPTER 6. "Do You Eat Cats and Dogs?": Student Observations of Racism in Their Everyday Lives 162

CHAPTER 7. The Interaction Order of a Poor Black American Space: Creating Respect, Recognition, and Value in Response to Collective Punishment 200

CONCLUSION Digging out the Lies by Making the Ordinary Strange 226

Acknowledgments 249

Notes 255

Bibliography 267

Index 281

INTRODUCTION

Racism Is a Clear and Present Danger

If you can convince the lowest white man he's better than the best colored man, he won't notice you're picking his pocket. Hell, give him somebody to look down on, and he'll empty his pockets for you. —Lyndon B. Johnson

Since the 1670s, fifty years after the first Africans were sold into slavery at Jamestown in 1619, racism has steadily and relentlessly wormed its way so deeply into the foundations of the American democratic experiment that we typically don't even notice it. Racism does not usually take an obvious form that we can see and prevent; rather it masquerades as the most ordinary of daily actions: as unnoticed and ever-present as the air we breathe. In this book we illustrate the many ways in which racism is coded into the everyday social expectations of Americans, in taken-for-granted Interaction Orders of Race (Rawls 1983, 1987, 2000) that create vast amounts of hidden unconscious—Tacit Racism—which most Americans are not aware of. Because it is institutionalized in our everyday interactional expectations, acting on this racism does not require conscious intent: actions are racist if Race is coded into them. This racism divides the United States, providing fertile ground for the manipulation of issues associated with Race (e.g., health care, guns, voting rights, and immigration) by wealthy special interests and foreign powers (López 2019; Metzl 2019; Saez and Zucman 2019), with Russia in particular exploiting Race to interfere with our elections (Wylie 2019; Maddow 2019), such that Race divisions pose a *clear and present danger* to the nation and its democratic institutions.[1]

In over twenty-five years of research, the authors have found that without being aware of it, *everyone* in the United States acts in racist ways just by doing ordinary things. In his book *The White Racial Frame* (2009), Joe Feagin shows that a 350-year-old racial gestalt shapes the way Americans view Race such that, as studies of implicit bias show (Greenwald and Krieger 2006; Jost et al. 2009), most Americans see and hear non-White Others in racist ways.[2] Since the birth of Black/White racism—which Theodore Allen (1994, 1997), in his two-volume magnum opus *The Invention of the White Race*, documents the beginnings of in 1670s Virginia—the myth of a dominant White Race has played a preeminent role in the social, economic, and political organization of the United States. According to Jonathan Metzl (2019) in *Dying of Whiteness*, Americans who identify as White, particularly White men, are literally dying for their investment in the mythology of Whiteness. The vast majority of Americans are being hurt by racism.

The irony is that *Race is not a biological fact.* It is a social convention, a "social fact" (a fact by social agreement). There is no White Race, no White civilization, and there are no White people, except as a matter of agreement. (Race terms—including "Race," "Black," "White," and "Other" when used to indicate a racialized Other—are capitalized throughout to highlight this social fact status.) Furthermore, each country has categorized differences between people in ways that suit its own needs, so Race categories differ by country. The Race issues we discuss in this book belong uniquely to the United States (Omi and Winant 1986, Allen 1994). Other important categories like Latinx/Hispanic and Asian not only do not denote Races the way the Black/White binary is intended to—even by agreement—they confer outsider status. Persons in these categories do not easily fit within the American binary. For Latinx/Hispanic, this is the case even though the oldest colonies in the United States were Spanish. The binary American Black/White category system that is taken for granted in the United States today is Anglo in origin. It was invented by rich English plantation owners in the Jamestown, Virginia, colony to trick poor Irish, Scotch, and English laborers into controlling African laborers for them (Allen 1994, 1997).[3] It was from the beginning a system predicated on the idea that everyone would be categorized as either Black or White and that all would be Anglo—a reaction to ongoing hostilities with Spain.[4] The invention of Whiteness was very simply a ploy by the rich to divide and conquer the colonial American working classes by Race, while also eliminating Spanish influence.

Corresponding myths about Blackness and the alleged violence and criminality of Black Americans have been used systematically to control White Americans since the late 1600s, encouraging them to remain in segregated rural areas and all-White enclaves; and when White Americans do rebel against this control and start speaking out in their own interest, powerful forces move quickly to punish them.[5] The myth of Black criminality and violence is as much a fiction as the myth of White superiority. Just as there is no White Race, there is no Black Race. Furthermore, studies of unreported crime suggest that the "real" White American crime rate is actually higher than for other categories of people. It has just not been recorded because the police do not patrol White neighborhoods the same way they patrol Black neighborhoods. White Americans have been made to fear the illusion of Black violence. But, as Michael Males (2017) reports, White Americans in predominantly White Republican counties are 50% more likely to die from violence than White Americans in racially diverse Democratic counties. It turns out that the biggest threat to White Americans is living in isolated White communities among themselves.

Nevertheless, on the basis of social fictions about a "criminalblackman" (Russell-Brown 2009) and Black-on-Black crime, Black Americans continue to be feared; shot by the police; denied jobs, education, housing, and the right to vote; and incarcerated at record rates for things that most White Americans do with impunity. Then when Black Americans do manage to secure high-status positions, they often find that the White Americans they work with do not recognize their legitimate status or competence, creating problems for them on the job and giving them back only "fractured reflections" of the identities they have achieved (Rawls and Duck 2017).

While many believe that Black Americans suffer from what Frantz Fanon (1952) called the "colonial mentality," leading to low self-esteem and impoverished cultural development, we note that it is primarily White Americans, not Black Americans, who are exhibiting the characteristics Fanon describes: in particular trying to emulate the wealthy White people who oppress them—a process that has become deeply invested in fantasies about Whiteness. Details about how voters were targeted by social media during the 2016 election suggest that those who designed the algorithms used to target susceptible voters understood and took advantage of the psychological correlates of this social condition (Wylie 2019).

We take the position of W. E. B. Du Bois (1903), who believed that because Black Americans have an experience of being seen by the White Other as inferior, while at the same time being blocked from emulating them, they have developed what he called "double consciousness," which has enabled Black Americans to create their own community that insulates them against the colonial condition. As Cornel West ([1982] 2002) noted, trying to emulate White Americans is detrimental to the well-being of Black Americans.[6] Our research shows that Black interaction order preferences tacitly embed this understanding. Thus, in the current crisis, it is ironically the colonial mentality of White Americans that threatens to overturn our democracy. In the words of Leonard Pitts (2019), "The Republican Party's appeal . . . stems largely from an implicit promise: Vote for us, and we will repeal the 20th century." However, while White Americans—egged on by the 1%—are trying to undo the civil rights reforms of the last century, Black Americans remain committed to a democratic future for every single American, and our research shows that Black American interaction order expectations reflect this commitment.

Powerful special interests are well organized to keep White Americans in thrall to an anti-democratic racial mythology that encourages them to continue trying to keep Black Americans "in their place" (Maddow 2019; Mayer 2016; Skocpol and Williamson 2011). Black American attempts to organize have also met with powerful political opposition.[7] But the primary objective has been to use Race to divide workers.[8] Each time White workers have begun to organize for their own benefit, special interests have quickly mobilized racialized counter-narratives ("you have no job because affirmative action gave Black people your jobs") in combination with political and legal action to stop them.[9] According to Kerri Merritt (2017), the need to put an end to the threat of a strike to end slavery by White southern laborers before the Civil War hastened the beginning of that war. Over the course of American history, the myth of White racial superiority has been the principal means of controlling White workers.

The question of why White Americans so often vote against their own self-interest has a simple answer: they do it to preserve their investment in the fantasy of Whiteness.

At this point of national crisis, we need to have a general conversation about Race to liberate both White and Black Americans from the myths that divide the nation. *Racism and democracy cannot coexist.* Racism is a basic failure to recognize the Other as a human being like oneself: a failure of empathy and reciprocity that impacts communication, social interaction, and the life chances of all citizens. Because most Americans now *believe* that racism is wrong, the discussion of Race we need to have *should* be possible. But a strong tendency to treat racism either as a matter of personal bias (whether overt or implicit), or as explicit bias in formal rules and laws, is getting in the way. First, the way we think about Race and racism will need to change. Not only does thinking about racism this way ignore the racism coded into interaction, but focusing on individuals and their attitudes creates the false impression that individual prejudice is a bigger problem than the tacit racism that has been coded into interaction that makes individuals and institutions act in racist ways in the first place.

This sets up the problem backward. It overlooks the most prevalent forms of institutionalized racism—which are tacit, not explicit—and obscures the fact that we all unknowingly act in racist ways. It also scares White Americans, who do not want to be told they are racist, and keeps them away from the conversation we need to have about Race. Ultimately, the biggest problem is not the explicit racism of institutions or individual racists and their attitudes—these we can see and deal with. The biggest problem is the racism we can't see that is structured into the fabric of American life, shaping the actions and implicit biases of all Americans in racist ways, encouraged by the powerful special interests and foreign powers that are taking advantage of our divided nation. Our country was built on a racist labor system that is still sustained by the many myths, lies, and fantasies about Race, and this has shaped our national culture. This is one of the reasons why we still need to talk about slavery. The preferred ways of interacting that have developed over time among Black and White Americans reflect the underlying racism embedded in our society. Given this background, how could we not be enacting hidden tacit racist codes every day?

In focusing on the Black/White binary and the two clashing interaction orders that correspond to it, we are not overlooking the existence of other categories of people identified by Race and/or culture in the United States who experience racism and exclusion. What we argue, however, is that they, too, find themselves positioned against the Black/White binary when they are in the US. The main category terms for such people are Asian, Latinx/Hispanic, and West Indian/African. We note that these are catch-all categories that can be offensive in themselves (i.e., Asian covers a broad range of countries including Russia, India, and parts of the Middle East, in addition to China, Korea, Japan, and Southeast Asia, while Latinx/Hispanic includes all of South America, parts of North America, and many islands, and the same is true for West Indian/African). Most of those so categorized self-identify by nationality or culture in ways that are not recognized in the US. West Indians and Africans, for instance, typically self-identify by nationality and often consider themselves White. But in this country, they are usually treated as if they were not only Black, but Black Americans. We note that members of the Latinx/Hispanic category in the US fall on both sides of the Black/White binary, splitting the community. Some are identified by Americans as White, while others are identified as Black, affiliations they struggle with. Outside the US, Latinx/Hispanic is not a Race category. But in the context of the US binary, it often functions as one—a complication that is beginning to draw some serious attention.[10]

We take the position that all racism (and misperceptions of Race) in the US are structured by the Black/White binary, and consequently that all other racial/cultural classifications *in this country* can best be understood in terms of their positioning in relationship to that binary. This ironically holds for the category Native American as well.[11]

The Black/White binary has been close to absolute for 350 years. Americans tend to be perceived as either Black or White, although who is considered White/Black shifted over the course of the twentieth century, with categories such as "Jews," "Middle Easteners," and "Italians" shifting from Black to White (Brodkin 1998; Maghbouleh 2017). Those who cannot be classified within the binary tend to be perceived as outsiders no matter how long they and/or their ancestors have lived here. Those who come to the United States from elsewhere are usually not aware of the way Race categories work in this country or how they will be assigned to (or excluded from) those categories by Americans. Nor are they aware of the expectations of the interaction orders of the categories to which they may be assigned. Students who arrive in the US from Haiti, the Bahamas, or India, for instance, typically identify as Haitian, Bahamian, or Indian. But they will be told by Americans in no uncertain terms that they are Black or Asian. Furthermore, the strength of the American binary leads to a strong unconscious tendency to perceive Black West Indians and Latinx/Hispanics as Black Americans (insiders), while perceiving those that are put in the Asian category as "foreign" and/or "exotic" (outsiders). As a consequence, Asian American citizens are typically perceived as not American, asked where they come from, and complimented on their command of English. If they answer that they were born in the US, they are asked where their parents and/or grandparents came from. Americans who perceive Asian Americans this way are typically unaware that they are engaging in a very prevalent and powerful form of racial exclusion. The same often happens to those Latinx/Hispanic citizens who cannot be easily categorized as either White or Black.

Because this "foreign" status accorded to Asian Americans and some Latinx/Hispanic and Native Americans is defined by the Black/White binary, it is against that binary that we seek to understand their experiences with racism and exclusion in the US. In chapter 6 we present observations of racism against Asians and Asian Americans that illustrate the tacit assumptions about being "foreign" that are at work (i.e., assumptions that Asians can't do ordinary American things like driving, walking, and talking), which reveal the positioning of this category against the Black/White binary. We also explore some of the complications of Latinx/Hispanic and West Indian/African identities through these observations. Then in the conclusion, we consider how racism and exclusion toward Latinx/Hispanic Americans, refugees and immigrants, are positioned not only against the Black/White binary, but also in the context of an old seventeenth-century Anglo/Spanish antagonism.

Our aim in this book is to examine how the legacy of the Black/White binary and its attendant anti-Asian and anti-Spanish forms of racism have been coded into ordinary social interaction in the United States—as tacit racism—so that we can stop pretending we are a democratic society and start becoming one. This will require achieving a level of awareness about Race among White Americans that we call "White double consciousness" in homage to Du Bois. Just as the experience of being seen as inferior has, he argued, enabled Black Americans to develop some insight about racism, we hope that an awareness of the many ways in which White Americans are acting out a false code of racial superiority will give them a corresponding insight into their own racism. Until we can develop a general awareness of the racism in our own actions, the defensiveness of Americans who identify as White, described by Robin DiAngelo (2018) in *White Fragility*, that leads them to deny they are acting in racist ways, will keep getting in the way of the awareness of Race and racism we need to achieve.

Organization of the Book

In the chapters that follow, we report on three decades of research on social interaction between Black and White Americans, the objective of which is to explore the nuances of tacit racism and explain how it works in social interaction. It is our position that this racism disrupts interaction and fractures society, demonstrating why equality is not just an ideal, but a necessity in a diverse modern society (Rawls 2019, 2020). As we studied the various tacit forms of racism, we watched it become more prolific and complex over time—burrowing deeper into the social practices of daily life. Ironically, as this happened it also became increasingly difficult to convince people that Race was a problem. After Barack Obama was elected, many White Americans were convinced they were living in a "post-racial" society and that Black Americans were exaggerating their problems. The dangerous fiction that racism could be overcome by being "color-blind," which Bonilla-Silva (2003) warned against in his book *Racism without Racists*, was also well entrenched. Most Black Americans knew racism had not gone away, but still remained optimistic that some progress was being made. It is only since the 2016 election that the fantasies of White supremacy have burst out in public to shock the nation.

What we found is that the institutional embeddedness of tacit racism had allowed it to become more deeply hidden and effective until, having burrowed its way into the most ordinary aspects of everyday life, it suddenly popped back up in public discourse in the backlash against Obama and the wave of White resentment that followed. While some White Americans were celebrating what they took to be a new milestone in racial equality, others had been secretly seething because what they disparagingly call "PC," or "political correctness," was preventing them from expressing their racism: their investment in Whiteness.

False narratives about Black Americans getting most of the benefits from government "safety net" programs, popularized in the 1970s, were used in combination with the new myths of the "criminalblackman" (Russell-Brown 2009) popularized under Ronald Reagan, and a growing fear of Black Americans as different and un-American, to convince a significant number of White Americans that the US government had been taken over by foreigners and "criminals," leading to the Tea Party movement (Skocpol and Williamson 2011: 78–79). In this context, the way we found tacit racism sustaining false narratives and myths about Race is a pressing concern.

Each chapter examines a form of tacit racism in detail. In describing and analyzing social interactions, where possible we also attempt to introduce the reader to the actual people involved—to give them a voice in telling their stories. We open in chapter 1 with an analysis of everyday tacit expectations about how people get to know one another, what they consider "personal" or "honest," and how what conforms to their ideas of "order" and "disorder" differs by Race. These differences make it difficult for Black and White Americans to even begin relationships, and frequently support the contrasting narratives that "White people are nosey" and "Black people are rude," the title of our first chapter. The second chapter explores how racial framings of identity interfere with the recognition of the high-status identity, legitimacy, and competence of Black men in the workplace, producing what we call "fractured reflections" of their presentations of self.

While many Americans believe that status offers protection against racial discrimination, we show how as Black Americans rise in the corporate world, tacit racism interferes with their work and obscures their achievements. In the third chapter, White and Black conceptions of honesty are contrasted, showing how differences in how "honesty" is understood as an interactional obligation can affect cross-racial relationships both in and out of the workplace. The fourth chapter documents interaction order misalignments in talk about health and responsibility that challenge conventional conceptions of Black masculinity (which we reconceptualize in terms of a democratic ideal we identify with a practice we call "submissive civility"). These interaction order issues are brought to bear on three distinct social contexts in the chapters that follow: a White/Black police/citizen encounter, primarily White college campuses, and a poor Black neighborhood.

In each case we document the interaction order expectations in these settings in detail and analyze how they clash. In chapter 5, we take up Du Bois's (1890) conception of the "Submissive Man" (foreshadowed in chapter 4), in the context of a police/citizen encounter, showing how the Black American preference for submission to the good of the whole (submissive civility) clashes with the individualism of the White "Strong Man" ideal, to produce misunderstandings that, in addition to a Black citizen's inability to get his identity recognized, are used by White police officers as a pretext for his violent arrest.

In chapter 6, we consider the impact of tacit racism on the academic life of several college campuses, finding that—even for White students—the racism of other White students and faculty is oppressive. Surrounded by racism, White college students realize they have been treating it as "normal." We refer to the constant daily downpour of racism they report as "Race pollution." Chapter 7 considers a poor Black neighborhood that has been the target of outside interference for decades. Here we find that contrary to what most people believe, drug dealers are valued insiders who are key to the stability and safety of the neighborhood, while the police and other outsiders are the main threat. There are other neighborhoods where the police have managed to so completely erode the local interaction order that drug dealers, often referred to as "gangs," do not have a positive function. But in this neighborhood, in spite of persistent outside interference, we find that the internal order—with the drug dealers at its center—is still better and stronger than the order that outsiders seek to impose.

In surveys, White Americans overwhelmingly say they believe in "fairness," but what they mean by fairness is highly individualistic. Many White Americans believe that if they could get rid of rules, society, and government, they would be free as individuals and things would be fair. Black Americans, by contrast, typically embrace a sense of "fairness" that acknowledges the sociological premise that humans depend on cooperation with one another for everything: for meaning, self, a sense of community, and even the achievement of individual autonomy, and that, as a consequence, freedom is only possible within a social organization that supports that possibility (Durkheim 1893; Rawls 2019, 2020). James Baldwin famously said that the "price" of becoming White was that Americans of European descent had lost any sense of community, which explained what he called a "remarkable" and "terrifying" "crisis of leadership" in the White community that had taken generations and a great deal of "coercion" to produce (Baldwin 1984). With White Americans favoring individualism and Black Americans prioritizing community, Race differences play directly into the current American political narrative, which pits strong man individualism against what is being called "collectivism," but is actually just the basic idea that human civilization can only develop and persist within an organized community.

Research by psychologists and Critical Race scholars is documenting high levels of unconscious racism. A rapidly growing stream of such research shows that White Americans literally "see" Black Americans in racist ways. Looking at a photo of a Black man, they are more likely to feel afraid or describe a criminal (Wise 2010). Given a description of a crime, they are much more likely to assume the perpetrator is Black than White (Dixon and Maddox 2005). Presented with a job application, White Americans are twice as likely to favor a White man they are told is a convicted felon with no college education over a Black man with no criminal record and a college degree (Pager 2003, 2008). Studies of medicine and law find that high levels of "implicit bias" are leading to unequal outcomes for Black patients and defendants (Green et al. 2007; Bagentsos 2007; Bennett 2010). High levels of implicit bias are found even among White people who identify as liberal and claim not to be prejudiced. Significant implicit bias is also found among Black Americans. Studies by Claude Steele (Steele and Aronson 1995), Joyce Bell (Bell and Hartmann 2007), and others also document the subtleties of stereotypes and raced speech.

While these studies are persuasive, they don't explain where unconscious forms of racism come from, why they persist, or how they work in everyday interaction. Our research is designed to answer these questions through a close examination of how differences in the racialized experiences of Black and White Americans are institutionalized in tacit interaction order expectations that differ by Race. We explain the differential focus on individual versus community. We also describe the social conditions that create and sustain these differences.

While it is clear that politics funded by "Dark Money" has been fanning the flames of racial resentment (Mayer 2016), if Americans didn't already have a Race problem, it would not have worked. A division between White and Black Americans that benefits only the very rich has kept the US from achieving democracy for 350 years. The clashing expectations we document have both emerged from and reproduced these divisions. As Anne Rawls (2000) has documented, racialized differences in expectations go so deep that even assumptions about the "definition of the situation"—that is, the understanding of what behaviors are appropriate and expected by type of situation—and the identities and meanings that such definitions make relevant in social interaction are not the same.[12] The White self organizes around status achievements, resulting in a "categorial" form of identity; while for Black Americans meaning and identity work are, by contrast, organized around the intrinsic value of being human in the immediate setting and resist categorization.

The two interaction orders are like mirror opposites. The separation by Race that both motivates and results from these clashing expectations reinforces existing myths about Race while continuing to generate more false beliefs and stereotypes that frame the way Americans think about Race and inequality and further divide the nation. While tacit racism originated in forms of racial exclusion associated with slavery and labor control in the early American colonies, we show how the tacit racism that is a staple of modern America *continues to create new forms of tacit racism and inequality:* becoming ever more sophisticated and more deeply coded into our daily lives.

Our Research on Tacit Interaction Orders of Race

Our research, based on fieldwork and the collection of narratives and audio and video recordings of interaction, documents the underlying differences in tacit expectations about interaction, different definitions of the situation, and the identities and expectations they embed, which are the foundation of sense-making for Americans according to their identification as Black or White. We argue that these interaction orders encode—institutionalize—the shared tacit rules and expectations that are used to coordinate daily sense-making—in the form of unconscious, taken-for-granted, "normally thoughtless" practices (Garfinkel 1967). These practices do not vary by individual, but rather by social and racial self-identification. When social expectations match and sense-making works, nobody thinks about *how* it works: and the process remains unconscious. However, when the expectations involved in this coordination do not match—and we show that with White and Black Americans they often don't match—sense-making cannot be coordinated.

When people have trouble making sense, we find that they stop taking interaction for granted, tacit coordination stops, and they begin to explicitly question each other's character, competence, and motivation (Rawls and David 2006; Rawls and Duck 2017). Interactional obligations—"Trust Conditions" (Garfinkel 1963)—require participants to use the same expectations as others in an interaction and to treat those others as competent to do the same. When one interaction involves two interaction orders without all participants being aware of this, these conditions are not being met. It is as if one person played checkers while the other played chess, but both thought they were playing the same game. The blame participants cast on each other for the resulting troubles generates narratives about Race that create new racial stereotypes, and reinforce old ones, generally making democratic public spaces impossible to achieve.

Our research documents how living separately and under different conditions, Americans who identify as White and Black have coded contrasting interactional expectations into their daily practices. A priority on individualism and social hierarchy that was characteristic of seventeenth- and eighteenth-century European thinking is coded into the White interaction order, while the Black interaction order, which developed in response to racism, is more modern in prioritizing equality, privacy, and democracy. The democratic character of Black American expectations will surprise those who assume that White American culture is superior.

That there are differences at all is a surprise to most White Americans, who tend to assume that all Americans have the same interactional expectations because they live in the same society. They are overlooking the fact that Black and White Americans have essentially lived separately in this country under very different circumstances for centuries. It would actually be *more* surprising if under such conditions Black and White Americans had developed the same social expectations. It is also not surprising that the expectations of White Americans preserve the seventeenth-century European upper-class priorities of the elite English landowners who first invented Whiteness to use as a manipulative tool. By contrast, Black American awareness of their own racial oppression, famously called "double consciousness" by Du Bois (1903), in combination with the strong racial binary that blocked them from aspiring to Whiteness, shaped the development of a very different set of interactional expectations that work as a shield against oppression, prioritizing equality and democracy and creating the possibility of living in a Black American community of equals. As a consequence, White American priorities preserve the inequalities of a pre-democratic seventeenth-century culture, while Black American priorities reflect a dynamic move toward modern democratic aspirations.

In contrast to the popular belief that Black American cultural preferences reflect an impoverished perspective that has been damaged by centuries of oppression, we find that the tacit interactional expectations of Black Americans embody a respect for equality, community, and personhood adopted as a creative response to racial oppression and exclusion that is largely missing from the tacit expectations of White Americans, who, we argue, are impoverished by this lack. The Black American expectations we document tend to be democratic in orientation, rising above Race, class, and gender differences, to deliver an oasis of equality to anyone who participates—Black, White, or Other—as long as they understand and respect the ground rules of the Black interaction order. White Americans, by contrast, remain faithful to an exclusive colonial status hierarchy that was designed to oppress and manipulate them, exhibiting a distressing tendency to value authority over freedom and status over personhood.

In a talk given in 1890, Du Bois introduced his conception of the "Submissive Man" as a Black American ideal that, he argued, is a needed counterbalance to the White "Strong Man" ideal (which for Du Bois was exemplified by Jefferson Davis, president of the Confederacy—but is also an apt description of Donald Trump's self-interested approach). The White ideal needs a counterbalance because the high value it places on individualism elevates the individual over the community, enshrining a dangerous degree of narcissism as an ideal. Whereas the White ideal places the highest value on the independence and self-interest of the Strong Man individual, Du Bois proposed that in response Black Americans place a higher value on democracy and the good of the community as a whole. In chapters 4 and 5, we identify a Black interaction order practice we call "submissive civility" and relate it to Du Bois's argument that the Black American grasp of democracy is stronger than that of White Americans because the Black American experience of racial oppression led to the development of a double consciousness about that oppression.

Because the double consciousness that comes with the experience of racial oppression has given Black Americans an awareness of differences between White and Black American interactional expectations, they can make allowances for these differences, although they often find the things White people do strange and/or immoral. White Americans, having no awareness of these differences, cannot make such allowances and consequently tend to attribute differences to the alleged inferiority of Black Americans and to characterize Black lifestyles as chaotic and disorganized. This mistake can be corrected by learning about Black interactional preferences and the moral standards they embed and by achieving an awareness of racism through a process that we call developing "White double consciousness." We suggest that White Americans stop trying to force Black Americans to assimilate and instead develop an awareness of how they, too, are oppressed by the priorities of Whiteness.

The overall objective of this book is to change the way we understand and talk about Race and racism. Treating Race as a biological reality and focusing on the individual as the primary location of racial bias are mistakes that prevent Americans from understanding how the ways of seeing and acting associated with Whiteness have become so deeply embedded in ordinary social expectations that we are constantly acting unconsciously in racist ways. Racism has been hiding in plain sight while it divides the nation, undermines our democracy, and provides fertile ground not only for the political manipulation of Race and issues associated with it, but also of issues that are falsely associated with Race (e.g., welfare, crime, drugs, guns, food stamps, etc.). Racism is a national problem that we are all responsible for. However, insofar as White Americans currently have more power to change it, they bear the greater responsibility.

At key points in American history when we might have overcome racial divisions, we have let the opportunity pass. Having failed to achieve racial equality at two major points in the past, we now have another chance, possibly a last chance. In his book *The Third Reconstruction*, William J. Barber III (2016) calls on Americans not to let this third opportunity pass. One mistake leading to the failure of the first two attempts at "reconstruction" was treating changes in formal law as if they could be self-sufficient without corresponding changes in social expectation. As a nation we made this mistake after passing the first Civil Rights Act in 1866 (which most Americans don't even know about), and again after the Civil Rights Act of 1964. Unfortunately, legal progress toward ending racism without a meaningful conversation among White Americans about why it was necessary only encouraged racism to burrow deeper into American social expectations—undermining democratic institutions and rendering American voters increasingly vulnerable to lies about Race. A second mistake is underestimating the extent of the structural racism that is coded into ordinary interaction and acted out unconsciously as tacit racism—an oversight reinforced by a general neglect of interaction in social research after WWII (Rawls 2018). A focus on mathematics and numbers, in sociology in particular, has all but displaced attention to what actual people do and how they do it. It turns out to matter a great deal how people draw inferences from the behavior of others during social interaction: a process that cannot be derived from statistics or reduced to mathematical abstraction. In focusing on this issue, we are inspired by Garfinkel's early pioneering work on Race (Garfinkel [1943] 2019, 1946, [1948] 2006, 1952; Rawls, forthcoming). As we show in chapter 5, assumptions about how an innocent person will react to police questioning can embed assumptions about Race such that a Black citizen's attempts to be cooperative, even though they are recognizable in the Black interaction order as submissive and civil, are treated by White police officers as grounds for suspicion and a pretext for arrest. The result in our example is a violent arrest that, in effect, legally punished a Black citizen for his culture.

The growth of both tacit and overt racism that followed the election of Barack Obama, the first African American president, ushered in a level of overt intolerance that most White Americans thought they had put behind them. The orgy of racism, inhumane treatment of so-called "Mexican" immigrants, and domestic terrorism inspired by Whiteness that has accompanied Trump's presidency has been a nationwide display of how overlooking racism and supporting the fiction of a "color-blind" society (Bonilla-Silva 2003) has damaged the White majority as well as racial minorities, and in the process come to threaten core democratic institutions, rendering the average American more vulnerable to manipulation by the special interests of the wealthiest 1% in combination with foreign actors.[13] As such, racism is a clear and present danger to the survival of our nation, the freedom and equality of its citizens, the public civility it depends on, and the autonomy of its sciences and democratic institutions.

Ground Rules for the Research

In crafting a conceptual approach to Race in terms of tacit interaction orders, we refer to expectations as tacit when they comprise expected—even required ("constitutive")[14]—aspects of social interaction that people don't think consciously about but nevertheless count on; and we refer to the contrasting sets of expectations we analyze as "interaction orders of Race" (Goffman 1983; Rawls 1983, 1987, 2000). Our argument is that these orders institutionalize the shared expectations people use to coordinate their daily sense-making as tacit, unconscious, taken-for-granted, "normally thoughtless" practices. These expectations make up the background against which people can draw shared inferences from the actions of others in interaction. For the process to work, participants must not only have access to the same practices, but must also have the same opportunity as others to use those practices and be seen as competent in so doing—a condition we call equality. We find that because Race inequality has led to differences in the tacit expectations they hold, White and Black Americans often draw different inferences from the same behavior and as a consequence misunderstand each other in fundamental ways.

Race as a social fact involves both social definition and self-identification. In this book we will often use the terms "identified as" or "self-identified as" White or Black to indicate this issue of self and other identification. Because Race only exists by social agreement, it also varies by social agreement. We cannot talk about what Race people "really" are. There is no such thing. Complicating this issue is the fact that Black and White American understandings of who is White and who is Black differ (and they also differ from the way Latinx/Hispanics and West Indians/Africans make that distinction). In one of the student observations presented in chapter 6, a Black male college student found himself talking to a White female student at a party. In telling him that she liked him, she added that it was "okay" because she considered him "White." This confused and upset the Black student, who had been having a good time talking and dancing with her up until that point. He does not identify as White and was insulted by that categorization, which she insisted he take as a "compliment." Understandings of who is Black also differ among Black Americans according to whether their ancestors lived in the United States and experienced the double consciousness that is a consequence of the American racial binary, or if they are more recent immigrants from the West Indies or Africa, where Race categories are quite different (Coates 2004; Rawls, Taylor, and Coates 2019).[15]

As with any social fact, the mutual accomplishment of Race requires participants to fulfill their commitment to the interactional obligations that comprise it. If we stop cooperating to make Race real in our daily interactions, it will cease to exist. People would still be different colors, but we would notice that they are thousands of different colors, not just two, and those differences would take on very different meanings. Therefore, that the Black/White binary is still going strong in the United States reflects a sustained, but tacit, continued commitment to it and to the interaction orders of Race in which these differences are made real again every day. How this happens is important. It is also important that these interaction orders differ by Black/White racial identification in ways that effect not only how Race is achieved, but also how identity and shared meaning are accomplished, or not, in interaction.

We use the binary categories Black/White almost exclusively in discussing Race and racism in the United States because the binary Black/White categorization system that developed in the American colonial context is the primary American classification scheme for Race. Other ethnic, cultural, religious, and class categories have been secondary to Race in the US ever since the invention of Whiteness. The exception is an "Anglo" vs. "Spanish" bias, also dating from the 1600s, which is enjoying a recent revival under Trump. We take that up in the conclusion in discussing the current treatment of Latinx/Hispanic so-called "Mexican" immigrants (many of whom are descendants of the original Spanish-American colonists and thus not true immigrants), the willingness to destroy Spanish-speaking families and children, and the shameful treatment of Puerto Rican citizens—the indigenous inhabitants of the first American colony.

In writing about Race, we follow the convention of alternating the terms Black American and African American, and keeping original terms such as "Negro" and "Colored" when they appear in quotations. There is one exception. We never say or write the N-word—even if it appears in an original text—and we ask all White Americans to do the same. We either write "N-word" or "N****r," although the latter is dispreferred and we only use it when the poetics of a phrase matter, as in one of our observations in chapter 6 (*"Nutcracker*, not the *Nutn****r"*). When Black Americans use the N-word among each other, it affiliates: it means "a person who shares my experience of racial oppression." But in racially mixed company, any use of the word is divisive. When a White person uses the word, it is always divisive and pejorative. Period.

Ultimately, we find that, although they are the consequence of inequality and exclusion, Black interaction order preferences serve an essential purpose in protecting Black Americans from Race inequality, and that they will need to do so as long as that inequality continues. This makes them different from White preferences, which prioritize status hierarchy and make Americans identified as White vulnerable to manipulation by the rich: these preferences need to change.

In spite of the positive value that Black interactional expectations have for Black Americans, however, the White power structure has the authority to act on misinterpretations of Black interaction through law, policy, and personal authority in ways that subject Black Americans to constant and severe punitive measures for acting on these preferences, and such actions frequently disrupt public civility.

Black American conversation is often misunderstood, Black identities are frequently not recognized, and Black places and actions are systematically treated as "disorderly" and "meaningless" by outsiders, when they are actually orderly according to the particular expectations of the place and its people. Trying to force an order on Black spaces that does not fit the existing order or needs of that place, and/or trying to force an interaction order on Black interactions that does not belong to them, is not only racist, it creates disorder. Outsiders trying to force "order" on Black Americans contribute to the mass incarceration epidemic, the school-to-prison pipeline, and many other racial inequities. The consequences of these intrusions raise the recorded "crime rate" for Black Americans independently of actual crime, and in so doing reinforce racist false beliefs: a vicious circularity. Black Americans—their interactions, identities, and neighborhoods—are not inherently disorderly or criminal; they just have a different order that is not recognized by White Others.

The Importance of Equality

Equality is necessary not only to sustain the reciprocity required for mutually intelligible social interaction; a stable economy and stable markets also depend on equality. This is a big argument that people cannot understand if they think that everything is working just fine now, in spite of the massive inequality in society. That everything is not working fine is one of the main points of this book. In the context of modern American capitalism, the popular belief—which is consistent with the White "Strong Man" ideal—that individual competition and economic markets work best without restraints is widespread (Fox 2009). But economists are issuing a loud warning that markets depend on a solid democratic foundation and that high rates of inequality make markets perform poorly (Stiglitz 2012; Krugman 2012; Piketty 2014). Science and technology also depend on a free exchange of ideas, and markets depend on science and technology. Not coincidentally, the 2019 Nobel Prize in economics went to three economists (Michael Kremer, Abhijit Banerjee, and Esther Duflo) whose research focuses on poverty, underscoring the growing recognition of the importance of inequality in economics.

Current political movements motivated by fantasies of Whiteness that aim to strip away the legal protections and social supports that over 90% of Americans rely on erode the democratic foundation that markets, sciences, democratic institutions, and cooperative social interaction all rely on.

The resulting increases in inequality are already negatively impacting those White Americans who support efforts to cut social supports. Recent research shows that White Americans living in racially segregated parts of the country (that are 90% or more White) are 50% more likely to suffer and/or die from violence at the hands of other White people in their own community. According to Males (2017), "Overall, white Americans who live in predominantly white and Trump-voting counties are 50% more likely to die from murder, gun violence and drug overdoses than whites who live in the most diverse and Democratic-voting counties. The more white and Republican a county is, the greater the risk for white Americans." Metzl (2019) documents high and rising rates of gun suicide among White men in staunchly Republican states that have eliminated restrictions on gun possession. Metzl also reports that when Republicans in Kansas decimated the state's public schools, the test scores and graduation rates for White students fell more than those of other populations. In the *US News & World Report* 2019 rankings of all fifty states on seventy metrics, nine of the bottom-ten-ranked states voted for Trump in 2016, while only two of the top-ten-ranked states voted for him. Research on the opioid epidemic in Trump-voting counties nationwide concludes that "support for the Republican candidate in the 2016 election is a marker for physical conditions, economic circumstances, and cultural forces associated with opioid use" (Goodwin et al. 2018). It turns out that racism is very unhealthy for White Americans.

Tacit racism is damaging not only because it creates and sustains inequality, but also because its hidden character sustains the false belief that we are doing just fine without equality. It should not be surprising to those who value the civility that comes with democracy that racism is self-destructive. But the recognition that White racial exclusion is more dangerous and creates more violence toward those who practice it than crimes by any other group flies in the face of prevalent *myths* about the dangers of Black crime and criminality, which have been used to justify a dysfunctional criminal justice system that has targeted Black Americans for decades. Given that studies also show a higher rate of unreported crime and drug use among White Americans, not to speak of higher levels of white-collar crime and money laundering, the concentration of police and criminal justice enforcement efforts in Black communities, and the resulting high concentrations of Black men, women, and children in our prisons and jails, not only endangers Black Americans—it *endangers the country as a whole.*

Racism and the myths that support it—including the belief that we are doing just fine without equality—have obscured our vision of the enemy, impairing our ability to protect ourselves from the actual sources of violence in our midst. Black crime and disorder are not the enemy. *Racism is the enemy.* And if the high rate of actual White-on-White crime and violence wasn't bad enough, White "outgroup intolerance" has been found to correlate with a declining support for democracy that puts our democratic social institutions at risk (Miller and Davis 2018). In other words, people who are racially intolerant are more likely to consider various forms of dictatorship to be acceptable, and to welcome foreign and illegal influence on our elections. It is hard to think of anything that would be more self-destructive than trading the fledgling democracy we have, imperfect as it is, for a dictatorship of violent White racists.

The argument that equality is required to sustain the growth of markets as formulated by Thomas Piketty, Joseph Stiglitz, and Paul Krugman parallels our argument that equality is required as a foundation for mutual intelligibility. When inequality becomes too great, the stability of the whole fails, and people are forced to organize into smaller groups for survival. This is what we document. Sense-making *within* such self-organizing groups and their corresponding interaction orders can be successful, and they can achieve a high level of internal cohesion and trust. But society as a whole is diminished by the division: the shared practices and mutual trust necessary for successful cooperation and understanding across groups, work sites, and scientific practices no longer exist. Without mutual trust, modern markets fail. When interest groups and organizations based on beliefs attempt to force their views on the whole society, science and occupations are no longer free: science itself comes under political attack, and "scientists can no longer participate in free public discussion" (Mayer 2016: 274). When the inequalities in question are racial, as in our research, people can end up in a permanent state of interactional segregation in which tacit racism produces a spiral of ever-increasing inequality for both White and Black Americans.

This is the current American situation. Understanding how Black Americans organize their interactions in the face of these inequalities and how that organization differs from that of White Americans is, we propose, fundamental to understanding this current state of division in our country. Given the mileage that well-funded interest groups are getting out of fanning the flames of racism and further dividing the country, raising awareness of how tacit racism works is particularly important in the present moment. As Abraham Lincoln famously noted: "A house divided against itself cannot stand." We cannot remain divided between privileged and poor, Black and White, valued and despised, without destroying the cohesion of the nation.

W. E. B. Du Bois's Double Consciousness Thesis Revisited

Coming to terms with why and how racism has managed to persist not only requires changes in how we understand Race and the history of racism; it also requires changes in how we think about Black Americans. The Black community is not fundamentally disorganized, and Black Americans do not suffer from the various ills—such as self-hatred, low self-esteem, low intelligence, criminal tendencies, or unwillingness to work—that racial stereotypes assign to them. Neither are Black Americans disadvantaged by a "culture of poverty" or "lack of values." It is White Americans who are more likely to have these problems. In our research we find that Black communities are organized to protect the persons who live in them and that Black interaction order expectations—forged in response to racism and oppression in a context of democratic ideals—are moral, rational, and functional: a model for White America that could balance out problematic assumptions about the feasibility of individualism that have resulted in increasing inequality.

Over a century ago, Du Bois (1903) argued that "double consciousness" had allowed Black Americans to survive the racism and humiliation that White America subjects them to without being destroyed by the feelings of alienation, low self-esteem, and self-hatred that Fanon (1952) argued are characteristic of the "colonial mentality" exhibited by other oppressed and colonized peoples. The incorporation of double consciousness into Black interaction order expectations involves a form of self-organization by the Black community that allows Black Americans to experience themselves both through the eyes of White society, which sees them as inferior, and through the eyes of their own Black world behind the "veil" of Race, in which they view each other as equals. Instead of measuring themselves by a White yardstick, according to which they would fall short, Black Americans adopted their own standards. While they are still oppressed, Du Bois argued that racial exclusion had given Black Americans an "emblem" of their own creation on which to build a Black "nation." Ironically, he said, this nation built on Race was organized to transcend Race. As a consequence, Blackness in the United States is a uniquely democratic conception.

Alone among the nations of the world, Du Bois argued, this Black American nation is egalitarian and democratic: transcending tribes, races, cultures, and countries. *While Whiteness excludes, Blackness includes.* Blackness in the US is unlike other ethnic, cultural, and class categories in its mirror-image opposition to the oppression against which it formed. While as Chris Hayes notes (2017), Black Americans are treated as the subjected population of a colony, rather than citizens of the nation, we find that the mutual commitments of Black American life embrace ideals of equality and fairness espoused by—but not practiced by—the larger community. Unlike other category groups, the solidarity of the Black community is not based on tradition (whether real or fictional), but rather on a democratic self-organization that originated in an experience of slavery, racism, and exclusion that is unique to African Americans. Occupied by an invading army of police—their young Black men on the run (Goffman 1974) and in jail (Alexander 2011); their families suffering grief and loss, unemployed, feared, criminalized (Russell-Brown 1998), and deprived of human rights—Black Americans responded by holding each other to a higher standard of equality, reciprocity, and humanity.

Our approach contrasts with discussions of double consciousness that treat it as a direct effect of the slave experience. Many peoples, including early White Americans, experienced slavery and colonial oppression without developing double consciousness. In fact, that is a large part of the problem. Most White Americans are also oppressed. Their communities are often poor, polluted, and without jobs. But they have not developed a double consciousness with which to protect themselves. Instead, they continue striving to emulate those rich White people who have actively organized to extort their loyalty (Mayer 2016). Reenacting centuries-old tacit social expectations based on Race, they fantasize that they have more in common with the rich White people who oppress them—because they have Whiteness in common—than with the Black Americans with whom they actually share common cause.

When the oppressed take on the perspective of their oppressors, confusion about their own identities and interests is inevitable. When White American workers and farmers embrace the objectives of the richest 1%, which cannot be their own, this kind of confusion is at its most destructive. The belief that rich and poor have the same interests because they are "White" has left those White Americans who believe it with few defenses. Black Americans, by contrast, have created a counter-narrative that can set them free from this kind of manipulation.

According to Du Bois, the experience of double consciousness that makes this counter-narrative possible can only happen if there is a separate and self-sustaining social context that can produce a positive side to the experience. Only Black Americans, he argued, have created a separate self-sustaining context that they control. It is ironically the rigidity of the American racial binary that made this possible. By contrast, while White Americans have developed identifiable "subcultural" contexts, few of these have allowed them to reject the standards of rich White people and adopt an alternate set of social standards and expectations that can produce feelings of equality and fulfillment. Labor unions have for short periods produced something close, but they have been actively suppressed. The hippie countercultural movement also offered a sustaining counter-narrative and lifestyle, but mainly for middle-class youth and only for a few years. Unfortunately, the mainstay of some of the poorest White subcultures remains the elevation of Whiteness, the Confederate flag, and the glorification of the inequalities of a slave system that benefited the 1%, rather than something transcending Race and inequality that would actually benefit working White Americans.

In exposing tacit racism in this book, we approach the conflicting social contexts of Black and White America through the tacit interactional expectations they exhibit, contrasting the expectations about interaction of the Black nation behind the veil, with the values and expectations that are characteristic of White American interaction.[16] We find these expectations so different, even mirror opposites, that they often prevent successful communication and identity work between Races. Without an ability to communicate and "see" the racialized Other in the identity and definition of the situation they see themselves in, there can be no empathy or understanding: only fear, anger, confusion, division, and violence.

The Invention of Race and the Conception of "Whiteness"

Race is a strange invention. Biologically there is no such thing. No pure White Race to defend or take pride in. No genetic core that all White people and only White people have in common. Improvements in the science of genetics have made this clear. There is no White culture either. Yet the binary Black/White social categories that developed between 1670 and 1725 in the early American colonies, as a way of manipulating and controlling English and African laborers, still play the defining role in creating racial exclusion, inequality, and political divisiveness in contemporary American life.[17]

The invention of "Whiteness" was a defining moment in the early American colonies (Allen 1994, 1997; Roediger 2007). The labels "White" and "Black" that we have inherited from this time period refer to important social facts: distinctions with legal and social implications. The exclusive binary nature of the American Black/White category distinction is unique (although it has now been exported) and goes some way toward explaining the singular achievement that is Black American double consciousness. Colonies in other countries dealt with the distinction between European, African, Asian, and Indigenous ("Indian") populations in quite different ways: each way of making distinctions developing in response to the particular labor-control issues in a given colony (Allen 1994). In colonies with very few White people, all of whom were rich landowners, status distinctions between African, Indian, Indigenous, Asian, and "mixed" people developed that recognized a broad range of categories, usually with possibilities for moving "up" and "down" between categories, depending on which categorization scheme worked best to keep laborers under control.

The American situation in the mid-1600s was unique in needing to transition from a majority of White unfree (slave) laborers to a majority of Black unfree laborers after the English treaty with the Dutch in 1654 first opened the African slave trade directly to England. No other colony in the 1600s had a majority of White slaves.[18] The use of "Whiteness" as a category distinction developed as a way of controlling the transition from White to Black slave labor and began to appear in legal documents around 1670 (a process that was not complete until about 1725 [Allen 1997]). The elevation to Whiteness gave former English and Irish slaves an incentive to keep Black slaves under control. Before this elevation, the primary social distinction in the colonies had been social class, not Race. In England, where the Jamestown colonists came from, the primary distinction was between the aristocracy and peasantry, and it was primarily English and Irish peasants who became slaves in the colonies. The industrial revolution that would create the modern middle classes was just beginning in the mid-1600s.

The invention of Whiteness allowed former English and Irish peasant/slaves to trade class status for Race in America, and after 1700 embracing Whiteness quite literally set them free. That the US is the only country in which Race replaced class this way explains why Americans are so little attuned to issues of class and status and so much attuned to Race (Allen 1994).

What the term "White" has meant over the years—who can successfully claim to be White—has involved a constantly shifting and expanding list of countries on the basis of which people can claim White ancestry. The first to be considered White in the American colonies were the English and Irish. French and German colonists were soon added to the list and then the Dutch. As late as 1920, however, Italian, Spanish, Greek, and Polish immigrants were *not* considered White. A student in the 1990s explained that her mother told her it was only when they left Poland and came to America in the 1980s that they became White. Jews were not considered White until after WWII, and the growth of White nationalism suggests that status is not at all secure. Who counts as White has changed a great deal over the years. Many Latinx/Hispanic and West Indian people who identify as White in their home countries discover that they are not White in the US. A person who was Black or "Colored" before WWII might wake up to find they had become White after the war ended. A Lebanese friend said he woke up after 9/11 to find that the color line had shifted again, and he was now on the wrong side of it for the first time in his life. The only constant has been that even a hint of African or Asian ancestry prevents a person from successfully claiming Whiteness in the US.[19]

There is nothing "natural" about racism. From 1609 to at least 1670 in early colonial America, Race was a relative non-issue. It was social class status that mattered. Africans were not initially enslaved because they were Black, inferior, or "pagan," as most Americans are taught. Anyone who could be purchased and forced to work was made to do so—a practice that continued with the buying and selling of English convicts until the American Revolution in 1775. Being Christian, White, or English was no protection. If a person was low enough down the social class ladder, they were fair game. The English sold their own peasant women and children into slavery. No Race distinctions were made. They called it "indentured servitude." But all forced laborers—whether African, English, or Irish—were sold on auction blocks, and colonial records show that English and Irish laborers were often sold as many as four or five times over a three-to-five-year period (Allen 1994). The death rate was high, nutrition and housing were poor, and punishment was frequent and severe.

The racism we are surrounded by today developed to meet the labor needs of the colonies. We like to believe that the English and Irish had special status as indentured servants, but indentured servitude was no special and considerate institution set aside for White people: it was slavery in most senses, and in early years was often referred to as such. The effort to clean up the terminology came later in response to the abolitionist movement in an effort to create a false narrative about Blackness to support the false claim that Africans had been enslaved because of Race. The indentured slave/servant system was not reserved for White people in any case. There were also African indentured servants who became free at the end of their terms of indenture, and before 1700 free Black people could and did own White people. The early colony had not developed the Race distinction that now divides us. It has become popular to believe that Race prejudice is natural because that belief absolves people of responsibility for it. But it can't be natural if there was a time in American history before Race prejudice had developed (Allen 1994).

Today we can say that the first slaves in Jamestown were White. But during the first seventy years of the colony, that Race distinction did not yet exist, and the few Africans in Jamestown labored alongside their English and Irish brother and sister slaves with whom they acknowledged common cause. Their unity and lack of racism was a problem, however, for their owners. There are many cases in the historical archives involving Irish, English, and African slaves helping one another to escape, steal food, and defend their families (Allen 1994, 1997). English and Irish laborers were sold on auction blocks near the harbor, just as Africans were. African bond laborers (who were mostly men in the early years) married English and Irish bondwomen and were encouraged to do so. There were even advertisements by plantation owners for African husbands for their Irish and English female slaves in the early years.[20] When African laborers became free, they could buy land and slaves to work it for them. Prior to 1700 there were a number of wealthy Black landowners in Virginia and Maryland (former indentured servants who had earned their freedom by serving out their terms) who were successful enough to buy English and Irish slaves to work their plantations. There was no special White status. Black and White slaves stood side by side during early uprisings and rebellions. It was the invention of Whiteness that put an end to this Black/White solidarity and the power it gave American workers to resist unfair labor conditions—leaving all American workers vulnerable to the demands of the wealthy.

The Need for a White Double Consciousness

Because the Black/White racial binary has persisted in American society for nearly four centuries and given rise to clashing interaction orders of Race, social inequalities of Race are likely to be created and re-created in interaction whenever Americans self-identified as Black and White interact with, speak to, or even look at one another. This is particularly evident in public spaces like workplaces and college campuses where Black and White Americans are often thrown together. In keeping with Du Bois, we find that Black Americans—who typically live in both the Black and White worlds—tend to be aware that White Americans are following different rules. As our analysis shows, they don't completely understand what these rules are, but they know *something* different is going on and that it negatively impacts them. White Americans, by contrast, seem to have no awareness of this "doubleness," assuming that everyone is trying to orient toward the same social expectations, but that Black Americans are just not doing it as well.

We equate the Black American insight in this regard with what Du Bois called "second sight" (a feature of double consciousness) and take up the paradox that in response to racism and exclusion, Black Americans have achieved enhanced insight and managed to turn discrimination into a means to prioritize equality—and this is the case regardless of social class status.[21] As a consequence, Black Americans have often led the way in the quest for equality (Ellison 1970).

For White Americans, by contrast, interaction order expectations have negative implications for equality that correspond to class status. The category-based introductory expectations preferred by White Americans that we discuss in chapter 1 inevitably reveal information that will exclude and shame lower-status White people who interact with higher-status White people. In a similar way, the White preference for diplomacy, discussed in chapter 3, is somewhat class based, such that lower-status White people are likely to feel constrained not to complain about things they need to complain about, one of the reasons many supporters have given for admiring Trump, who complains without restraint. The only significant class/status differences we found for African Americans is that those of higher status are more likely to have extensive experience with the White American interaction order (often negative) and, therefore, to have a better understanding of its expectations (which they nevertheless do not adopt).

Any person who succeeds in identifying as a Black American, whether male or female, rich or poor, will experience the forms of racial exclusion we describe, and most will orient toward the expectations of an interaction order we identify with the Black community. By contrast, a person seen by others as Black who tries to identify as White may experience the "colonial mentality" that we have identified with White Americans. Furthermore, in trying to be like White Americans, they will likely experience the oppression of racism without the benefit of double consciousness that comes from the affirmation of a Black American self-identification. Such persons will lack an awareness or second sight about racism. Trying to emulate their oppressors as White Americans do, these Black Americans will typically experience the self-hatred and alienation of the colonial mentality, and will often act in overtly racist ways toward others like themselves.

That White Americans are more likely to suffer from the colonial mentality is not as strange as it may at first seem. The first White slaves in America were bought and sold by the colonial elite: they were a colonized people, and as Scots and Irish, many had also been colonized by the English before being shipped to America as slave labor. But unlike their Black American counterparts, who developed double consciousness, the invention of Whiteness encouraged these former slaves to emulate their rich White oppressors. Consequently, White Americans created no separate nation of their own that could use Race divisions to transcend Race. In fact, current attempts to raise up a "White Nation" are, ironically, based on a 350-year-old racial categorization scheme that *increases* the class and economic disadvantages that working White Americans face rather than transcending them.[22]

The uniquely Race-based character of American society explains why the class-based labor movements of the mid-twentieth century that swept Europe have had little traction in the US among White Americans. Powerful interests have kept White laborers preoccupied with Race, and Race has been skillfully used to subdue White labor movements when they have arisen. Recent scholarship by Kerri Merritt (2017) suggests that the timing of the Civil War was precipitated by the urgent need to squash a growing White southern labor movement in the 1850s that challenged slave owners' monopoly over the southern job market and threatened a general strike of White laborers to end slavery. Having declared war, the White laboring class was immediately conscripted to fight that war (to preserve the slave system they opposed), putting an end to any talk about a strike.

We propose that *White Americans develop their own double consciousness.* It is the experience of being seen as different by those one is trying to identify with while also experiencing a competing positive affirmation of your personhood that creates the experience of doubleness. The research we present in this book is designed to start that process.

Conclusion: Exposing the Fantasy of Whiteness

The 2016 election initiated an outpouring of overt racism and violence toward Black Americans and Latinx/Hispanic "Mexican" immigrants, refugees, and asylum seekers (who are actually from various Latin American countries), accompanied by an intense media discussion of White "discontent" and where it came from. A significant number of White Americans are determined to eliminate privileges and entitlements they falsely believe Others have at their expense. As Metzl (2019) and others have shown, in order to hurt Black Americans (and "Mexicans"), working White Americans are stripping away their own social safety net. The investment in the fantasy of Whiteness that has left many White Americans acting like a "colonized" minority caught the general public by surprise. But it really should not have. Poor, middle-income, and rural White Americans have been the backbone of the modern conservative effort to eliminate their own social services since the 1970s—a modern extension of their colonial role—and they have been very effective in getting rid of every social support they had. Of course they are unhappy. Studies show that since conservatives began dismantling the social safety net and loosening government regulations, the health and longevity of poor and middle-income White Americans have significantly worsened, while their problems with drugs, violence, and incarceration have increased. As a result of these factors, the CDC reported in 2018 that the life expectancy of Americans had declined for three years in a row, with White men experiencing the largest drop. Their racism—their allegiance to Whiteness—fuels an effort to hurt Others that is backfiring on themselves.

The real question is not why so many White Americans are angry, or why they have been so easily manipulated by the 1%. Rather, the question is why Black Americans are so clear about where their interests lie. Why don't Black Americans pretend, as White Americans do, that their interests are the same as those of rich White Americans? (And why is it so easy to recognize the absurdity of the few who do?) The resiliency of the Black American ethos cannot be explained through comparisons to anything else. As Du Bois maintained (1903), the Black American experience is unique. Because of the rigidity of the racial binary it encounters, the experience of double consciousness, and the interaction order it gave rise to, the Black American experience prioritizes democratic principles of inclusion and equality that transcend oppression.

We argue that it is the uniqueness of the Black American experience and the contrast between the interaction order expectations it prioritizes and the status priorities of the White majority that explain both White denial/discontent and Black self-awareness. These contrasting interaction orders correspond with historical aspects of Race as a system of social control in this country that remain deeply embedded in tacit interactional practices in contemporary life.

As processes of racialization in the US became less explicit and more tacit over time, obscured by a thin veneer of "political correctness" and what Eduardo Bonilla-Silva (2003) calls "color-blind racism," the barriers to equality and the exercise of legitimate authority that are deeply embedded in the interaction order expectations of everyday life also became increasingly problematic. Buried deep in the stereotyped assumptions of White Americans, and institutionalized in the taken-for-granted practices of daily life, tacit racism grew stronger.

One of the things that has allowed tacit racism to avoid detection is a research focus on conscious attitudes and formally institutionalized types of racism that ignores what happens in social interaction. Research on conscious attitudes and biases can only measure what people are aware of, and even then it is largely based on statistics and surveys, which obscure the existence of the tacit racism in interaction. *This needs to change.* Not being able to show how racism works in actual interactions makes it difficult to demonstrate that the glaring racial inequalities in American life are the result of institutionalized racism; even given the stark statistical realities involved in "mass incarceration" (Alexander 2011).

Critical Race researchers have documented that unconscious racism and implicit bias are much more prevalent than anyone had thought. However, even this research does not examine the interactional preferences through which unconscious racism is enacted and perpetuated. Our research is designed to reveal how tacit aspects of racism have been institutionalized in everyday interaction in ways that have allowed Race inequalities to reproduce unchallenged. Many people think that if they are not conscious of racism and do not "hate," they are not doing racist things. But they are wrong.

Race inequalities are produced any time the definitions of the situation participants use to make sense together incorporate expectations about interaction and identity that embed Race. These differences are social, not psychological, and they institutionalize tacit structures of expectation that are not individual. That tacit interactional processes are forms of institutional racism is not a new idea, already evident in Everett Hughes's (1945) observations of how racial expectations limit the identities African Americans can hold, thereby limiting their life chances. But in the current context, in which racism is typically defined in terms of individual hatred, conscious intent, or implicit bias, understanding how unconscious forms of racism enact deeply institutionalized racial inequalities in everyday interaction has become increasingly important.

The tacit nature of the problem makes ethnographic and qualitative studies that focus on interaction orders (and the cultural framings they embed) essential. Statistical and psychological research is not enough. More research is needed that exposes racism where it lives in interaction and documents how it works. Using different definitions of the situation, Black and White Americans use different social processes in interaction to achieve different social facts: they literally *see* different social objects and recognize different realities, and, in doing so without awareness, reproduce racial inequality. The many definitions of the situation that comprise the foundation of everyday sense-making and the various racialized "framings" of identity and meaning they contain have deep histories. They are the result of centuries of slavery and segregated living in conjunction with the American Black/White racial binary, and they have carried old ideas and frames of reference about Race into contemporary interaction.

We look closely at how the interactional expectations that developed among Black Americans support a robust independent and egalitarian domain of self, sense, and community in the context of these restrictions, contrasting these expectations with those of the White majority, which embed the values of a society based on hierarchy, individualism, competition, and financial success: treating the rich and successful as more valuable, interesting, and deserving than the poor ("losers"). We take a close look at what happens when Black and White interaction order expectations clash, arguing that when they do, and self and sense-making become problematic, racial categories are given fresh life and racism is reactivated, further dividing the nation (see also Rawls and David 2006).

Pretending the problem doesn't exist, pretending to be "color-blind," makes it worse.

Before we can have an effective national conversation about Race, before we can effectively accomplish the needed "truth and reconciliation" that could repair our divided nation, we need to understand how tacit interactional racism works. An obvious first step is to develop a general awareness among both Black and White Americans that clashing institutionalized structures of social interaction exist. White Americans need to stop being defensive about this and develop some self-awareness—some White double consciousness—that living in a society founded on racism we are *all* reproducing racism. For White Americans, learning to see their actions through the eyes of Black Others will be a life-changing experience. This experience of double consciousness is where self-awareness and empathy start.

That is what this book is about.

CHAPTER ONE

"White People Are Nosey" and "Black People Are Rude"

Black and White Greetings and Introductory Talk

When I acted White she said I was the friendliest Black person she had ever known.
—Black college student

In this first chapter, we examine greetings and introductory talk in interactions between Black and White Americans, treating the differences as an illustration of the conflicting interaction order expectations manifest in tacit racism. We find that African Americans prefer introductory talk to respect a firm boundary between public and private that treats all status information as private, also preferring information to be volunteered rather than asked for. These preferences render introductory talk between Black and White Americans problematic because White Americans place a premium on sharing information about social categories at the very beginning of a conversation or relationship, even between strangers, and they prefer to ask and be asked via direct questions, rather than waiting for information to be volunteered. As Thomas Kochman (1981: 97–101) noted decades ago, White speakers seek information. Black speakers, on the other hand, place a premium on personhood and egalitarianism. This is still the case.

Thus, the title of this chapter: from the perspective of Black interaction order preferences, "White people are nosey"—the name we gave the narrative that initially afforded access to the whole realm of interaction order differences we present in this book. It was a lucky break that a Black colleague finally complained to Anne after a long series of questions about what Race differences look like in interaction: "You are just like every other White person, Nosey." His reluctance to answer the information questions White speakers prefer made him seem "rude" from a White perspective, whereas he experienced Anne's White interaction order preferences as "nosey."

In studying introductory sequences between Americans self-identified as Black and White, we found significant differences in expectations about talk and interaction that render mutual understanding between Americans identified with different Races not only problematic, but *impossible* in many cases. Because these expectations are largely tacit—unconscious—people don't realize they have them until they start observing interaction. We refer to these interaction order expectations as *constitutive* because the meaning of the interaction is constituted, or cooperatively created, using these expectations. We also refer to interaction order expectations as *preferred*, by which we mean that they are not just the expected way of doing things, but are required and considered better—even morally better—such that violating the preference not only interferes with sense-making, but conveys negative connotations about moral character.

The interaction order preferences about introductory talk that we identify as White take the form of seeking information about social categories: residence, occupation, marital status, and education top the list. White speakers prefer to locate information about these categories as "things in common" that they can then use to build a conversation on. The interaction order preferences we identify as Black, by contrast, protect category and status information, producing a kind of status equality in the Black community that Black Americans do not often experience elsewhere. Even volunteering status information violates this preference unless the information is needed for the clarification of something in the immediate context of an interaction.

Interaction orders have a strong moral dimension because the mutual coordination of interactional practices is necessary for the social achievement of self and mutual intelligibility, both of which are essential human goods without which we are not recognizably human (Goffman 1959; Garfinkel 1963; Rawls 1987, 2017, 2019). Orientation toward an interaction order is therefore a moral obligation of both self and sense. But because the moral demands of the interaction order preferences of Black and White Americans are different, they often violate one another's moral sense. The Black self faces an additional challenge. As an individual self who is forced to achieve sense and self in two conflicting interaction orders, Black selves are simultaneously held to two different and conflicting sets of moral demands. In order to recognizably construct practices in the White interaction order domain, which is the taken-for-granted mode of interaction in most social institutions in the US, Black Americans need to violate the moral obligations of their own domain. These conflicting moral requirements confront the African American self throughout American society. Satisfying the White Other (as, for instance, by adhering to the expectation to ask for status categories) comes at the expense of violating their own moral commitment to equality. Thus, in addition to racism and exclusion, the Black American experience involves a high degree of moral tension, and this is in addition to the stigma of not having one's talk and identity recognized and understood by White Americans.

The White practice of seeking category information is not random or individually motivated, and neither is the Black reluctance—even refusal—to answer. Both are social obligations within their respective interaction orders, and each makes sense in historical context. Interaction order expectations render interaction stable and meaningful for those who share them in common. While these preferences are not individually motivated, however, when asking questions or refusing to answer them violates the Other's expectations, the violation tends to be explained through narratives that focus on individual (and group) motivation. As a consequence, interaction orders themselves and the role they play in tacit racism are obscured, while the motives that are inappropriately attributed to individuals and/or to entire racialized groups rise to prominence—perpetuating stereotypes about motives and the importance we place on them.

Instead of focusing on attitudes and stereotypes about Race that are the consequence of interactional problems, we argue that the key to understanding racism lies in the interactional details that generate those attitudes and stereotypes. The problem can be stated simply: Because African Americans prefer to avoid categorization, while White Americans prefer to build their conversations by eliciting categories from one another, the way White Americans go about formulating their greeting and introductory sequences constitutes a direct violation of African American interactional expectations and their underlying moral commitments. The same is true in reverse—when Black Americans don't ask and answer questions, White Americans feel they are being rude and unfriendly on purpose. The difficulty is in coming to an understanding of what this looks like, and why it matters so much, that does not lose sight of the unconscious tacit interactional dimension in which it takes place.

The Quest to Document Tacit Interactional Differences

Our search for a way of understanding how and why Race is enacted in social interaction began in the late 1980s. Committed to the idea that all social facts must be achieved during interaction, Anne realized that people must also be enacting Race and challenged herself to find it.[1] At Wayne State University in the early 1990s, a research team was assembled to undertake that work.[2] After some preliminary field research that proceeded via observation and the collection of narratives about Race, we began making audio and video recordings of the sequential details of the interactional preference orders that were being described in the narratives.

The research proceeded in a number of different ways: we did fieldwork, conducted interviews, held focus groups, led alumni and community groups, and videotaped the interactions. The videos from which the transcripts of Black and White introductory sequences in this chapter were made came from a research project in which student volunteers of the same gender participated. The transcripts of introductory talk are from two pairs of women. We avoided mixed-gender pairs so as to keep the focus on Race. We settled students in a room in pairs—White/White, Black/Black, and White/Black—explained the research design and had them sign a permission waiver for us to videotape. We turned on the camera, told them to get to know each other, and left them in the room to talk for five to ten minutes.

The narratives about "nosey White people" that we had already collected had alerted us to the importance of the very beginning of introductory sequences. The challenge was to create a context in which these beginnings would occur as naturally as possible. We had heard some introductions in passing. But getting them on tape was tricky. For any two people, an introduction only happens once in a lifetime and it goes by quickly. We also knew that because the interactional preference orders in play are largely tacit—and unconscious—only coming to consciousness when they fail, the narratives we had collected were likely to have focused on failures, leaving open the question of what successful introductory sequences would have looked like. We wanted to see what it would look like if two Black speakers did a greeting sequence without violating one another's expectations. We also wanted to see what it would look like for White speakers. The introductions we contrived for the research project were designed to show us what kind of talk Black and White speakers preferred, so that we could understand why the variations by Race that were reported in the narratives had been so upsetting.

There is an additional bonus to looking at introductions. People meeting for the first time are strangers (unless they have heard about each other before). The meaning of an interaction between strangers must be achieved over the course of that interaction without recourse to prior knowledge. Participants cannot rely on prior knowledge about each other that they do not have or on symbolic meanings they may not share. Grammar and syntax alone are not sufficient to settle on a single meaning in most cases. Under such circumstances, strangers are forced to cooperate in the use of finely tuned (turn-by-turn) interaction order expectations even more than people ordinarily are. Failure to coordinate this interactional dimension can leave an interaction with no mutual meaning and many negative impressions.

If introductory talk is not produced with an orientation to shared interactional preferences—that is, if it doesn't exhibit an orientation that is recognizable as an orderly practice to all parties—it cannot be mutually understood. This is the strong sense of "local order" involved in the conception of interaction order: a practice is only mutually intelligible insofar as it can be recognized by all parties to an interaction, and mutual recognition requires that a practice be *witnessable* in its orientation to a preferred order in a way that can be recognized by others. The weak sense of social order, typically indicated by the term *norms*, says only that aspects of social practice are typical, valued, or representative, not that they are necessary for or "constitutive" of understanding. In this sense, the constitutive expectations we examine are much stronger than norms because the penalty for violating them is built-in: they are self-organizing (Rawls 1989, 2019).

Because the constitutive interaction orders we focus on are local—and emerge *from* the needs of interaction rather than being imposed *on* interaction by large-scale "macro" structures—they take a different form in different places and situations. Because Black and White Americans rarely have extended interactions with one another, the interaction orders they are familiar with will have emerged separately without much contact between them. As Du Bois (1903) noted, Black and White Americans inhabit separate worlds side by side. We argued in the introduction that the "doubleness" involved in experiencing both social worlds is something African Americans are aware of, while White Americans for the most part are not. Not only do White Americans typically not see both worlds;

they often believe that "seeing" Race is itself racist—committing themselves to *pretending* they are color-blind—when the society they live in and the practices they engage in every day embed racism at almost every turn. What we need is to see more of the Race in our actions—not less.

White Greeting and Introductory Sequences

We collected many Black and White introductory sequences and narratives we were told about them. For reasons of space, we chose to focus on one transcript of each kind—referring to them as illustrations of a type. Following these illustrations, we examine a selection of the narratives we collected about problems with introductory talk in order to explore the differences further. Obviously every introductory sequence is different in many ways. But we argue that there are preferred characteristics of what we refer to as the Black introductory type and the White introductory type that are essential to achieving mutual understanding.

In presenting and analyzing these transcripts, we follow the conventions of conversation analysis and the Jeffersonian transcription system.[3] The first transcript we present illustrates a White introductory sequence of the preferred type that was videotaped during the research project at Wayne State University. As soon as the researcher left the room (line 7), the two White female participants (Sue and Mia—both pseudonyms) began to establish categories that they fit into: Where do you *live* around here? (line 9); What are you *majoring* in? (line 21); What *year* is this for you? (line 25); What are you doing for a *job*? (line 30); So what do you *major* in? (line 38).

It is important to note that the information exchange proceeds via asking category questions, not by volunteering information. White speakers do not generally volunteer information that is not asked for. They prefer to ask and be asked. Black speakers, by contrast, prefer to volunteer information. To say that these are preferences means that the occurrence or non-occurrence of "volunteering" and "asking" has implications for both meaning and the assessment of moral character and mutual commitment. Preference means that the expectation is constitutive of understanding such that the implications of the same "move" are different in a Black introductory sequence than they would be in a White introductory sequence.[4] White speakers *should* ask. If they *don't*, it means something and is "accountable." Black speakers *should not* ask. And if they *do*, it means something and is "accountable."

"WHITE PEOPLE ARE NOSEY" AND "BLACK PEOPLE ARE RUDE"   39

Two White Women (R is the researcher)

1.	R:	Okay, so why don't you grab a seat here and just—um—take a
2.		few minutes to get t'know each other and I gotta check on the
3.		other—um—students and I'll be back.
4.	Sue:	Okay
5.	Mia:	Okay
6.	Sue:	Allrye
7.	Mia:	Hh hh hh: ((sound of door closing))
8.		(2.0)
9.	Sue:	So um: (.) do you live around here
10.		(1.0)
11.	Mia:	Ah: (.) yeah (.) no
12.	Sue:	no
13.	Mia:	No, I have t'drive but I don't, like, live here—I live in Canton.
14.		Where do you live?
15.	Sue:	Um, Dearborn.
16.	Mia:	Oh really?
17.		(1.0)
18.	Mia:	Hmm . . .
19.	Sue:	On da west side origh:[t hh hhh]
20.	Mia:	[hh hh hh]
21.	Mia:	Yeah what you're majoring in?
22.	Sue:	Um, I'm not really sure, probably social work
23.	Mia:	Oh reall[y]
24.	Sue:	[yeah]
25.	Mia:	What year is this for you?
26.	Sue:	Well I have a BFA in, umm, natural Fine Arts in literature (and theater)
27.		and I'm just, um, pre- ( ) so I'm (planning) t'hh back to schoo::l
28.		I think social work but—um—my job doesn't allow me
29.		to really go full time right now.
30.	Mia:	What're you doing for a job?
31.	Sue:	Um, I work at Second City.
32.		(0.5)
33.	Mia:	Oh do you?
34.	Sue:	Yeah so I'm tired. It's just demanding of time and [energy]=
35.	Mia:	[Right]
36.	Sue:	=and so is the social work department so I can't do both s[o]
37.	Mia:	[hh heh heh heh-hh]

38.	Sue:	So what do you major in?
39.	Mia:	Dietetics.
40.		(2.0)
41.	Sue:	Cool.
42.	Mia:	Yeah.
43.	Sue:	Like, for the nutrition[n]
44.	Mia:	[y]eah.
45.	Sue:	Cool.
46.		(1.0)
47.	Mia:	Yea[h]
48.	Sue:	[a]nd ah how far are you in it?
49.	Mia:	Ah, this is my—um—I started in the fall.

It is characteristic of a White introductory sequence that the two women begin by taking turns asking a series of questions of one another. After Sue asks where Mia lives (line 9), Mia answers (lines 11, 13) and then asks a series of questions. Then Sue takes over again at line 38 and asks basically the same series of questions (which continue past the end of the transcript). Neither woman self-discloses information about something she has not been asked about.

In this typical White sequence, there is only one apparent exception (lines 14–20) where Sue volunteers information (line 19). However, it is not actually an exception. Sue volunteers information here. But only after Mia has made two assessments of her answer and then paused (lines 16, 17, 18), which indicates that she is having trouble understanding Sue's answer about where she lives (line 15, "Um, Dearborn"). The topic is sensitive. In fact, it involves Race. The assessments and the pause prompt a clarification. Better information is required. Some local background is also needed here. Dearborn is a large area that is predominantly Arab. Sue, who is White, appears to have identified a Black/Arab location as where she lives. Her eventual clarification that she lives on the "west side" is an indication that she is aware of the racial overtones of the "confusion" Mia is having, and that she does live in a White area. But she also understands the racial implications of the question and resists them. Sue requires three prompts before she volunteers this information that she has not been directly asked for. This indicates both her awareness of what is at issue and her unwillingness to volunteer a clarification. She is making Mia ask for it. It is interesting that in the context of a racial sensitivity, Mia was also reluctant to ask a direct question that is otherwise preferred.

In the transcript of a Black introductory sequence that follows, there is a similar apparently dispreferred turn sequence: another exception that proves the rule. It is also a request for information following confusion. That this direct questioning is dispreferred is indicated by the apology (line 33). This is what it means to say that asking questions is dispreferred and therefore an accountable matter among Black speakers.

Whereas the African American preference is for avoiding information that would locate persons in a social hierarchy, White greeting sequences like the one between Sue and Mia focus on what might be called category information: that is, information that aids in placing people into status and role categories. As Goffman maintained, the meaning of many words and actions depends on the *definition of the situation* one holds and the *role* or *identity* one assigns to a speaker. White interactants focus on getting the information they need to settle identity issues and place people in a White-dominated status hierarchy, and White interaction order preferences reflect that. In a study that focused exclusively on White college students, Douglas Maynard and Don Zimmerman (1984: 309) even suggested that "categorization sequences are required conversational and cultural forms for generating 'personal' or autobiographical talk among unacquainted parties in such settings." In the absence of shared biographical information in conversations among White college students, they argue, categories are necessary to provide shared context. They noted (1984: 309–11) that when such information was either not forthcoming or not asked for, there were noticeable troubles in sequences between the White college students they studied. There were long silences, topics changed frequently without going anywhere, and the expected "*sensitivity* to co-participants" was not displayed.

This is an illustration of the unnoticed role that Race and racism play in social research. Not taking Race into account as a possible factor, Maynard and Zimmerman have mistaken a White preference for a necessity. Black American speakers routinely interact without exchanging category information, and they do so without experiencing the troubles that the White college students in their study experienced. This shows that category information is *not necessary*. It is merely preferred by the White interaction order, which is structured around such information.

African American Greeting and Introductory Sequences

African Americans do not exchange category information the way White speakers do, and they do fine without it. Moreover, when categories (particularly status categories) are exchanged, they tend to be volunteered, rather than asked for, and only volunteered when they are immediately relevant to the discussion. The Black American greeting and introductory sequence prefers to proceed on the basis of talk about immediately available public matters, rather than category identifiers: what we can see, hear, smell, and so on, in the immediate surroundings. Whereas, according to Maynard and Zimmerman (1984: 304–5), talk that focused on the immediate setting seemed to function as a technique for avoiding intimacy and maintaining anonymity in the conversations they observed between White college students, African Americans report that talk which focuses on the immediate surroundings is respectful of them as persons and therefore preferred. It is easy to see how this would lead to problems in cross-Race interactions. The quest for category identifiers is treated by Black Americans as devaluing their personhood, while the avoidance of category identifiers is treated by White Americans as avoiding intimacy. *The Black preference in this regard is the complete reverse of the White preference.* Avoiding categories leads to intimacy among African Americans, whereas it is treated as a way of avoiding intimacy by White Americans. The consequence of this difference in interactional expectations is that a Black American doing a preferred introductory sequence would be seen as trying to avoid intimacy by a typical White speaker in a typical White introductory sequence.

While it is necessary for all parties to orient toward the same interactional expectations in order to make sense together, it is *not* necessary to do so by establishing categories as our White students Sue and Mia did. Conversations can proceed on other grounds as long as the preference is shared. The process only requires all parties to make a commitment to the *same* orders of preference combined with an interaction order that is sufficiently egalitarian to support the required reciprocity. By not relying on category identification as the foundation for conversation, Black Americans are engaging in a purer form of reciprocity that allows for more equality because it depends more exclusively on exhibiting preferences and moral reciprocities face-to-face and move-by-move.

The transcript below illustrates a preferred Black introductory sequence from the same Wayne State University research project. In this sequence, after the researcher makes the introduction and the two women exchange names (lines 6–7), the two Black women participants (Rita and Tania—both pseudonyms) focus their introductory talk on the immediate interview setting (lines 9–21). It is not until line 29 that any category information (age) is asked for—and then only because a piece of information that was volunteered (first year at school, line 26) conflicts with what is observable in the immediate setting.

Two Black Women, Rita and Tania (R is the researcher)

1.	R:	Sit right here. We'll be back in a few minutes, but sit across from here.
2.		You guys get to know each other and I'll be back.
3.	Rita:	OK
4.	Tania:	ok ((softly))
5.	Rita:	Hello
6.	Tania:	Hi. I'm Tania.
7.	Rita:	I'm Rita. How you doing?
8.	Tania:	Fine. How are you?
9.	Rita:	A'right(.) I'm curious as to what this, um, what this—questions
10.		that we're doing ...
11.	Tania:	What's this interview about?
12.	Rita:	I don't know.
13.	Tania:	Oh.
14.	Rita:	I don't know either ((laughter))
15.	Tania:	What's they got the tape on? ((whisper))
16.	Rita:	Um, we're being filmed in audio and video.
17.	Tania:	Uh oh. We on TV? He he he he
18.		(1.0)
19.	Tania:	How they s'posed to stop us if they not in here?
20.	Rita:	The lady came in and just started it so I'd assume that's how she
21.		wants it to be.
22.		(1.0)
23.	Tania:	You in this class?
24.	Rita:	Mm.
25.	Tania:	Oh. Ok.
26.	Rita:	Well, this is my first year at school—, at school.
27.	Tania:	Really?
28.	Rita:	Mn.
29.	Tania:	You just graduated high school?
30.	Rita:	No please, girl, I'm 29. [I'm almost 29]
31.	Tania:	[Oh I was about to say]
32.	Rita:	I'll be 29 in two days.
33.	Tania:	Oh, ok.

34.	Tania:	I blew that one. Huge ((nervous laughter))
35.	Rita:	Mm.
36.	Tania:	What, you was goin' somewhere else?
37.	Rita:	No, I just started back to school. This is my freshman year.

Rita and Tania introduce themselves at lines 5–7 by greeting each other and volunteering their names. At lines 7, 8 and 9, they exchange a ritual "How you doing?" "Fine. How are you?" "A'right." Then following a slight pause, Rita (lines 9–10) volunteers that she is curious about the project they are participating in. Tania responds (line 11) with a question that echoes lines 9–10, "What's this interview about?" to which Rita (line 12) responds, "I don't know." They continue focusing on the immediate situation, making comments and asking questions about the project, the room, the "lady," and the "class" they are both in, until they get to line 25.

They don't ask any of the White category questions that Sue and Mia asked. The question asked at line 22, about whether Tania is in the class, is relevant to their immediate participation in the setting. But then Rita (line 25) *volunteers* a status—that this is her first year at school. This statement creates a confusion that makes other category information (age) relevant. Rita does not look that young. The confusion elicits an assessment from Tania "Really?" (line 26), clearly expressing disbelief. The assessment implicates a category, age, that wasn't already established, but Tania doesn't directly ask for it. Rather she hints.

Kochman (1981: 99–100) refers to the process of hinting that information is desired as *signifying*.[5] This practice of signifying enables Black speakers to get information when needed without having to ask a direct question to get it (which they would not do if asking was preferred). In this transcript, the question that initiated this sequence (line 22) is not about an unknown category, age, but about an already-established category, "member of the class." The information volunteered at line 25, however, "this is my first year at school," creates confusion. The response by Tania (line 26), "Really?," and then the query (line 28), "You just graduated high school?," work as assessments of a category already in play, "first year" in college. Rita responds (line 29), "No please, girl, I'm 29." Tania then says (line 33), "I blew that one," which is followed by nervous laughter. On line 35 Tania again asks a question: "What, you was goin' somewhere else?" which continues the search for an explanation of Rita's age as a first-year student. It is important to note about this series of questions that they are pursuing a *clarification* of information that has already been volunteered, and even then they use fairly open-ended questions. Tania does not directly ask Rita for a category, and Rita *never does supply one*. Her answer, "No, I just started back to school," which minimally addresses the age factor without explaining the interval between high school and college, is treated by Tania as adequate and she drops the issue.

Even though from a White interaction order perspective a lack of category information might be said to have caused a problem of the sort that Maynard and Zimmerman predict (lines 28–33), the confusion is occasioned by a statement that conflicts with the way Rita looks, not by a lack of category information. Furthermore, the speakers continue speaking and resolve the issue without asking for categories. Unlike White Americans, who tend to ask more category questions to solve such problems, African Americans resort to signifying and other subtle ways of letting the other know when missing information is confusing them (Kochman 1981: 99–100). In this case, category information was volunteered: college student, freshman, age. But it was not asked for. And those categories were all available in the immediate setting. Take age, for example. Age was made relevant by the contrast between "first year at school" and what the speaker, Rita, looked like (too old to be a first-year student). The conversation makes it clear that this inconsistency was *visible* to both participants in the immediate setting.

Whereas the preferred White sequence has several clearly identifiable elements that usually come up (where you live, what you do, education, marriage, children), although the order may vary, there are no such identifiable elements of a preferred Black introductory sequence. Because of its focus on the immediate setting, it will change a lot from setting to setting. What can be said is that the participants, avoiding the use of institutional and bureaucratic categories, will focus on things in the immediate environment that offer themselves as possible topics of conversation, such as "You in the class?" "What's this interview about?" "How you doing?" One African American woman, in commenting on a White introductory question that she found offensive ("What brought you to the conference?"), told us: "If that White person hadda talked about how they had been brought together, it might get a better reception because we are dealing in the here and now from there." What she was objecting to was being asked why she was there, a question with status implications. While Maynard and Zimmerman (1984: 304–5) found that between White college students, a focus on the local setting was treated as a way of avoiding intimacy, we find the mirror opposite in a Black greeting sequence: *a focus on the here and now of the local setting is preferred* between African Americans.

"White People Are Nosey": The Initial Narrative

The first clue to these interactional differences had been the complaint from a colleague that "White people are nosey." Recognizing it as an account about trouble, we began to look for the source of the trouble. When we said this to Black people, we could see that it meant something to them, and it usually made them laugh. To a White researcher, it meant nothing at first. We found that we could say "White people are nosey" to Black friends, secretaries, and students, and they would laugh about it and then tell a story. We were using the "coat hanger" method devised by Harold Garfinkel (2002) for getting access to the details of interactions that the researcher does not understand. The story is the coat hanger on which others can hang their return story. If "White people are nosey" meant something to a person, they would tell us a story and we would learn something more about what it meant. If not, we would get a blank look, heads turning from side to side, bewildered expressions, shoulders shrugging, and that would tell us who didn't know about it. The Black people we said it to *all* had stories for us, and the stories had a common feature: White people asking them for information in ways that made them uncomfortable. No White person we told it to gave us back a story; they didn't know what it meant.

One Black student was a teacher at a private school for wealthy White kids. She stood up in class to tell her "nosey" story and said that on Monday mornings the kids are always nosey. What did they do? Well, when they walked in the door Monday morning after the weekend, they would say, "Hi, teacher. What did you do this weekend?" The other Black students in class immediately indicated that they understood the problem. The White students looked around in a bewildered way. They had no idea why this would be a problem.

The young Black teacher telling the "nosey" story did not recognize "Hi, teacher. What did you do this weekend?" as a ritual greeting. To her it was a request for information. She did not have the option—in her interaction order—to just say, "It was great; how about you?" From her perspective, a question that appeared to be asking for information *was* asking for information. Because asking for information violated her sense of moral propriety, she began thinking about why the students would ask her for this information. She explained that she had decided that because they were all rich and White, they were making fun of her because she was poor and Black and had done nothing that or any other weekend. We explained that in the White interaction order, it was a ritual greeting and that probably none of the students had done anything much themselves most weekends. They were probably not expecting her to give them the details of what she had done. More likely, they were just being "friendly." This possibility came as a big surprise to the Black students in class.

Over and over again in our research, we found that Black students, professionals, teachers, and friends had been sharing narratives about White behavior. They shared these narratives because they were trying to make sense of behavior that they found "strange." It is when interactions are "troubled" (expectations do not match, turns falter because participants are not sure what is being said) that narratives and stereotypes are invoked. While these narratives were widely shared in the Black community, however, what they described had little to do with White behavior as White people understand it. Trying to understand how Black Americans were seeing and interpreting White behavior was the beginning of what we call developing a White double consciousness. Although it took a while to understand this, Black Americans were correct that the orientation of White talk *was* toward revealing status categories. In a preferred White introductory sequence, elements of social status are quickly revealed such that low status and other stigmatizing identity issues (like unemployment, single-parent status, homelessness, mental illness, drug addiction, and prison experience) are exposed. It is not the conscious intention of a White greeting sequence to shame people. The revelation that it does so was upsetting.

The White Americans we talked to seemed to have no idea that there are two ways of doing things, and they attributed interactional troubles they encountered in cross-Race interaction to the *inadequacies* of individual Black participants. Black Americans, who were aware that White Americans do things differently, had developed narratives about *why* White people do what they do in interaction, but these narratives were usually wide of the mark. When we explained that asking category questions was just a normal and expected White way of being friendly that used categories to build common ground, Black participants were surprised. The discussions became very interesting at this point. But in the end, most Black participants thought that the practice was just wrong: immoral.

Acting White for a Class Assignment

Anne asked students to complete an exercise that involved imagining that they changed Races and then engaged in an interaction using the interaction order expectations of the other Race. Black students should imagine orienting toward a White interaction order, and White students should imagine orienting toward a Black interaction order. One Black student who described herself as *very* skeptical that there really was a difference in interactional preferences had an interesting experience with the assignment that she wrote up and reported back to the class. She did not believe we could be right about the interaction order differences we described. In particular, she couldn't believe that anyone would consider the White preference for asking personal and category questions to be normal. It wasn't normal to her. She decided that one way to challenge us was to not just imagine an interaction, but to have an actual interaction using the White interaction order as we had described it in class and see whether a White person would really consider her "White" behavior to be normal.

For her exercise, this Black woman sat down next to a White female student in the student center and initiated a conversation—something that she said she would not have done otherwise. Because we had told her that White people get to know each other by asking a series of questions—and she was pretending to be White—she began by asking questions. She said it made her feel weird, but she did it. At points in the conversation where the White student asked her for personal information (that she would *never* normally have given), she either gave real answers or made stuff up based on relevant life experience (if the real answers made her too uncomfortable), just to see what would happen. At the end of an hour-long conversation, she reported back to the class that the White girl she had been talking to turned to her and said, "I hope you don't mind my saying this, but you are the friendliest Black person I ever met." It was a really interesting class. This student had started out to prove us wrong. But when she used what we had described as White interaction order preferences, her Race was not the barrier to conversation across-Race that it often had been in the past. Even though she understood this, however, she felt so strongly that the preferred White way of talking was morally wrong that she said she would not adopt it. This is very important, it goes back to the moral foundation of double consciousness in creating an egalitarian community in the face of racism.

Luckily, it is not necessary for Black people to act White or for White people to act Black to bridge interaction order differences. What *is* necessary is to recognize that more than one set of expectations are being used, and that it is the clash between them that is leading to misunderstanding. Understanding this, we can step back, stop attributing motivations to each other when things go wrong, and focus on how we have violated each other's expectations. In this sense, information about interaction orders and their relationship to tacit racism is an essential foundation for the national conversation about Race that we all need to have. Why is asking for information offensive to Black Americans? Why is refusing to answer a problem for White Americans? Having had many conversations and led workshops and sensitivity trainings focused on these issues, we know that discussing these questions does lead to mutual understanding.

The African American Focus on the Immediate Setting

The preference for focusing on the immediate setting was highlighted when African Americans were asked to role-play a Black greeting and introductory sequence with a stranger. These role plays occurred both in the classroom and in research settings. The invariable response from Black participants was "Where are we?" Before they could initiate a greeting and begin an introductory sequence with a stranger, they needed to know what setting we were imagining they were in and what was going on around them. We described a variety of imaginary settings for the role plays: a line for pizza at Little Caesars, a line at the bank, a table in the cafeteria, and so on, in all of which we had overheard White people engaging in introductory sequences. To most of the settings we came up with, Black participants responded that they would never initiate a conversation with a stranger in that setting. So they couldn't do the role play. We had to keep brainstorming to find imaginary settings in which they could conceivably even begin a conversation with a stranger.

By contrast, when we asked White participants to role-play, they would immediately begin to produce a preferred White greeting and introductory sequence without asking for any information about the setting. We could tell them someplace we imagined they were, and they didn't need to know anything more. They would just begin talking. We had heard conversations like these on campus. One of the most memorable was between two White women standing in a line at Little Caesars whom Anne heard introduce themselves right after they got into the line—so we knew they didn't know each other previously. The wait might have been as long as five minutes. By the time we stepped away from them to order, they had compared academic majors and families, discovered their mothers had both died of cancer, and begun comparing their experiences taking care of their fathers and siblings while also going to school full-time.

It was an amazing conversation—all in less than five minutes. But when we described it to Black students, they all told us that this would never have happened with them. It's not just that the personal topics (health, cancer, mother dying, taking care of father) were taboo and would never have been shared with a stranger. The bigger problem for them was that they would not have initiated a conversation with a stranger in the first place in such a setting.

In response to our prodding, Black students would suggest places where they felt they *might* engage in introductory talk with a stranger. There were some common themes. The setting must be rich in potential conversational topics, because the topics must be drawn *only* from what is available in the surrounding environment. Therefore, Black participants would look for such potential topics in the immediate environment before they would initiate an interaction. The potential topics must be "public" and focus only on what is present *here and now*. One pair of African American women chose for their role play a line in which they were waiting to register for courses (back before this was done by computer). They were then able to role-play a conversation about the university and their respective courses. They explained that they were able to do this because the *purpose of the line* made these topics *immediately relevant*. The long multi-hour wait also made conversation with a stranger more than ordinarily welcome.

The importance of a focus on the here and now was often mentioned by participants in our research scenarios as an essential element in an African American introductory sequence. One Black woman who lived in a wealthy White suburb and was on the board of directors of several White suburban organizations with one of the authors explained that the differences between preferred Black and White greeting and introductory sequences continued to be a problem for her, even after many years of serving on such boards. When White people approached her with a typical White greeting involving what she referred to as a "string of questions," she understood that she was expected not only to answer the string of questions, but also to ask a string of questions of her own in return. She could manage to answer the questions. However, she balked at asking the kinds of questions she knew White Americans expected of her. Instead she employed the strategy of substituting a vague question like "What would you be doing if you were not here?" for a question like "What do you do?" She also described using strategies for bringing the conversation back to the here and now—getting it off of the string of questions—so that she felt more comfortable.

Another Black woman who participated in one of our workshops illustrated her frustration with trying to be friendly with White people through a narrative about an experience she had attending a conference (mentioned at the beginning of this chapter). During a break she found herself with other participants at a table with a coffee machine and pastries. One of the White attendees whom she did not know initiated conversation with her in this setting, asking, "What brought you to the conference?" This Black woman told us that she was insulted by this. She asked us, "Why did she need to know why I was there? Wasn't it good enough for her that I am a person and I was there?" and explained that what she expected was to have her "personhood" respected. From her perspective, asking her *why* she was there raised questions about her job and the legitimacy of her attendance.

We asked her what she would have done differently. She said she would "come up with a comment" about what's going on, or "I will say, 'Let us talk right now.'" The question "What brought you to the conference?" was asking about things that were not available in the immediate environment. This was a problem for her. She told us:

> I had to find a way round it because *it was very intimidating*. Um, whatever reason I am here, or if I have been selected to be here, or whatever reason they brought me here, the fact is that I am here. So, accept me as this. There's never—*the acceptance is not there.*

This woman referred to questions seeking basic introductory information as "very intimidating" and expressed the feeling that the legitimacy of her presence was being questioned. White participants, by contrast, would typically treat such questions as seeking category information on which to build a conversation—without realizing that such questions do ask them how their social status got them there. However, for this Black woman, a question about *why* she is at a conference, which is by implication about her *job*, is immediately recognized as a question about her qualifications to be there—which to her indicates that she is *not accepted* as a person. Her preferred emphasis is on what is happening "right now." In that setting, questions about the coffee, pastries, or the talk they had just heard would have been preferred from her perspective.

When she explained her reaction as "Don't ask me why I am here. Let us talk right now," we could imagine that the White response to this might be a bewildered "But we are talking right now?" From the African

American perspective, however, talking "right now" means *sticking to topics drawn from the immediate environment*, without reference to categories or roles. It means not asking *why* she is there, which requires her to identify her job, role, or scientific/business interest. It means finding things that can be immediately *seen* and *heard* to talk about. For this Black American woman, category questions come across as intrusive and intimidating. It is important to her to bring the talk back to the here and now in which participants exist as equal and uncategorized human beings at this moment. She emphasized this conjunction of "here and now" and "human beings" a number of times. That is what constitutes acceptance and "genuine" conversation for her. African Americans do sometimes exchange information about jobs and residence. But they do so on a voluntary basis and only when it is relevant to the immediate setting they are in. If the information is not volunteered, it is often never exchanged (even over the course of a long friendship).

The typical category questions White Americans prefer were referred to by Black participants as questions about the "past" or about one's *private* or *social* life, as opposed to what is happening "right here, right now" in *public*. This preference for avoiding categories and direct questions is not only *typical*—it is *preferred* and *constitutive*. When questions are asked that violate this preference, African Americans do not recognize them as casual introductory talk. They have described such introductory sequences to us as *insults* and *interrogations*. Because the casual and ordinary character of White introductory talk is not recognizable, African Americans, when speaking with White people who ask category questions, often fall back on interpretations and narratives about the motives of White speakers in trying to make sense of the interaction.

African American participants invariably reported trying to figure out "why those White people can't accept me the way I am." Or they try to figure out "why *they* want to know so much about *me*." One Black man who participated in a workshop on Race we put on for alumni of Wayne State University told us the discussion had given him a new way of understanding a troubling incident that happened to him at work where he was the only Black person. The employees were all looking forward to a group retreat at a beach. He was also looking forward to this day away from the office. Then, he said, "They got me in the car and started pumping me for information." He had arrived at the conclusion that the retreat had been arranged for the sole purpose of getting him into a situation that he could not escape from and then interrogating him. He came to this conclusion, because, he said, as soon as "they got me in the van" to travel to the retreat, they began to "interrogate me." The White participants at this workshop were amazed. From their perspective, the questions were just attempts at "being friendly." From his Black American perspective, however, the category questions were violations of his expectations that must involve a motive. He felt like he had been kidnapped.

The category questions that White Americans prefer do reveal status and stigma. When Anne tried at first to explain that these questions didn't seek to discriminate between categories of people, the response from the Black person she was talking to was "Okay, you are at a party asking your questions and you find out you are talking to the janitor. What then?" Of course the conversation would take a very different turn from there. The White practice of building a conversation on categories people have in common sorts people quickly by status—shaming some and elevating others. It is not an egalitarian practice. But it is so deeply ingrained that this is difficult to accept.

Narrative and Stereotype as Consequences of Miscommunication

When interaction order preferences clash, ordinary conversational "moves" cannot be recognized. Not producing a recognizable version of what is expected prevents the achievement of mutual understanding and calls into question the mutual commitment of participants to each other and to the interaction itself. White participants question the commitment of Black participants and vice versa. When tacit attempts at mutual intelligibility fail between Black and White Americans in the ways described, these failures lead to conscious interpretations and attributions of motivation to the racialized Other (Rawls and David 2006). These interpretations in turn generate more narratives that are shared between those who have the same interaction order preferences and therefore see problems the same way when interaction orders clash. By contrast, when things go as expected, the interactional process remains tacit and taken-for-granted. It is not stereotypes that produce the initial misunderstandings. It is the tacit misunderstandings that produce and invoke the stereotypes. In other words, when tacit interaction orders of Race prevent mutual understanding, they do so in ways that produce, reinforce, and invoke stereotypes.

While we disagree that society consists primarily of narratives (Maines 1993) and would argue that a focus on narrative has tended to obscure the underlying tacit interaction orders without which narrative orders would not be possible, narrative is very important. We think that narrative is especially important in modern society because whenever people who cannot recognize one another's interaction order practices interact, they produce miscommunications that generate narratives. In such cases, narrative interpretation, which is *not* necessary when interactional practices are recognizably produced, does proliferate (Rawls 1987; Rawls and David 2006; Sacks 1992; Garfinkel 1967). When expectations are violated by people whose interaction order preferences are different, conflicting narratives are invoked. Black participants will invoke one set of narratives, while White participants will invoke a contrasting set. Racialized narratives result. Because this sort of conscious interpretation only occurs when recognition fails, however, it operates without benefit of the interaction order practices we ordinarily rely on to make sense. Narrative tells a story about what went wrong that falls back on shared beliefs to make sense of the unexpected. This drives people even further apart when their beliefs are not shared.

In order to end this vicious cycle and understand why cross-Race interactions are going wrong, we need to focus on the tacit interaction order practices of Race—the clashes between that are leading to the problems that generate the narratives.

Conclusion

In this chapter we showed how Americans, divided by the social categories Black and White, but speaking the "same" language and apparently occupying the "same" geographical space, can be divided by Race in such significant ways that they are not able to achieve mutual understanding. If people do not talk and act in ways others can recognize, they cannot understand what Others say and do. This in turn jeopardizes the entire interaction and calls into question the motives, identities, and moral commitments of all participants. In the case of interaction between Black and White Americans whose interaction order expectations are different, each side will have violated the other's expectations. But neither will realize that this is what happened. Instead they will make judgments of the Other's moral character, competence, and motivation.

White Americans, lacking awareness of racial differences in interaction, experience Black Americans as disorganized, less intelligent, and rude—typically ascribing whatever misunderstandings occur in an interaction to shortcomings on the part of the Black Other. While Black Americans are more aware than White Americans that there are differences in how White and Black Americans communicate, and might be said in this regard to have what Du Bois referred to as "second sight" because they are forced to interact in both worlds, they are not clear about how they are being seen by White people, nor are they aware that the problems are due to differences in how interactional expectations are structured. Black Americans typically experience White Americans as nosey and not accepting of their personhood and humanity.

In arguing that these Race differences are tacit ways of acting that have become institutionalized forms of interaction, we are urging the necessity of *a new way of thinking about Race and racism*. We want to shift the focus from the large "macro" structures of inequality and their manifestations in the individual as conscious or unconscious prejudice that have preoccupied the popular imagination, to the embedded expectations of social interaction that render those inequalities consequential over and over again in interaction every day. Black Americans have orderly communities and lives that should be—but are not being—respected. Until that much is understood, tacit racism will continue doing violence to Black Americans and their interaction orders, and the equality and mutual respect needed to achieve racial equality will remain as elusive as ever.

There is an urgent need for White Americans to develop a sense of double consciousness about what is going on: to understand and accept how their actions and identity performances are being seen through Black eyes, and to accept that they really are reproducing a social order that is individualistic and hierarchical rather than egalitarian. As long as White selves are aware of and accountable only to White interaction order expectations, they will not understand what is going on in cross-Race interaction. We all need to know how these interactional preferences differ and why. Everyone needs to know how the two social worlds of interaction are different. And most particularly, from a White perspective, it is important to acknowledge the value of the egalitarian forms of association that are characteristic of the Black American interaction order.

One side of the racial binary is oriented toward promoting solidarity and equality in the face of external oppression and displaying loyalty of the self to the group, while the other is oriented toward the display of individualism in a status hierarchy. This results in two distinct forms of self-presentation—what we call the *categorial self* and the *egalitarian self*—and two different types of community: the community of *competitive strategic individuals* versus the *egalitarian solidarity community* (Rawls 2000). These two forms of self and community not only respect conflicting boundaries between public and private, but ideas like honor, honesty, and equality that are essential to one are not so important for the other.

While there is a great deal of inequality in the world of formal institutions, corporations, and other macro structures, we maintain that at the level of interaction orders, not much inequality is tolerated. Our research on greetings and introductory talk demonstrates the sort of problems that occur in interaction when inequality is too great. The fragility of self and mutual intelligibility require protection. If they don't get it, society will continue to divide and fragment. When persons standing in grossly unequal relations form contradictory interaction orders, they cannot cooperate to make sense together. Thus, mutual intelligibility across interaction orders that have formed as a result of political oppression and inequality is inherently problematic.

As Emile Durkheim argued in *The Division of Labor* ([1893] 1933), without open equal access to what he called "constitutive practices" in modern life, democratic society will fail (Rawls 2012, 2019). In the current context of high levels of political, institutional, and economic inequality, the possibility of open and equal public spaces becomes even more important. Diverse modern societies cannot make progress in science and business, or provide the exchange of ideas needed to support that progress, unless everyone can participate in scientific, educational, political, and work spaces. Without the possibility of interaction across social boundaries in open and equal public spaces, people are forced to fall back on communities of shared belief and narrative in order to communicate. Democracy simply doesn't work under these conditions.

In modern societies, we argue, the interaction orders that make it possible to exchange ideas with strangers have largely replaced traditional beliefs and values as the primary means of sense-making in the public domains of science, business, and work. When those tacit interaction orders are also tasked with handling institutionalized racism, they can't function across group boundaries the way a modern society needs them to. If we cannot get racism out of our daily interactions, we are going to end up back in the seventeenth century.

CHAPTER TWO

"Fractured Reflections" of High-Status Black Men's Presentations of Self

Non-Recognition of Identity as a Tacit Form of Institutional Racism

I didn't answer because I don't trust him. —High-status Black man

This second chapter examines how tacit expectations about Race—which have become institutionalized in an interaction order—can frame how we see Black men and women who perform high-status occupational identities. This framing, we find, leads to many occasions on which their high-status identity performances are not recognized. Americans do not expect Black men and women to have high status (Chou and Feagin 2014). So, they often don't see it. This Non-Recognition of identity is not a small thing. It threatens basic processes of sense and self-making, prevents mutual understanding, threatens the Black achievement of self, and forces the Black men we studied to take evasive action—which we call a "Null-Response." We focused on men to make sure we were seeing a Race effect that was not entangled in gender bias. Because these Black men can retreat into their own interaction order to confirm their sense of self (a process that generates shared narratives), they are not destroyed by Non-Recognition. But it makes their jobs more difficult than they should be. They are constantly faced with inappropriate responses to their high-status identities that test their creativity and ingenuity (Anderson 2011; Moore 2007). The institutionalization of tacit expectations about identity in our everyday working lives means that occupational advancement in the United States is based on Race and not merit. The experience of this inequality in turn reinforces interactional divisions between Black and White Americans that make public spaces difficult and dangerous for everyone: making it impossible for America to function as a democratic society.

Our objective in this chapter is to articulate the empirical contours of what we call "Fractured Reflections" of self-presentation, as a type of interactional event. This event occurs when the person presenting a self gets back from the Other(s) an unrecognizable reflection of their identity performance, not only once, but so often that they come to expect it. Because they expect it, they don't treat it as accurate feedback about something they are doing wrong—but, rather, as feedback they must ignore. We elaborate on the theoretical relevance of this phenomenon given our assumption that self and identity are social facts that must be achieved through what Goffman (1959) called the "presentation of self" in interaction. Approaches that treat the self as a given—as more durable—will miss the significance of this interactional event. As with the shared experiences that Du Bois (1903) drew on for his conception of double consciousness, the phenomena of fractured reflection and null-response that we analyze are currently known primarily as "experiences" about which high-status Black men and women exchange narratives. Little consideration has been given to what it looks like as an interactional event, or to its theoretical, methodological, and political implications.

We argue that as an interactional event, "fracturing" illustrates what happens when people are not using the same definition of the situation, or orienting the same interaction order expectations, and as a consequence can't meet the involvement obligations required for mutual sense and self-making—which include cooperation and reciprocity with others. We propose that the essential back-and-forth process of mutual reciprocity necessary for achieving self and identity turn-by-turn has become racialized, and sense-making has been damaged, by the systematic non-recognition of self by Other(s) in interaction.[1]

When a person enacts an identity that Other(s) are unable or unwilling to see them in, that failure to confirm identity is negative feedback. Ordinarily, people are expected to take negative feedback into account and repair their presentations of self. However, when the feedback is due to an unequal distribution of expected identities by Race, it is a form of institutionalized racism, and Black Americans often refuse to repair their self-presentations when confronted by such negative feedback. While self and sense-making must be continually achieved through mutual recognition and commitment to the constitutive reciprocity conditions of an interaction order (Goffman 1983; Garfinkel 1963; Rawls 1987), Race, gender, and other "categories" can become embedded in expectations about identity such that inequality becomes institutionalized in the expectations that are structured into interaction. Under these circumstances, for a self to take the fractured reflection as an accurate reflection of identity work would mean accepting a racist assessment of self.

While everyone may experience some disconfirming reflections of self, we propose that there is a threshold of frequency beyond which what Garfinkel called "Trust Conditions" (sharing interaction order expectations and trusting that others do as well) cannot be maintained, such that defensive strategies of null-response become likely, particular interactions are broken, and the possibility of future interactions may be jeopardized.[2] Too much negative feedback threatens the integrity of the self and requires defensive action. We argue that most Black Americans experience that threshold and that the practice of null-response is a development of Black interaction order preferences that can protect the Black presentation of self in such instances.

Narrative accounts of this problem circulate widely in the Black community among men and women of all social statuses. Waverly attended a bachelor party at which exchanging narratives about this problem was the main topic among the high-status Black men who attended. We focus on the problem as it is reported by high-status Black men because there seems to be a general belief that high achievement can at least mitigate the experience of racism. We find that it does not. We argue not only that the high-status Black men we studied experience racism on the job, but that the tacit expectations about identity we document follow Black men and women wherever they go no matter how successful they are. In fact, we find that the problem is likely to increase with status, rather than decrease, because of the greater proportion of interaction with White people that high status requires. There are two factors at work: One is the need for a Black boss to be able to count on the tacit acceptance of his superior position and authority by his White subordinates; the second involves the resentment many lower-status White people feel when they see a Black American rise to a higher level of success than they have achieved.

There is an essential moment in the process of the *presentation of self* when a presentation of identity has been made before Other(s) and it is the turn of the Other(s) to recognize, respond to, and ratify that presentation. It is a basic tenet of the interactionism of Charles Horton Cooley, George Herbert Mead, Erving Goffman, and Harold Garfinkel that the integrity, legitimacy, and, in fact, the very existence of the self *as presented* depends on (and can be changed by) that response. The self in this regard is a social accomplishment that requires mutual cooperation from others. Failures to recognize and ratify competent presentations of self, which were reported frequently by the high-status Black men we talked to, threaten to strip them of the social identities they are entitled to and the dignity, power, and authority associated with those identities. This is not only an injustice in the conventional sense, but violates fundamental interactional obligations that Garfinkel (1963) summed up as the trust conditions that undergird the cooperation required to achieve self and mutual understanding. In other words, fracturing violates the requirement that participants use the same definition of the situation, orient the same expectations/rules, extend benefit of the doubt to each other, treat the other as competent, and ratify competent presentational work in order to make sense.

If there is no place in White American society where a Black American, however accomplished, can expect to have their competence and qualifications recognized, then the foundation of the American democratic way of life is fundamentally broken.

Combining Ethnography and Ethnomethodology with a Narrative Approach

The narrative data in this chapter come from interviews with Black men who are all salaried employees with high-status corporate careers. We made a strategic selection of interviewees based on our theoretical concerns relative to Race and high status. Poor Black men are also perceived in negative identities they don't claim for themselves, seen as out of place, told to go back where "they belong," and mistaken for identities they do not claim. Katheryn Russell-Brown's (1998) conception of the "criminalblackman" as an omnipresent framing device is a case in point. But, in spite of earlier research documenting the problems faced by the Black middle class (Bell 1973; Feagin and Sikes 1994; Delgado and Stefancic 2001), there is still a widespread perception today that successful Black middle-class professionals are able to escape from such racializing experiences, at least at their professional worksites.

Our own experience with fracturing suggested the reverse: that, in fact, high-status Black men are very likely to be experiencing fracturing with some frequency; maybe even greater frequency because of the mixed-Race environments in which they work. This is a problem. The question Everett Hughes (1945: 359) raised back in 1945 about Black professionals remains relevant: "In what circumstances can the person who is accepted formally into a new status, and then informally kept within the limits of the kind mentioned [racial limits], step out of these limits and become simply a lawyer, foreman, or whatever?" The answer is with extreme difficulty and at great cost to both the Black self and the Other with whom they interact.

Following an initial experience in the field with a fractured reflection witnessed by both authors, Waverly initiated discussions with nine high-status Black men to explore the phenomenon. When all nine men indicated that they recognized and were familiar with the experience we told them about, we increased the sample, identifying and talking to more than three dozen high-status Black men about the problem of fracturing and non-recognition. It was happening to *all* of them.

Participants were selected based on their executive or professional status and authority. We relied on the networks of the men we interviewed to identify additional men to interview: a "snowball" sampling method. High-status Black men who were known to us were interviewed first and then asked to recommend other high-status men who should be interviewed for the study. All were from the Midwest and Northeast United States. Most were in their mid- to late forties: the youngest was twenty-eight, the oldest sixty-one.

In soliciting their narratives, we used the method described in chapter 1, whereby an initial story becomes what Garfinkel (2002) called a "coat hanger" for collecting similar stories. It is a method for use in exploratory fieldwork when the researcher does not share the situated practices and definition of the situation of the subjects being studied. An initial story is presented and if the person recognizes it, they will tell a similar story. Thus, the method avoids the problem of assuming a shared set of social facts where there may be none. Garfinkel used it to study problems in laboratory science that were beyond his own scientific understanding as a researcher. Employing the method successfully gives the researcher access to narratives that highlight problems in the social interactions through which the social objects and understandings they are interested in are achieved, adding empirical contours to matters that are otherwise inexplicable.

Anne had used this method in earlier research (Rawls 2000) on interracial interaction that we report on in chapters 1 and 3, to turn up a rich vein of narrative about Race issues in interaction that were otherwise invisible from a White perspective (and distorted from a Black perspective). In this case we used it to generate narrative data about a Race problem that we had already observed. If people don't recognize the coat hanger story, they will say nothing, ask for clarification, look puzzled, and so on, as the White people had to whom we told the "White people are nosey" story. The Black men Waverly told the fractured reflections story to all launched immediately into similar narratives, thus indicating their recognition of the phenomenon.

Two stages of interviewing took place. The initial goal was to confirm our sense that the problem is well known and widespread. Every one of the high-status Black men we approached recognized the phenomenon and told us stories about similar experiences of their own, sometimes taking the experience so much for granted that they immediately began talking about "it" and how they deal with "it." In response to our narrative about fracturing, we found they could talk for hours. There was no contradictory information.

The men participated with the intent of discussing their experiences as white-collar professionals: authority figures in predominantly White workplaces. They shared extended personal narratives about being leaders/supervisors in their various occupations. Most of the participants were affluent and well educated; they included corporate vice presidents, physicians, attorneys, architects, engineers, and school principals. While exceptional by any standards, these men nonetheless tended to downplay their accomplishments (which is consistent with Black interaction order preferences).

We followed up with a second stage of more extensive interviewing with nine men to deepen our ethnographic understanding of what fractured reflections look like across a collection of their narrative accounts of various situations. These interviews took from one to six hours, were recorded, and consisted of an extended reexamination of issues raised in their first interview about workplace dynamics. Our initial interviews had established that all of the men were familiar with the phenomenon of fracturing. The extended interviews collected detailed accounts of fracturing as an interactional event.

The narratives we selected for this chapter are intended to exhibit the empirical contours of this fracturing process. We did not distill a theme from the data or select one theme from many. But rather we aimed to present fracturing as the men explained it to us. Their narratives were powerful, consistent, and repetitive. Because the narratives are extensive, each involving essential contextual detail, keeping them intact and in sequence to the extent possible was a priority. The context and sequence of events offer insights into what expectations were violated and how a sequence of such events led the men to expect additional instances and to develop defensive strategies over time. In the interest of preserving contextual and interactional detail, and considering the high degree of consistency and redundancy across narratives, we settled on an extended discussion of narratives from three interviews.

It is a matter of both theoretical and ethnographic significance that the high-status Black men we talked with *all* reported adopting the defensive strategy of null-response to protect themselves from fractured reflections. These men do not take fractured reflections as accurate indicators of their own competence, as they would if they accepted the legitimacy of the Other's response to them. Rather, they treat these responses as distortions for which they hold the Other responsible. They perform a null-response in the face of non-recognition of their identity performances. These null-responses range from refusal to acknowledge or ratify the Other's response to them, to complete withdrawal from interactional reciprocity, and even refusal to acknowledge the Other's presence. Remaining committed to the constitutive requirements of interaction would require them to take responsibility for the distorted reflection of themselves, which would result in damage to self. Because of the racism and lack of reciprocity involved (White people unable to see how their responses look through Black eyes), the trouble is not reparable. So these Black men withdraw. This is one of the big differences between the Black American experience of double consciousness and the colonial mentality (discussed in the introduction) as it is treated in the literature on colonialism by Frantz Fanon (1952) and others. These Black men do not—cannot—measure their competence by the same yardstick their White coworkers use.

The stories that circulate about this process of non-recognition and null-response have the virtue for the researcher of exhibiting points of violation, or breach. These violations can be seen by all parties. But each side will make different sense of them according to their different framings, interaction orders, or definitions of the situation. Operating without benefit of trust conditions or shared background expectations, the problems at these points cannot be resolved by participants through mutual effort; they lack the means. In the narratives we collected, the men report subjecting these problems to repeated analysis, which further underscores their irresolvable character. We argue that these points of breach, *where things don't make sense*, are essential data for understanding how processes of racialization work tacitly in interaction and how they can do so without conscious intent. Moreover, the narratives we collected represent only the tip of the iceberg—a widespread sharing of narratives about identity problems among high-status Black men and women who confront a common problem.

Conventional ethnographic and qualitative methods are likely to overlook these points of breach and violation, taking meaningful social objects and identities for granted as if they just existed. What is needed is to recognize their character as mutual achievements that need to be accomplished through cooperative action (in observable empirical details) each next time. An approach like ethnomethodology that regards violations as clues to the underlying expectations and definitions of the situation people are using to make meaningful social objects together—to make sense together—treats the existence of a corpus of such narratives in a community as important information. Indeed, the existence of a large body of these narratives suggests a recurrent problem that is serious enough to be repeatedly talked about.

Empirical Contours of Fractured Reflections

The narratives recount situations in which the high-status Black men we talked with had trouble getting their identities recognized: employees did not recognize their status as the boss, did not do the work they were asked to do (or checked with others first to see *whether* they should do it), and/or would not follow their instructions. Various accounts of why this might be happening also appear in the narratives, highlighting the inability of these men to make sense of the events in a normal taken-for-granted way. Their attempts at interpretation are revealing of how failures to achieve shared meaning can reinforce group stereotypes about Race. Some parts of the narratives relate the Black executive's own interpretation of why it happened. Other parts report accounts they were given by their White employees. The latter exhibit the White employees' uncertainty as to whether or not the Black executive is the person who should be telling them what to do (Kochman and Mavrelis 2009). The narratives all involve situations in which an employee's definition of the situation does not include the Black executive as an identity with the authority to give them instructions. By contrast, the definition of the situation the Black executives are working with (and the one their bosses are working with) *requires* these Black executives to manage and give instructions to their own employees.

These high-status Black executives describe unexpected and inappropriate responses to their identities that they learn to "ignore" and "brush off": White people treating them as interchangeable with other Black people is something they learn to "expect." They describe various ways in which they are treated as incompetent and emphasize the importance of vigilantly "not trusting" those whose responses confront them in ways they consider unfair and disconfirming. They describe being constantly "on guard" in interactions, both at work and with White people more generally. While they are all successful and do not detach from the organizations they work for, they express some feelings of alienation and might be said to suffer from what is being called "racial fatigue" and "racial battle fatigue" (Smith 2004): the constant need to monitor both sides of the "veil" that separates White and Black Americans is tiring especially when, as Du Bois pointed out, the White majority these Black men are surrounded by do not even recognize the existence of the problem they face, and consequently cannot cooperate with them to solve it.

While we argue that fracturing is a racialized experience, the men all initially tried to discuss their troubles in a way that downplayed Race. Nevertheless, they offered Race as a contributing factor once they had gotten into their narratives. However, they made it clear that this was a topic they avoided discussing with coworkers, approaching it as an interactional "hot potato." Furthermore, they told us their authority was sometimes questioned by Black employees as well as by White employees—although when this happened, they expressed surprise. The prevalence of a White racial framing of all Black people means that Black employees can adopt the same institutionalized sets of expectations about racialized identity that White employees have, although *most* Black employees are also aware of the importance of racial solidarity as a defense against racism. If we had just asked these men whether they experienced racism on the job (as in a conventional survey), they *would likely* have said no. With a large sample, this could have led to the false conclusion that high-status Black men are not experiencing racism on the job. We are sure that this sort of false result occurs.

From the beginning they were all certain *something* was amiss in their interactions and described both recognition failures and disengaging from those interactions using null-responses.

First Narrative: Robert, Corporate Vice President

The Black male vice president (mid-forties) of a large corporation, whom we call Robert,[3] described problems he has at the office with people who do not recognize his identity and status as a competent vice president. To deal with this, he has developed what he calls "strategies" for getting his job done. These involve expecting the sort of troubles he describes, not treating the non-recognition he gets as a reflection on himself, and not trusting those who respond to him in ways he considers inappropriate.

Robert: His Assistant "Second-Guesses" His Instructions

Robert has a White female office assistant who he says will not do what he asks without "second-guessing" and "checking" to see whether his instructions should be followed. The person she checks with is his boss—the president of the company. Robert expresses his belief that his assistant wants him to succeed. But when he gives her an instruction and she checks with the president, she is implicitly refusing to recognize his identity and authority, which creates problems for him. Robert has already talked to the president and knows what he expects. Thus, if his assistant checks with the president, this makes Robert look incompetent.

Data Excerpt #1: Robert

Okay, the most frequent interactions that I have are with persons who report to me and I have given them either an assignment or I have been given an assignment from my superior and I ask for them to do certain kinds of things where that assignment is concerned and they have a habit of going around me and asking my, actually asking the president of the company, if this is something that he really wants done, or is this the way that he wants it done. And it is couched in, "Well, I wanted to make certain that I was protecting you by asking how the president wants this accomplished." Now I've already been told how the president wants it accomplished and I've already shared that with the person who reports to me, but it is not good enough. She, for instance, in many instances, needs to get it from the president. And I have not witnessed her doing that to anybody else. And then she gets patronizing and says, "I was just doing it to protect you." I don't need her protection, you understand what I'm saying, and so what she does is, she tries to couch her, in my mind insurrection and insubordination, she tries to couch it in being responsible for me.

His assistant's non-responsive behavior indicates to him that she doesn't recognize his identity as company vice president. He considers her behavior patronizing because she acts as if she needs to protect him and as if she knows more than he does. But he is the boss. He considers her response *insubordination* because it denies his identity as her supervisor and refuses to acknowledge the legitimacy of his instructions. Because Robert rejects the relevance of her response for his own identity and competence, however, her non-responsiveness does not damage his self-esteem. However, it does make it difficult for him to perform competently in his role. His own boss may wonder what is going on, and it will make achieving mutual understanding with his assistant increasingly problematic.

Robert: Not Trusting as a Defensive Strategy

When asked what effect this non-responsive behavior on the part of a subordinate might have on Robert's willingness to trust them, he responded vehemently, and with many repetitions (for emphasis), that it leads him not to trust them.

> **Data Excerpt #2: Robert**
> I never trust you. I never trust you. I never ever trust you. I always second-guess your motives. This person, one of these people who reports to me does an outstanding job, outstanding, every "i" is dotted every "t" is crossed, it's outstanding. But the process by which she has gone to do it, she causes me not to trust her, not to trust her. So it becomes exceptionally convoluted, you know, the relationship becomes one of somebody where I need somebody whom I need to be trusting but I can't, but someone who gets her job done and does it exceptionally well, but I still have to question the motivation and all of that. So no, I don't ever trust her.

Robert is describing a *broken interactional process*. He has responded to his assistant's non-recognition of his identity by withdrawing from trust relations with her. When he asks her to do something for him, he does not trust that she will do it, or that she will respond to him as a competent supervisor and vice president. He withdraws trust even though he believes her motivation is to help and protect him. Refusing to ratify a person's presentation of self has negative consequences no matter what the motivation.

Unfortunately, withdrawing from trust relations, although a useful protective strategy, interferes with Robert's ability to deal with these issues directly. Repair work requires trust and mutual commitment. His assistant, who probably can see clearly that he is not happy with her, is likely as a consequence to do more and more to "help" him. Her increased efforts to help, in turn, will again tell Robert that she does not think he is competent, and the cycle will continue. Because trust is lacking and definitions of the situation don't match, the inability to effect a *within-interaction repair* will perpetuate the cycle.

Robert: White People Refuse to Accept That a Black Man Is Competent

Although initially telling us that his problem was not racial, Robert went on to formulate the problems he experiences in terms of the unwillingness of White people to recognize a Black man in a competent identity. He told us that at least he had not had to resort to negative sanctions for the non-responsiveness of employees. If that became necessary, he said, he would have to be meting out negative sanctions to "all kinds of people."

> **Data Excerpt #3: Robert**
> Because one of the things that I have come to realize is that particularly White folk, White people, and I don't know if I'm being too graphic here, but White people simply refuse to accept that a Black man could possibly have the kind of intellectual acumen to get things done without their striving to do those things for us. You know, there's the sense that they are superior.

Like the other men we talked to, Robert is reluctant to express things in terms of Race. Nevertheless, once he got going, he said explicitly that in his experience "White people simply refuse" to accept that a Black man could have the "intellectual acumen to get things done" without their help. He says he senses that White people feel "they are superior."

Second Narrative: George, Corporate Newspaper Executive

George is a young (mid-thirties) up-and-coming executive with a major newspaper. He told us about a number of what he called "strange experiences" of non-recognition with his White coworkers. He was for years one of only two Black executives working for the newspaper and was often mistaken for the other man, his mentor, who was twenty-five years his senior (being mistaken for other Black executives was a frequent complaint from the men we spoke to). After five years with the company, a third

Black executive was hired, and many people congratulated George on his new job. Of course, it was not his new job. People he had worked with for five years could not recognize George or distinguish him from the new Black executive.

In addition to such literal recognition problems, George told stories about trouble he had getting people to recognize his role/identity and to do as he requested. He said he realized early on that his White coworkers didn't think he had earned his position through merit. Following a temporary promotion to acting director of his department (to replace his vacationing boss), he experienced a combination of face-to-face challenges and employees refusing to do what he asked. Although George said he had expected trouble, he was still surprised by the extent of it.

George: Problems as Acting Manager

George's narrative of his two weeks as acting manager of a team of twelve employees includes people in other departments refusing to do the work requested by his department: "not processing paperwork, not processing the client's ads, pushing back on us things that should have been produced to make things stressful for me."

Data Excerpt #1: George
I had a manager who was going on vacation for two weeks.... He chose me to be his acting manager because I was doing such a great job and he felt I could handle the job and the team always really respected me. It was a team of twelve of us. So he put me as the acting manager in his absence for two weeks, which was again, unprecedented, because I was the young Black kid. What happened is, after, you know, while I was in my acting manager's position for those two weeks, a lot of people in the company were not happy with that, and they had no problem making it known by messing with all of the people who worked out of my department, not processing paperwork, not processing the clients ads, pushing back on us things that should have been produced to make things stressful for me, to make me think that "Oh it's so stressful, I shouldn't wanna do this." So they kept making it harder.

While members of his own department (mostly African American women) were working hard for him, his directives were being ignored by employees in other departments. When they didn't run ads as requested, they said things like "Well, we didn't know if they were supposed to run."

We asked George how he found out that people in other departments were not doing the work he had asked for and not placing the ads he sent over.

Data Excerpt #2: George
Oh, it got back to me because the employees who I was over at the time were telling me that things weren't getting processed, their ads weren't getting—some people's ads didn't appear in the paper, some people's online advertising didn't start and they were confused as to why it didn't happen. And then with me being the acting leader, I had to call and check into it, and then as I started calling and checking with people, like, "Okay, what happened with these clients' digital programs?" And they were like, "Well, we didn't know if they were supposed to run." You know, they gave me explanations that did not justify not putting them in, and then I explained to them that, you know, I let them know that I could tell that their reasoning wasn't appropriate for not taking the actions that they should have. So they was really trying to stir up problems, you know, missing ads, which cost the department money, which made me look bad under my leadership.

According to George, they said they "didn't know if [the ads] were supposed to run." He considered that their "explanations didn't justify their actions." This made him think "that this was something against me personally."

Data Excerpt #3: George
I was finding these things out as I made calls to see what was going on, because I didn't delegate it, I stood—because it was on my name I made sure I got in front of the people who were doing these things. I handled the problem . . . and then as I would talk to these different departments and people I could hear that they were messing my stuff up, or messing stuff up in my department on purpose, with no justifiable reason. And then that's when I realized that they were, you know, that this was something against me personally. Because then, as I said, the explanations didn't justify their actions. Any other time they would have processed everything or put this through or billed something correctly, but within the time frame that I was—they wouldn't process it, they wouldn't bill it correctly. They wouldn't design the ads for my salespeople—everything, everything was just like, "No, no, no, no, no. We can't do it." Or, "We didn't wanna do it." Or, "We didn't know what to do, so we just didn't do anything."

George: "Most People Like George Are in Jail"

An explicit face-to-face challenge to his identity occurred when a White worker from another department walked into his department. George's immediate subordinates told the man what a good job George was doing and said that they would like to be more like him. The man's response to their enthusiasm was "I don't know if you wanna be like George, because most people like George are in jail." Race is not mentioned directly, but the invocation of the "criminalblackman" stereotype is obvious (Russell-Brown 1998). George describes initiating a complete interactional break—or null-response—at this point.

Data Excerpt #4: George
The guy, he was about fifty-five, fifty-six, and he had been there for like thirty years doing the same job and now I was the acting manager and he was mad because he just didn't believe that I was—because I wasn't part of the good old boy system, he didn't believe I should have had that opportunity. And so he came into the department and with a very comedic type of attitude was talking to me about, "Oh, so I hear you're in charge over here. Oh wow." So when he said that, my subordinates were like "Oh, yeah, yeah, George is in charge. We're trying to be more like George. He's making goals, he knows his processes, he's sharp, he's all of this." And then that's when he tells the group, "I don't know if you wanna be like George, because most people like George are in jail." And that's how he worded it on the floor, in front of everybody. And then, I just, I just turned from him and just walked away. Well, actually, he was at my desk, so I really turned from him and just went back to my work. So it would be like you standing over me and then I just stop looking at you, I don't give you my attention anymore, and then I went back to my desk and just started working.

George said he turned away and *didn't give him his attention anymore.* In our terms, this is a total null-response. Even though the White man was standing right "over" him, George backed out of reciprocity relations and removed himself from the interaction. It is this removal from interactional reciprocity that we want to highlight. We came across it repeatedly in the narratives. The way the situation played out is that George's staff (primarily African American women) "spoke up" for him while he ignored the situation.

Data Excerpt #5: George
And then my staff, who part of them were, mostly they were African American women, some were African American women, some were White women, some were White men—they just all started, you know, well, actually the African American women really spoke up. And they were older than me. So they really

like, I mean, they were more, I would put them in their forties, and they were more boisterous to him for that attack on me, than anyone else in the group because they know that I was doing good things, and so they were pretty much defending me. And I just asked the ladies to let it be. "It's okay, don't worry about it, we don't need to, we have other things we have to do. He said it, please let's move on." And so, that's kind of how I ended it. And then I went back to my work and he left with pretty much egg on his face that this came out. And I did a good job, and I did a good job and I ended up being promoted a couple of months quicker.

In George's view, his null-response was effective and he came out of this interaction the winner. The man who insulted him "left with pretty much egg on his face," and George got a promotion.

George: Knowing Your Enemies and Not Trusting Them

George explained that it is important to know who is in your corner, know who is against you, and not trust the enemy. He is clear in his view that there are enemies in the workplace and he needs to figure out who they are *so that he can discount their responses*: "They was really just trying to frustrate me by just telling me that what I was doing was wrong but wouldn't give me any answers as to how or what."

Data Excerpt #6: George
I, um, I could tell. I could tell when I felt my enemies would always speak to me in very abstract terms. You know, not giving me any, well you know, my enemies would say that I did something wrong but wouldn't tell me exactly what I did wrong. For example, just saying that "You know what, all of this is wrong." And then, just don't wanna give me any specifics as to what components of it is wrong. Those are the people who I immediately just looked at as my enemies, because they didn't, weren't trying to help me do something better, they was really just trying to frustrate me by just telling me that what I was doing was wrong but wouldn't give me any answers as to how or what. So those people who would say things and then, yeah, usually the people who I didn't trust, the little ones who would try to make things—I just—if their actions or their words were to make things harder for me then I didn't trust them.

George refers to "the ones" who "I didn't trust" as those who would try "to make things harder for me" and considers it important to identify such people. Then he would "either put processes in place where they had to do whatever I asked them to do" or figure out how to work around them. The prospect of working amidst enemies and people who can't be trusted because they are hoping to make things so hard for you that you give up is staggering. We heard from other men about White people who would give criticisms that were too abstract to be helpful. Nonetheless, George treats it as what he expects and what he needs to deal with to succeed.

Third Narrative: Simon, Corporate Advertising Account Executive

Simon is an account executive selling advertising space for a major newspaper. When we told our initial coat hanger story, he indicated immediately that he was familiar with what we described by taking "it" for granted and immediately began telling us how he dealt with "it." According to Simon, he is at a point in his career (early forties) where he has had a number of different positions and sufficient experience to "learn to deal with it." He said, "I think experience teaches you how to deal with it and act maturely."

Simon: "I Don't Know If It's Necessarily Race Related"

At the beginning Simon offered the disclaimer that he did not know whether any of his experiences with "it" were Race related. Nevertheless, he explicitly formulated his problems getting subordinates to do as he asked in terms of what he called a Race and gender "double standard." The question of whether problems were Race related he called "a gnawing feeling in the back of my head." Ultimately, though, he said it didn't matter because there was nothing he could do to change it.

Data Excerpt #1: Simon
I don't know if it's necessarily race related. I mean, I don't ever wanna say something is definitely race related unless someone says it for sure, but it's always a gnawing feeling in the back of my head, and it gets to the point of what are you gonna do about it? You know what I mean, and it's almost a rhetorical question.

Simon: Subordinates Challenge His Authority and Will Not Do as He Asks

Simon went on to tell us about subordinates who don't do as he asks. It has apparently become necessary on many occasions for Simon to "assert his authority" to get things done. Assistants tell him they are busy with other projects. He is not recognized as an authority figure.

> **Data Excerpt #2: Simon**
> But I've had situations where I've had to tell subordinates, remind them of who the authority figure was, namely myself. I had an assistant once who I asked to do something and, you know, she told me she was working on something else and it was a priority and to me that was just, that was mind blowing, and I had to remind her that I set her priorities and that what I asked her to do, which was something that was coming from my own boss, was urgent and needed to be done and that just, that was mind boggling.

The need to assert authority to get things done is not only an indication of a problem, but Simon recognizes that it can become a problem in its own right. If he needs to deal with too many situations forcefully, Simon worries that he may come off as "arrogant."

Simon: It's Like a "Double Standard"

While he is reluctant to say that his experiences have anything to do with Race, Simon refers to a "double standard" and says his own situation is analogous to when "men who are aggressive are applauded in the workforce and women who are aggressive are called a very derogatory term."

> **Data Excerpt #3: Simon**
> I had other situations where you hear feedback from people and some of the words that come up, you know, whether someone is saying that you're perceived by your coworkers or colleagues or subordinates as being arrogant or not approachable or something like that, which again, I think that was kind of mind boggling. It's a double standard where I can see, you know, white males in a similar position and maybe exhibit the same behavior I did or do and they don't have that same kind of feedback. It's almost like the situation where men who are aggressive are applauded in the workforce and women who are aggressive are called a very derogatory term, and it's kind of like that double standard,

and again, I think just with experience you just kind of learn to deal with it or brush it off and figure out a way to approach the situation that's not going to negatively impact my own career.

Feeling that he is being forced to be aggressive by employees who don't recognize his identity, Simon worries. It is the same double standard that keeps them from recognizing his identity that also forces him to be aggressive. At the same time, he recognizes the likelihood that others will not applaud aggression on his part. He may find himself in a position analogous to that of an aggressive woman being "called a very derogatory term." So he prefers to "brush it off" and deal with "it" in a nonconfrontational way.

Discussion: Null-Response as a Protection against Fractured Reflections

Because high-status Black men often don't get back a reflection of the self they have actually presented, they learn not to treat such fractured reflections as true assessments of themselves. In order to maintain high status and self-esteem, they deny the validity of such responses—by giving a null-response and sometimes completely withdrawing from interaction. The experience of invisibility and non-recognition reported by the men in our narratives is reminiscent of the problem Ralph Ellison (1952) called attention to in *The Invisible Man*. You know you are participating and talking, but the feedback you expect is either missing altogether or not (in any sense you can make out) a response to, or an affirmation of, the identity you are presenting. Such failures of mutual intelligibility and recognition of self would normally be corrected or repaired within an interaction. Correcting presentations of self in the face of the Other(s)' response is an essential and ongoing part of achieving and maintaining self.

However, correction cannot occur without cooperation from others. Furthermore, continued attempts at repair that fail would create a sense that the problem is due to a personal failing. While these men may be doing something wrong in the context of the Other(s)' definition of the situation, they are not doing anything wrong in the context of their own. Because of the frequency of the problem, their priority must be to preserve the integrity of their own identity in the face of what they are experiencing. The men we talked with reported breaking off reciprocity and falling back on stereotypes and motivated accounts as a way of making sense for themselves of these troubled interactions. They do this while refusing to acknowledge the relevance of the Other(s)' response.

A good "attitude" toward Race and/or a commitment to racial equality doesn't lessen the effect of a failure to recognize identity and competence, as Robert's discussion of his assistant illustrates. She has (in his view) a good attitude and wants to help him. She is not trying to be racist. The problem is that in trying to *help* him—in being extra "nice" to help him—she is challenging the legitimacy of his identity. It is not bad attitudes about Race that lead to these interactional failures, although such attitudes may lurk within the interaction order expectations and racial frames that render people unable to see Black men in high-status positions.

The problem is tacit racism and the constancy of it. We propose that those who experience frequent and unpredictable failures by Others to affirm the self they are presenting will at some point cross a threshold where they must either begin refusing to make corrections and repairs or be damaged themselves. We see this with Robert, who has stopped treating his assistant's responses as having anything to do with the competence of his own performance. We see it also in the narratives of Simon and George, who talk about the need to "ignore" and "brush off" responses they do not recognize as relevant to their own conception of themselves. *The effect of continuing to make a full commitment to interactional reciprocity requirements would be a damaged conception of self.* These men are able to use their understanding of racism to protect themselves.

In spite of the problems they describe, the men we talked with are all achieving a high degree of success. That success, however, comes at a price: it requires skilled use of adaptive strategies that are not required of those whose physical characteristics fit racialized expectations, and it requires them to succeed without access to interactional tools available to their White competitors. They must do *extra work* to manage their employees, which they worry carries the danger that they will be seen as arrogant or bossy. Operating without the benefit of information conveyed by feedback about the self they *are* presenting is also problematic. Fractured reflections come from participants who they *should* be able to count on to reflect back an accurate assessment of how they are doing. Needing to reject distorted reflections of self leaves them without reliable feedback for assessing their performance. Ultimately, their need to frequently break off reciprocity relations undermines the trust relations that are constitutive of self and sense-making. It will make workplace friendships difficult as well. Instead of receiving the cooperation and reciprocity they need from others, they are forced to fall back on *guessing* and *imputing motives* (often using stereotypes and shared narratives like the ones we collected) as a way of gaining some purchase on how Others are interpreting them.

When Black men and women are forced to resort to such self-protective measures, they lose access to essential interactional resources. Others, in turn, lose access to mutually meaningful interaction with them, and we all lose the possibility of democratic public spaces.

Conclusion

The presentation of self is a fragile process that requires a great deal of mutual attention. As theorized by Goffman (1959), it requires participants to cooperate in maintaining a "social contract" or "working consensus" about their mutual obligations in interaction. Garfinkel (1963) proposed that trust conditions and commitment to a specific shared set of background expectations (including a shared definition of the situation) are also required in each interaction. These shared (but situated) resources must be used cooperatively to achieve social self and mutual understanding, a process that depends on interactional commitments being met at each next point.[4] Interaction orders that meet these conditions—rather than formal rules and institutions—are how order and meaning are achieved in diverse modern social contexts in which people have little else in common.

Not only is the process fragile, but, as Garfinkel and Goffman demonstrate, it depends on a cooperative sharing of practices and information. Everyone depends on others for information—feedback—about their interactional performances. Feedback on performance depends, in turn, on information about which identity a person is performing: and the identities available to be performed depend on the definition of the situation and the interaction order that is in play. Accordingly, there is a shared need for information about the identities of other participants, and the interactional resources they will be using, on the basis of which inferences about interactional "moves" can be made. Next moves are made on the basis of how prior moves are interpreted and can reflect back new meaning onto them. This is what Garfinkel meant by "reflexivity."

Goffman's point is that identifying "who" a person is—which identity they enact—helps to determine "what" definition of the situation is in play. Goffman (1959: 1) opens his argument in *The Presentation of Self* with an emphasis on this shared need for information:

> When an individual enters the presence of others, they commonly seek to acquire information about him. . . . They will be interested in his general socioeconomic status, his conception of self, his attitude toward them, his competence, his trustworthiness, etc. . . . Information about the individual helps to define the situation, enabling others to know in advance what he will expect of them and what they may expect of him. Informed in these ways, the others will know how best to act in order to call forth a desired response from him.

Stereotypes and racially framed assumptions about identity are intrinsic to this information-gathering process. "If unacquainted with the individual," Goffman (1959: 1) says, "observers can glean clues from his conduct and appearance which allow them to apply their previous experience with individuals roughly similar to the one before them or, more important, to apply untested stereotypes to him." Because recognition of performed identity often depends, as Goffman says, on "stereotypes" and "previous experience with individuals roughly similar," inconsistencies between stereotyped expectations and actual performed identities are barriers to recognition. A failure to recognize an identity as presented can, in turn, call the whole definition of the situation into question, leading not only to momentary embarrassment, but to enduring failures of meaning and trust for everyone involved.

We argue that failures by Others to recognize presentations of self by high-status Black men are such events and that they have become institutionalized in the way we see people by Race. We refer to this process of non-recognition as a fracturing—not of the self—but of the reflection of that self that comes back from the Other (what C. H. Cooley [1902] called the "Looking Glass Self"): a "fractured reflection" as if from a broken mirror, with consequences not only for the performing self, but for the whole social interaction and all its participants.

It is our position that such fractured reflections of identity work are evidence of a broken interactional process in which multiple definitions of the situation stand in fundamental conflict, in which clashing interaction order expectations about identity and competence make it impossible to achieve mutual understanding.[5] There are consequences at many levels. The exercise of legitimate authority by Black men is certainly compromised. But, at a deeper level, the involvement obligations that facilitate mutual cooperation for all participants are violated. As a consequence, the situation in which these interaction order conflicts occur can become confusing to everyone, and because trust conditions are not being met, shared resources for achieving resolution are not available. Because self and meaning are fragile achievements, a broken interactional process is dangerous and threatens the coherence of modern public spaces. White Americans can avoid the problem by avoiding interracial interaction, which is a distinct pattern in American life. But high-status Black men and women, who wield their authority in predominantly White environments, and poor Black citizens subjected to constant surveillance by White intruders cannot do so.

The injustices that Black selves experience in interaction are tacit and thus not apparent to those participants who employ a White racial frame (Feagin 2009) and thus cannot see them in the identities they perform. Having not "seen" the problem in the first place, those working with a different definition of the situation and orienting a different interaction order may consider the practice of null-response uncalled for—even rude. These Black men are after all refusing to respond. So, it is important to realize that the practice of null-response is the main resource these men have to achieve and protect high self-esteem, maintain personal dignity, and wield power in spite of persistent non-recognition. It enables them to escape from negative evaluation. *They need to do it*. However, there are consequences. Beyond the incomprehension it produces for White Others, research shows that withdrawal from reciprocity relations in interracial interactions can escalate interactional troubles related to Race (Rawls and David 2006).[6] There may be damage to the interaction itself, and to mutual understanding, accompanied by a reluctance to trust participants of other Races (Rawls 2000).

Thus, while a null-response offers protection, it also creates new problems, and the constant need to employ such strategies can result in what is being called "racial fatigue" and "racial battle fatigue" (Smith, Allen, and Danley 2007). As Elijah Anderson (2011) explains in *The Cosmopolitan Canopy*, Black Americans all too often learn that it is dangerous to adopt an egalitarian approach to interaction: an approach Anderson calls "cosmopolitan" or "cosmo." Such an approach leaves them open to damaging racialized moments that can happen at any time and thus are impossible to anticipate. In other words, while a cosmo approach that treats everyone as equal is highly desirable and even essential to public civility in modern democratic publics, Black Americans (and others who experience persistent fractured reflections of their identity work) may find an approach embedded in their own ethnicity or community of values less risky. As a consequence, a protective ethnic and cultural stance is frequently adopted in addition to tacit interaction order differences. Although this is often necessary for Black Americans, doing so negates the trust and reciprocity that are necessary for mutual intelligibility across Races. This problem illustrates again that when inequalities that are built into the social distribution of identity expectations make trust and mutual reciprocity dangerous, modern democratic publics cannot be achieved.

CHAPTER THREE

Clashing Conceptions of Honesty

*Black American "Honesty" in the
White Workplace*

White people must have been dishonest for hundreds of years because they don't even remember what "honesty" means anymore.　　—Black American Fortune 500 corporate executive

Oriented toward different conceptions of self and community—one individualistic, the other egalitarian—Black and White interaction orders embed clashing expectations of what "honesty" requires as an interactional practice. For African Americans, honesty is not only about telling the truth. It involves a commitment to completely and accurately express how one feels in the moment—with a particular focus on expressing feelings about trouble—combined with a commitment to sticking with an interactional trouble until the problem is fixed. White Americans find the Black practice of honesty both intimidating and puzzling. Black Americans find the White American version of honesty, which involves being "diplomatic" and withholding anything that would be problematic, to be dishonest: "plastic." When Black Americans do withhold in an interaction, as in the null-response discussed in chapter 2, it is because trust relations have broken and they are either taking self-protective action or have given up on an interaction completely. The Black American focus on creating a space for equal personhood here and now, which we explored in chapter 1, leads to an expectation that the feelings of participants in the moment should be expressed. In an inversion of what White Americans consider personal—Black American interactional expectations treat a person's feelings as part of the immediate public situation in which they occur—while the information about job status and social category that White Americans consider public is treated as private.

The Black conception of honesty aligns with the overall Black interaction order orientation toward equality and mutual responsibility. In order for persons to meet authentically and equally face-to-face, a full disclosure of feelings about what is going on is required, while at the same time category information should be avoided. However, the commitment is often quickly abandoned with White people who indicate that they are not to be trusted. The White practice of first identifying the status categories relevant to a person when first meeting them and then carefully not saying anything negative about any categories relevant to that person, which White Americans often call being "diplomatic" or "politically correct," is considered extremely hypocritical from a Black perspective.[1] Black Americans would not make category assessments in the first place. And among strangers, no category topics or assessments are made unless they have immediate relevance to the situation in an egalitarian way. This preserves equality, while at the same time does not require avoiding any particular categories.

But especially when people are not strangers, African Americans expect that they will say what they personally feel without worrying about the relationship between what they say and the social category or social status of the person to whom they are speaking—even if it is their boss. In more formal settings when, for example, the boss or supervisor tells an employee to do something they do not want to do, the Black American notion of honesty seems to require that the employee speak their mind. In order to be in compliance with this requirement, for instance, Robert's assistant (chapter 2) should have told him to his face that she was not sure she should do what he asked her to do. They could have talked it out there and then. However, this would have required her to explain why she didn't think she should do what he asked, and trying to explain that directly to him would likely have alerted her to the inappropriateness of her actions and made her aware of the tacit assumptions she was making. In other words, honesty would have exposed the racism.

The same expectations with regard to honesty seem to apply in interaction with other authority figures, including the police (see chapter 5). In the Black interaction order, it is important to let authority figures know they are making you feel disrespected, which can be seen in video after video. One Black Fortune 500 corporate executive told us that when White coworkers criticize such practices, he tells them that "White people must have been dishonest for hundreds of years because they don't even remember what 'honesty' means anymore."

From a White perspective, by contrast, being careful about category statements and the expression of feelings is considered "diplomatic" and "smart" and is not only socially expected but required. White Americans are much more likely to tell their *true* feelings only to close friends and family in private: they "unload" when they get home. In public, and particularly with persons of higher status, what they would call "diplomacy" and careful control of the outward expression of their feelings is the accepted practice. In a hierarchical setting, it is considered suicidal to tell the boss that you don't want to do as they say—or to tell them they are making you feel angry or disrespected. The employee is not the social (and workplace) equal of their boss, and the White interaction order expects status deference to control the expression of feelings in such circumstances. Expressing one's feelings in such a context may be brave, take courage, and be in some existential sense more honest, but from a White perspective, it does not fulfill the role expectations of the position the employee has assumed. It also doesn't respect the role expectations of the boss. Yet African Americans judge harshly those who make a "compromise" with regard to this issue, and some told us that every Black American who succeeds in American society must have "compromised" their honesty in this way.

Of course, the notion of honesty doesn't make sense if it is interpreted literally to mean the immediate expression of every thought and feeling. It is necessary to draw the line somewhere. As Harvey Sacks (1992) demonstrated in "Everyone Has to Lie," when people are asked "How are you?" as a form of greeting, the literal truth would be a description of their state of mind or health (i.e., a long description whether of troubles or happiness). However, the long description is not what people expect in either the Black or White interaction order. Those people who do respond with a full disclosure are seen as deviant, and they will likely not be asked the question again by the same person (who may also warn others about them, in the process generating narratives about people who tell you how they really feel when you ask, "How are you?").

Black Americans also understand and follow this rule. The person doing the greeting does not expect, or want, a literal or complete answer in return, and Black Americans do not offer one. Black honesty is not full disclosure. It involves ritual social expectations just as White honesty does. The complication is that Black and White interaction order expectations about that ritual are different. The White conception of honesty serves an interaction order that supports a categorial self that is competing in a hierarchical framework with other categorial selves. The Black notion of honesty supports an egalitarian self who is cooperating with others in an egalitarian community united against oppression.

Many social practices in both interaction orders require discretion. Discretion is not the problem. A line always needs to be drawn between the things it is possible to say and what should be said. It's not literally that White Americans are being dishonest, while African Americans are telling the "truth," although it can look that way from a Black perspective. Rather, members of the two groups are drawing the line between honesty and dishonesty in different places, in a different social ritual, with very different expectations and consequences. Black Americans don't do full disclosure—it is not possible—they are following a different rule about hierarchy and concealment. In the Black interaction order, respect for hierarchy is avoided, and a Black American is much more likely to express their feelings to an authority figure, whereas in the White interaction order, hierarchy and authority are important objects of respect from which discontent should be carefully concealed. The reverence among many White Americans for the individualistic "Strong Man" ideal is related to this orientation. As we discuss in chapters 4 and 5, the Black American ideal rejects this individualism and its status orientation, instead elevating the practice of submission to the good of the whole—which we call "Submissive Civility"—over the individual: elevating the common good over the individual strong man.

The commitment to being open and sticking with a problem until it is either solved or the interaction is broken is another important part of Black American honesty that White Americans say they find intimidating. From a Black American perspective, it looks as if White Americans want to run away when things become difficult. The consequences of this difference are always serious. However, the consequences in the White workplace can be particularly dire. Workplace misunderstandings affect the ability of individual African Americans to compete successfully in the job market and may seriously hamper not only their access to promotions, but even their ability to keep the jobs they already have. When differences over the conception of honesty impact relations in the workplace, Black American employees will not understand why they have received negative evaluations from White employers and will protest that the employers must be racist. These employers will not understand why an employee who from their perspective is "not conforming to standards of behavior" and has been "complaining about doing their job" doesn't understand why they got a bad evaluation. The problem is tacit racism: White employers are enforcing a racialized standard of conduct they are not usually aware of.

The African American Conception of Honesty in the White Workplace

How does it happen that a Black employee—in a relatively low-level position and not a vice president as in chapter 2—believes they are doing a *good job*, while on the basis of the very same information about their performance, their White employer thinks that they are *not doing their job*. We maintain that the answer to this question is often related to the conflict over conceptions of "honesty" and the Black interaction order preference for expressing one's feelings and sticking with an issue until it is resolved. Between White bosses and Black employees, racialized expectations about what should be expressed and what should be concealed are often violated.

Observational research on a variety of interracial workplace relationships—combined with interviews, workshops, and focus group discussions of these issues—reveals that African American employees say "no" to work assignments or express frustration and concern with them when White employees would not, and that they do so for very different reasons. Black employees also do openly things that White employees carefully conceal (like playing with video games or accessing Facebook on their computers). Evidence to support this comes from self-reports of White and African American employees and from field observations of workplace behavior (some on videotape). In group interviews, Black employees consistently maintained that saying "no" to their supervisors was a "right" that they felt it was essential to their dignity as human beings to exercise. As one Black employee explained in response to a video we showed of a Black employee "expressing" her feelings over a workplace assignment:

> I don't know if she *should* say "no." Okay, I think that she had a *right* to say, "Now this is happening and this is happening and this is happening." For you to understand that.

The idea of a right to say "no" expresses the sense of equality that characterizes what we have called the egalitarian self. In the Black interaction order, everyone has the right to say how they feel about what is going on "right there, right then." Status relationships in the workplace are no exception. The employer has the obligation to listen and understand. Furthermore, honesty requires that both parties say exactly what they feel and be willing to discuss it until everything is mutually understood. These obligations often lead to conversations in which African Americans confront one another with conflicting feelings and viewpoints. The expectation is that once the feelings are expressed, a solution agreeable to both parties will be arrived at. Parties will stick with the interaction until the trouble is resolved. The problem comes in cross-Race interaction. White bosses (and employees) do not expect this kind of "expression," and the White expectation is to quickly retreat from such an interaction, considering the "expression" itself embarrassing and "low class."

According to Kochman (1981), the Black American expectation that issues will be talked through "on the spot" often leads to the perception by White speakers that African Americans have a confrontational and intimidating style of speech. In the workplace, in public forums, and in chance encounters, Black speakers will insist on seeing an argument through. From a Black interaction order perspective, this is expected. It is honest. But it can take a good deal of energy and make for drama that violates White expectations. White Americans often complained to us that Black people are "loud" and told us that they had been scared or intimidated by such encounters.

On the other hand, because sticking with an issue until agreement is reached is treated by African Americans as a sign of mutual respect and commitment to one another's personhood, the White American practice of retreating from or being "intimidated" by such "scenes" leads Black speakers to assume that their White coworkers have something to hide. They interpret retreating from minor problems in the interaction as "running away," a sign of dishonesty and cowardice (Kochman 1981). Black Americans only withdraw from the interaction as a last resort when the interaction is broken—as in the null-response described in chapter 2. When White Americans withhold expressing their feelings, in order to keep up "appearances" or maintain their role, African Americans report experiencing them as *fake, dishonest,* or *plastic.* Ironically, one could argue that in continuing to "express" their feelings in encounters with the police, Black Americans are trying to show them respect—which the police invariably interpret as a lack of respect (see chapter 5).

What White and Black Americans are intimidated by is not at all the same. African Americans report feeling intimidated by a standard White greeting sequence that asks them for category information. White Americans, on the other hand, report feeling intimidated by African American "confrontational style," or honesty. This is a claim that Black Americans are aware of but do not at all understand. When White Americans make this complaint, African Americans tend to chalk it up to a basic dishonesty on the part of White people. The fact that White Americans often find Black Americans intimidating is known to both Black and White Americans, although Black Americans don't understand it. However, that Black Americans often find White Americans intimidating goes generally unrecognized by White Americans, who have a deep-seated belief that they are the polite ones who are being intimidated by loud and overbearing Black people.

During ongoing research on another project, a situation developed between a White female post-doctoral research fellow who was supervising the work of a Black female graduate research assistant in a research project under the direction of Anne, who was the ultimate boss and mentor of both. The White supervisor felt that the Black graduate assistant was being insubordinate, refusing to take direction, and generally "making excuses" to get out of doing her work and complained to Anne about it. The situation she described had many of the characteristics we have identified as indicative of interracial miscommunication. We knew the Black graduate student researcher was working hard and suspected that her responses to her White supervisor were being misunderstood. Furthermore, we suspected that if we could videotape the way she was expressing herself, and then show it to different groups, the responses of African Americans and White Americans to the interactions between the two would be completely different.

In order to test this idea, a video recording was made of an interaction between the Black female graduate research assistant (whom we will call Sarah) and Anne, who was the overall boss/mentor for both Sarah and her White supervisor (whom we call Joan), with Sarah's prior permission. The videotape was of a routine interaction that would have occurred anyway, during which Sarah was asked by Anne to do something, and we expected her to express herself in the way we thought was bothering Joan. During the videotaped interaction, Sarah was told that she would be traveling to a conference in Florida with the whole research group to present papers on our research, and that she would be expected to present a paper herself. This would be the first time she had ever done such a thing. Sarah responded immediately and vigorously that she would not go, could not present a paper, and was already doing too many other things. This was her normal response, which Anne never took literally, but thought it was this likely expression of feelings that Joan was complaining about.

In fact, Sarah did travel to Florida and present a paper at the conference. She never meant that she *wouldn't* do it, and she said so during the interaction on video. What she meant was that she did not *want* to do it and was feeling overwhelmed by the responsibility. This was exactly the sort of response that Joan had reported interpreting as insubordinate and complaining.

Just by chance, Joan came into the room as Anne was reviewing the videotape with Sarah, who had just been explaining the importance of honesty, and that what she had been doing on the tape was trying to be honest about her feelings, not refusing the work assignment. Sarah had explained that when she came to graduate school, she had promised herself that she would not become plastic like White people just to get ahead, and now we were trying to force her to be dishonest. It was just after she had finished explaining this, and Anne had assured her that we did not require such a compromise—which was why we had made the tape and were having the discussion—that Joan came to the door and watched about a minute of the tape. Then Joan said, "See that is exactly what I have been telling you about. She is making excuses and complaining about her work." It was amazing to see the two versions of the interaction juxtaposed so neatly.

We worked hard in that workplace to get both employees to see that they were each misunderstanding the other. Sarah did finally realize that a different standard of honesty was at work—although she still judged it harshly. However, we made little headway with Joan, who continued to say that it looked to her like Sarah was just lazy and refusing to work. Having argued that stereotypes are often generated by these misunderstandings, this remained both interesting and problematic. Sarah was very smart, hardworking, and diligent. She always went above and beyond what was required. But this was not the only time that she was labeled lazy and even "stupid" by a White person who refused to reconsider that judgment. And the fact that Sarah was very culturally Black adds to the importance of what we found.

The tape of our interaction was played for many different interracial groups. Some were public community workshops on interracial miscommunication. Twice we used it in presentations to Wayne State University Alumni groups. On a number of occasions, we presented it in the classroom or in small focus group sessions. Many of these sessions were also videotaped. After playing the videotape for a group, we would ask participants for comments on the interaction. At several of these presentations, Sarah was also present and participated in the group discussions about her own interaction. In addition to our research, we had the practical aim of alerting the people who came to these sessions to the fact that these differences by Race in the expectations about how and when people should express themselves could be leading to trouble in the workplace.

The tape was very effective in generating responses. White participants often responded first and invariably remarked that Sarah was very loud and confrontational. They said this freely even when Sarah was present. They interpreted her comments, particularly the repeated saying of "no," as a refusal to do the work assignment. They had no sense that a Black cultural issue could be involved, or that their judgments involved tacit racism. The fact that Sarah said "no" was astonishing to White Americans. As one White woman said:

> I would never be like "I've got this to do there's no way I can do it." I would never talk that way to my boss. I say "yes" and I mean "no." But I *say* "yes." And then I'd go home and say, "I can't believe she asked me that."

That White people would say yes and mean no was not problematic to them. But it was to Black participants. Following such assessments, African American participants invariably came to Sarah's defense. They did not find anything offensive in the loudness and firmness of her response. In contrast to the White participants' expressions of disbelief, Black participants characterized the response as typical. It was interesting watching them listen to one another. One Black woman said:

> I'm used to that. Hers was just a typical response.

Some African American participants were aware that the White supervisor might be offended. But they still did not see this as a problem with the employee's behavior. Rather, they found fault with Joan for expecting Sarah to be dishonest.

The responses to Sarah by Anne (who was leading the discussion with the alumni group) were also frequently described by Black participants as patronizing and inconsiderate. Phrases that from a White perspective have the flavor of a "pep talk"—"It will be good for your career" and "I know you can do it"—were met with cries of "Typical White response" and "White people always think they know better than Black people what they should do." Black participants had no hesitation in saying this directly to us either.

> Well, see, I saw a lot of things that she [the boss/mentor] did do that happens often, nurturing . . . telling you to do what's *good* for you. "You folks jus don't try hard enough" and then I kinda saw you [Sarah, who was present for the discussion] giving in a little bit.

Sarah, the African American research assistant, is encouraged not to give in. From a Black perspective, the complaint is about the White employer who continues to press the request to go and present the paper in the face of the employee's response. Black Americans comment that it is wrong for the employer to have decided for someone else what they were going to do. The employee should be able to decide whether to take on an increased workload:

> It seemed to me in the first place she had a lot of work to do. She was working hard in getting this stuff done. And here you come, giving her something else to do. And it's like, where as her advisor, how could you do that? Knowing what's going on with this woman and you had to know because you're her advisor. And then to take on this other project. I felt sorry for her.

While equality is a human ideal, and an important part of the Black presentation of self, it is not an expectation of most modern workplaces. It would be more humane if workers could dictate their own workloads. There is something essentially dehumanizing about having one's labor owned by others. However, claiming this as a right within the current context of work is foreign to the White American understanding of workplace relationships. Furthermore, in a professional setting in which the employer/employee relationship is essentially one of apprenticeship (as it is in graduate school), and the eventual success or failure of the employee/student will be almost entirely determined by their employer's evaluation of their competence, a failure to follow *all* of an employer's suggestions can end one's career. The employer does, in fact, know better than the employee what the job requires in many cases.

In the case in question of a graduate assistant and the professor they are doing their dissertation research with, the situation is not merely hierarchical; it is in essential respects feudal. It is certainly not egalitarian. The Black graduate assistant is in something like an apprenticeship with her White mentor, and her success will depend on her mentor's ability to convey that to her.

In contrast to Black participants, White participants expressed their amazement at the what they called the "boldness" of the Black employee and considered the response of the White employer to be very "patient" and "nurturing":

> I thought you were really much more *patient* with her with all her *excuses*. I mean they just went on and on and on and she was really a master at it.

From a White perspective, Sarah's protests are seen as *excuses* that she invoked to manipulate the White boss/mentor, while the mentor herself is evaluated as patient to an extreme. Sarah, on the other hand, is characterized as being a "master" at making excuses.

Black participants, however, saw things differently. From a Black perspective, Sarah was not making "excuses" at all, but rather expressing facts.[2]

> I didn't see them as excuses. I saw them as *facts*. She had this paper to do and that paper to do.

There is a very significant difference in perspective between the two groups. White participants said things like "Oh my god, if I ever talked to my employer like that, I'd get fired," and "If anyone ever talked to me like that, I'd never ask them to do anything again." Clearly, they found such behavior *intimidating* and *offensive*. African Americans, on the other hand, saw it not only as their right, but their obligation to let others, including their employer, know just how they feel. Black American participants explained that if Sarah did not tell her employer how she felt, it would be *dishonest*. Feelings *should* be communicated. When it was suggested that it would be more "diplomatic" to keep one's feelings to oneself, one Black woman responded:

> That's what's wrong with White people. They are dishonest about their feelings. When they are upset about something, they will *pretend* everything is all right, and now you want *us* to do it *too*.

The problem in terms of Black/White workplace relations is compounded by the fact that an African American who is a very hard and committed worker, like Sarah, is even more likely to say "no" than a Black American who really is trying to get out of doing the work. In other words, the White interpretation is backwards. Because the obligations with regard to "honesty" are reversed in the two interaction orders, the background expectations against which inferences can be drawn about what behavior means are also reversed. Among Black Americans, the one who always says "yes" is much more likely to be the *insincere* and *dishonest* worker, which White Americans simply do not understand.

But when White participants argued that refusing work assignments might jeopardize their positions in the workplace, African American participants responded that sometimes refusing work was part of doing a good job, and *they are right about that*. If they were working hard on a task that had already been assigned, and were then assigned additional work that might interfere with accomplishing the first task, they said that they would need to let the employer know that they felt the additional assignment threatened the quality of the work they were already doing. For example, one Black woman said:

> If you're new to the system, you're thinking, "I want to do my best at what I'm working on. But don't give me something else." You don't have resources. Don't have anyone else to go to for help.

This woman went on to talk about how difficult it was to learn about these White expectations because when an African American gets a job they are usually fairly isolated and don't have anyone showing them the ropes:

> If you don't know the rules of the game, like you say, *you* would say "yes" because you think in the back of your mind, you know, "I want that promotion," or because maybe you seen that's how someone else got it. But if you're new in the game, you don't have the examples and you don't know "Oh I'm supposed to say 'yes' if I want that promotion."

In other words, the idea that saying "no" might not be a good move is not immediately apparent from a Black American perspective. A White mentor would need to explain this carefully. But the isolation that Black Americans typically experience on the job would tend to keep this mentoring from occurring. Even if an African American did become close friends with a White employee, however, who could show them the ropes, that White employee would likely not realize that a Black American needed to be told not to say "no" to the boss. From a White interaction order perspective, the point is so obvious they would likely not explain it unless they overheard the exchange. The conversation would in any case be difficult. The taboo against saying "no" is obvious to a categorial self and is simply taken for granted among White employees. But it is not obvious from the perspective of a Black egalitarian self, and the Black employee might respond that she was being told to lie, as Sarah responded.

There is a further complication with regard to "learning the ropes." It has been pointed out by several successful Black corporate executives that their success in a corporation has depended on the sponsorship of a White mentor. They explain that they will only be able to rise to the level of their mentor, because the mentor will not have the power to raise them above their own position. Given the importance of the mentor relationship, there are two problems to consider: First, in the videotape of Sarah and her White boss/mentor, it was a mentoring relationship that was being described by Black participants as patronizing and insensitive. If many Black employees respond to White mentors in this way, then that all-important relationship will rarely develop; and, second, it is one's mentor who generally shows them the ropes. That is what was happening in the videotaped interaction. If African American employees often respond to being told what the ropes are by rejecting and criticizing the advice the way participants in our research said they would, their mentors will not succeed in mentoring them. In any case, there are very few White mentors who will understand what is going on and want to continue acting as a mentor after encountering a typical African American response. Most will react the way Joan, did in the case we have been discussing. *Thus, tacit racism will make the very conversation in which White employees/mentors might be telling Black employees about "the ropes" highly problematic and likely put an end to the relationship.*

Most importantly, however, even when African Americans do figure out what is expected of them, they face the dilemma that Sarah expressed. The expectations that White Americans have of workplace behavior do compromise the personal integrity and racial identity of the Black American worker. The question is to what degree can they comply with White expectations without compromising their own identity and integrity as a person with egalitarian Black interaction order commitments? Many African Americans in corporate and white-collar positions have expressed these concerns to us.

One story that we were told early on in our research illustrates this point. In the Department of Social Services in Detroit, there were both Black and White social workers. They all had paperwork to do. The White workers, we were told, would make sure to spread their work out on their desks and take a long time doing it so that when a supervisor walked by, they always looked busy. Black social workers, by contrast, would finish their work as quickly as possible and then play video games on their computers (this was before Facebook). Of course, the Black workers were sanctioned for this behavior while White workers were rewarded. We had to agree that as a matter of workplace efficiency what the Black workers did made more sense. We could also see their point about dishonesty. The White workers were pretending to be busy when they were not. But given the high priority given to hierarchy and deference to authority in the White interaction order, it all makes sense. But we couldn't say that the White practice was honest or even good business practice.

When White Americans respond to this dilemma by saying, "That's how it is. They'll just have to learn," they are using their White interaction order expectations to evaluate African American behavior. They are assuming that hierarchy and authority are more important than equality and honesty. But does it actually have to be this way? This is another case where the development of a White double consciousness would be helpful. Black interactants are being held to two sets of standards, while White people are accountable only to one. This is a disadvantage to Black Americans in the workplace. And White Americans have an additional advantage, in that the expected practices are known to them, while most African Americans do not know them but are nevertheless sanctioned for not conforming to them. It is impossible to conform to standards that one does not know about, and still difficult when you realize that those standards require moral compromise.

Honesty and Personhood vs. Hierarchy and Bureaucracy

The premium that African Americans place on personhood, honesty, and self-expression is at odds with White expectations regarding status relations in the workplace. A White boss expects their employees to comply without explanation. Many successful Black bosses do too. Employees should do a task because they have been asked, or because the bureaucracy needs them too. We saw in chapter 2 that successful Black male executives also expect this. Things are not going to go smoothly in the workplace if employees don't do what they are asked to do. The difference is that a Black boss is likely to understand what is happening. To African Americans who work hard to neutralize hierarchical relations, status hierarchies are not a very good reason for doing anything. A Black American boss should be more willing to explain why it is necessary if they are asked. African American values are oriented toward personhood and mutual responsibility. Given this orientation, they are not likely to develop respect for a person's wishes just because that person is higher up the status ladder. The boss will have to achieve their respect without appealing to status claims. This is something successful Black executives will understand about their Black employees. *What they don't understand is why White employees say "yes" and then don't do the work.*

The Black American understanding of what is expected from an employee may change with exposure to White employers over time, creating a degree of class variation, with more successful Black employees understanding better what White bosses expect. Nevertheless, African Americans of all social classes, and with all degrees of experience with White Americans in the workplace, have told us that they would say "no" whenever they felt they should. Instead of becoming used to what they are expected to do, it seems that the further up the status ladder a Black employee gets, the more onerous they find the increasing demands for what they consider to be dishonesty. The following are reactions from Black professionals:

If it was me? I might not say "yes."

You just pre-assumed that you were just gonna walk in and you were gonna tell her this and she was gonna say "okay."

I would with no uncertain terms say "no."

In fact, when White participants in these discussion groups described how they would just say "yes" when they didn't want to, African American participants were consistently incredulous that they would really say "yes" when they feel like saying "no." Black participants asked, "Why would we go home and complain to our spouses and family about a situation at work?" They want to know "why would we let ourselves be overworked?" And they asked White participants, "Why don't you just say 'no' when you realize that it is too much work, you can't do the job, or have some other problem with the request?"

These are good questions. Recent research has shown that stress on the job is one of the biggest health problems in America. So, while it may seem obvious from a White perspective that Black employees need to change their behavior and "act more like White people" in order to succeed, maybe a reevaluation is in order. Maybe an occasional "no" would relieve some of the stress that White employees feel. Maybe expressing their feelings would even improve the quality of their work. As one White male participant commented:

> Um, I think it's very interesting because, um, one of the things I'm trying to work out is to say "no" and it's very difficult. I'm used to just saying "yes" and end up upset with a chip on my shoulder and say, "How the hell can you load all this stuff on me, what do you think I am an ox? Or something to carry all this burden." I'm learning it because I have to, and I'm learning that if there is a good reason you can *get away with it*. But, another perfect example, a fellow I've known for several years, one of his student employees was leaving and he was always telling them don't disagree with the boss and *that's the culture*.

This White man would like to learn to say "no," and his point is that he is trying to learn to do so. However, his use of the phrase "get away with it" makes it clear that even while he argues that saying "no" might be a healthier and more courageous thing to do, he can't escape the feeling that from his perspective it is "deviant" and wrong to do so. From a Black American perspective, by contrast, it is not deviant but expected—more honest and hence a strong preference.

Having the courage to confront situations as they emerge is very important to African Americans (Kochman 1981). Even when a Black employee is being *very* careful not to cause problems on the job, they may assert their "right" to refuse work. The following response by an African American man is interesting in this regard because he began by challenging our claim that Black Americans say "no" more often than White Americans and described himself as being very careful at his worksite not to give anyone a reason to find fault with his work. Yet he ends up asserting that he would say "no" to his employer himself.

> Not to be negative, but I don't think that Black people necessarily have to tell their superiors how they feel and also at my place of employment there's a difference. I'm the only Black employee and I'm treated different. I don't know why, but I'm treated different, so I don't say anything really to anyone at work. So I don't really, I don't joke with anybody because I don't want to give them any reason to slip or do anything wrong. So, I don't joke with them. I just go on with my work. *However, when I'm assigned a task which I feel is unfair or anything, I won't go on a tirade, but I will with no uncertain terms let my boss know that I don't feel that this is for me to do, and the work is to be spread evenly and whatever.*

While this man claims to be stating an exception to the Black/White cultural pattern we proposed, what he says actually reinforces it. He has become so sensitive to his position as the only Black employee that he describes himself as refraining from any interaction at work so as not to give offense to the other employees (which likely is offending them). Then, although he says that African Americans don't *need* to let their employers know how they feel and that he would not "go on a tirade" to do so, he ends his narrative with the assertion that he *would* say "no" in "no uncertain terms" to his boss. This pattern of beginning with disagreement and ending with agreement is likely another Black American mirror-opposite interactional preference (which we discuss below, page 99).

Although this Black employee challenged our claim that Black and White interactional preferences are different, his story actually reinforces our claim. It is also clear from his response that he does not understand what the White expectations with regard to workplace behavior are. Like many African American participants, he expresses the belief that he is being treated differently because he is Black, and in many ways *this is probably true*. However, not for the reasons he thinks. He offers this as one of the reasons why he is so careful about what he does and says at work. But his version of being careful involves refusing to interact at work—which will violate the interactional expectations of his White coworkers. If we examine his statement carefully, we find that the way this Black man goes about being careful is highly problematic from a White perspective. He says, "I don't joke with them." He avoids the very sorts of casual interactions that might further integrate him into the workplace because he is trying so hard to do a good job—and to preserve the Black American separation between personal and public, which would require him to conceal personal category information at work. Then, after violating White expectations about casual communication, he says he will also "in no uncertain terms let his boss" know if he feels he should not be asked to do something. Because he does not understand what White interaction order expectations are, his "care" not to offend is likely achieving the opposite effect from what he intends.

In terms of this Black employee's interactional practice, he is not just being treated *as if* he were different—he is in fact *acting differently*. However, it is quite apparent that he has no idea that this is the case. Even though Black Americans are more aware of racial differences in expectations about interaction, the way White interaction order expectations actually work is as much a mystery to most African Americans as Black interaction order expectations are to White Americans. This makes it difficult to accurately interpret cross-Race interaction. This man has likely encountered problems trying to get to know his coworkers, like the ones we examined in chapter 1. He has also probably mistaken White diplomacy for a lack of courage and honesty, which would not encourage him to respect or trust his White coworkers, while they in turn will likely interpret his African American honesty as intimidation and his hard work as an unwillingness to be friendly—in fact, they likely view him as "rude."

The high premium placed on honesty and full disclosure leads to the assumption among African Americans that between honest persons, problems will be articulated publicly. Therefore, if a Black American has offended a White American, they expect that person to tell them what they have done "wrong" on the spot.[3] Certainly they expect that if what they have done was so upsetting that steps are going to be taken as a consequence, someone would have said something to them about it *during the encounter:* not just said something, but confronted them with it and *made* them listen; *right there, right then*, not later. As with greeting and introductory sequences, the emphasis is on the here and now. But White-run bureaucracies, by contrast, tend to deal with problems invisibly and after the fact through human resource departments.

The Black American Preference for "Seeing It Through" Face-to-Face

The Black Americans we talked to in our research insisted that their model of communication is more honest and authentic than what White Americans do. During some of the extended group discussions, many White participants expressed the wish that they could express themselves the way African Americans do; but they remained afraid that to so do would cost them their jobs. Adopting the Black American ideal would relieve them of a great deal of stress. All participants would get to say what they feel, and an eventual consensus could be reached without anyone having to repress their views (Kochman 1981). Participants come to respect the force of each other's positions by listening carefully and seeing how important the other's perspective is to them. It is a sort of conversational "taking the role of the other toward oneself" in literal terms: a practice that works well in an egalitarian setting. But it requires that positions be stated and defended between cooperating equals on the spot—and in White America there are few equals.

We have observed in conversations between groups of African Americans, both young and old, students and middle-class professionals, that when a topic is raised over which there is some difference of opinion, they see it through to resolution. One particularly striking interaction occurred at a board meeting of the local NAACP, where all board members (with the exception of Anne) were high-status Black professionals. There was an important topic on the floor. As speakers vied for turns, each next speaker spoke more loudly than the last. They each began with a point of disagreement (which is the opposite of the preferred White "Yes, but" turn response, and we suspect is another Black interaction order mirror-opposite preference). After several people had spoken and the conversation was becoming very animated, the next speaker would rise slightly out of their chair and lean over the table as they began to make their point. The conversation moved around the table in a circle, increasing in momentum, energy, and volume as it proceeded. Each next speaker opening with a "No, but" format. As the last several speakers spoke, half of the group were partway out of their chairs speaking at the same time. When the last speaker finished, they all sat back. The conversation stopped. They were done. They had reached an agreement, and everyone had taken an active part in reaching that agreement. Therefore, everyone's obligations to the group and to the topic were fulfilled.

From a White perspective, it looked like they were all disagreeing with each other. The typical White reaction would have been that the participants were angry and yelling at one another (Anne, who was present, had to ask them whether they were agreeing or disagreeing, which they thought was funny because it was so obvious to them that they were agreeing). But, in retrospect, it is clear that the conversation wasn't even competitive. Everyone got their turn—in order around the table—and everyone said their piece. When all was said and done, the group was satisfied, and a consensus was reached. Positions were modified. The process was very democratic. No one was allowed to be a dominating force, and, in spite of the high volume and significant speech in overlap, there was little actual emotion expressed. The point is that everyone contributed and said how they felt. It was a discussion, not an argument, and in spite of being what a White person would call "loud," there was no anger. Most importantly, it was a discussion in which all took an active part and in doing so demonstrated their solidarity, reciprocity, and commitment to the group. Of course the potential for anger is always there, but it is also just below the surface of White diplomacy, as the prevalence of workplace stress, political intrigue, assault, genocide, war, torture, and violence both in the family and in public among White people should attest.

During focus group discussions between Black and White students, Black students expressed their feeling that whenever a conversation became the least bit confrontational, White people would back out of the conversation. The White students in the room saw this as diplomatic behavior. Not so the African American students, who felt strongly that if you care about the person you are speaking to, you don't just back down and pretend everything is fine when it isn't. Pulling out of reciprocity is a defensive measure taken by Black Americans only when they feel personally threatened or see that the interaction is already too broken (i.e., one-sided, status driven) to participate in. White Americans, by contrast, typically back down at the first hint of trouble, saying "yes" when they mean "no." For African Americans, this is not diplomacy—it is pretense (Kochman 1981). Honesty in the Black American interaction order requires a commitment to both expression and seeing things through.

Diplomacy vs. Honesty and Their Suitability to Modern vs. Traditional Social Forms

Although the White American interaction order is in many ways modern and has developed in response to economic and political developments since the seventeenth century, we argue that the Black interaction order is actually a more modern development. It is a mistake to treat Black interactional expectations as traditional. Their origins are more recent historically (in post–Civil War America), and the circumstances of Black American life in which these expectations arose were from the beginning more culturally and ethnically diverse and democratic than the White social context has ever been. We find that Black Americans are way ahead of White Americans in their pursuit of democracy.

Looked at historically, it turns out that diplomacy does have origins in the pretense and political intrigue involved in the lives of European royalty and highly placed diplomats (Elias 1939). In the watered-down version of diplomacy that characterizes White interaction order expectations in contemporary American interaction, we forget that diplomacy has its origins in secrecy and intrigue, and we have come to think of it as "normal" behavior. It feels authentic because it has become a taken-for-granted everyday practice—an expected part of the categorial presentation of self. As Goffman argued, this presentation can be strategically manipulated, but it *should not* be manipulated, and there is a moral requirement that one not do so. However, from a Black perspective, diplomacy looks just like the pretense and intrigue it is descended from.

This is also one of the aspects of the White interaction order that is likely to be class sensitive. The preference for diplomacy seems to be much higher among middle- and upper-class White people—and the historical context for the development of diplomacy would suggest why: they need to prevent the White working class from openly challenging their status and privilege. However, this means that the White working and lower classes may not share the same commitment to the value of diplomacy—viewing it instead as an unnecessary constraint on their feelings. This could leave them feeling much like Black Americans do about the dishonesty of the restraint. But without something like the Black American commitment to equality and seeing it through to anchor their interactions, getting rid of restraint might lead to a free rein of open resentment and insult by White Americans. This could explain the popular orgy of saying nasty and undiplomatic things out loud that was ushered in by Trump.

In thinking about the differences between the Black and White American perceptions of diplomacy, the function of diplomacy in a society based on individual status competition should be contrasted with what its function would be in a society that was actually oriented toward democratic equality and mutual respect. Diplomacy had as one of its original goals to facilitate complex and delicate negotiations between elite persons in strict status hierarchies (and between nations) without offending anyone. This required treating people differently according to their status. However, in a democratic society that put the good of the whole before the individual, one might engage in careful diplomatic relations with outsiders who threaten the group, but this would not be appropriate with insiders. Careful protocol could also be observed between certain social roles—like mother-in-law and son-in-law, and president and Congress—but these are not general status issues, and would be understood as exceptions for select and difficult role obligations.

In high-status levels of Western society from about 1,000 to 1900 AD, the enemy was in most cases a member of the family. We sometimes forget that the various queens and kings of Europe who fought so many wars with one another over territory and honor were usually members of the same extended royal family. The danger, in European society, was rarely from outsiders. It was more likely to come from members of one's own family. The elaborate court protocols and "diplomacy" that developed should be understood as originating in this context.

As originally practiced, however, diplomacy was between formal roles and not between private selves. As Western society industrialized and the distinction between private and public collapsed into the categorial self (Rawls 2000), the development of diplomacy took a new turn (Arendt 1958). As ordinary individuals in society became more influential in political and economic relations, they began to pose important economic and political threats both to one another and to the larger community. In a competitive individualistic society, each next individual is competing with everyone else for opportunities. Skill in the competition becomes not only necessary, but also valued and appreciated. Many novels have represented diplomacy as an interactional skill that White practitioners appreciate. Two quotes from an early twentieth-century British novel illustrate the point:

> Revell perceived that the discussion, for the time being, was over, and he could not but notice and admire the ease with which the other resumed his earlier manner. Nerves or not, he certainly had them well under control. (Hilton 1931: 25)

> "Come along and have tea with me one afternoon, if you can spare the time. So long." It was the pleasantest, politest, and most effective way of saying: "Don't bother me anymore just now"; and Revell, who himself specialized in just such pleasant, polite, and effective methods, appreciated the other's technique. (Hilton 1931: 36)

Among categorial selves, diplomacy is a skilled social practice that is appreciated by others who share the skill. It is not seen as dishonest but rather as a game with rules and expectations. Everyone who understands the rules knows what is being said or not said. This skill with which things are said without being said is the essence of diplomacy. To the degree that all parties understand what is *really* being said, diplomacy as a practice does not, in fact, *conceal* but rather *conveys* information. One might say that diplomacy conveys unwelcome information in a face-saving manner; that, in its modern guise, it is responsive to the presentational needs of a categorial self. However, understanding what is being conveyed requires knowledge of the relevant interaction order preferences and their details.

From a Black American perspective (and likely for many working White Americans), the rules are unfamiliar and therefore no information is conveyed. When White people are being what they think of as diplomatic, from a Black perspective they are "really" pretending they are *not* upset about something which *is* upsetting them. For White Americans, on the other hand, direct references to unacceptable behavior are embarrassing and threaten the aspect of the self that Goffman (1959) called "face." Anyone familiar with the preferred social practices of White Americans would be able to pick up the subtle signs of disapproval. White Americans (or at least those in the middle class) consider it a virtue to sublimate one's feelings for the good of what Goffman referred to as a "surface veneer" of consensus (an emphasis that likely increases with social class status). African Americans, by contrast, typically feel that this is dishonest and often refer to it as "plastic" behavior. Sticking with a conversation, and saying what you mean, is not just a matter of commitment to the conversation and loyalty to a friend, but also a measure of a person's honesty and character. Black Americans don't want friends and acquaintances who will "pretend" everything is fine when it isn't. The consensus *should* be real and explicit, not a carefully managed fiction that allows people to save face.

Black Americans who view compliance with White norms as compromising their honesty often assume that White Americans feel that they have similarly compromised their honesty. But because the interactional orientation of the White self is different in the first place, and the rules and expectations are different, they are not as likely to feel compromised— which probably also differs by social class. The point is that for those who understand the practice, information is being conveyed, so the question of honesty is not the same. They *are* expressing themselves. The signs are usually there for a skilled practitioner to "see." For lower-class White people who are less familiar with the practice, however, and who are likely to be more coerced by it into doing things they don't want to do, it may be as frustrating as it is for Black Americans—with the difference that they don't have an alternative Black interaction order practice to fall back on.

The White categorial self orients toward the performance of formal bureaucratic roles and social categories. A lower-class categorial self is never treated as an equal in this game. But a categorial self is not supposed to feel that they have given up any ultimately real, more human identity or feelings in order to take on, or "play," categorial roles. In suppressing "feelings," a categorial self is trying to make a better role performance.[4] It is trying to make the performance "true" by getting it to totally envelop the self. This is the opposite of what African Americans expect themselves to do. The White individual is trying to become *equivalent* to the role. The African American is trying to maintain their *distance* from the role and continually assert the "real" human self that is not equivalent to any public role except "equal person": or citizen.

Furthermore, because the White self is an individualized categorical self, and has been for two centuries at least, White Americans do not abandon their group when they present their self in this way. *There is no group: no White community*. White Americans have a different relationship between the self and forms of association in society to begin with. However, it is as hard to see that from a Black perspective as it is to see the Black sense of self from a White perspective.

Because of the tacit racism African Americans face, Black identity, solidarity, and community are more important than ever. There are many misunderstandings that seriously effect Black achievement, recognition, and upward mobility that are due to assuming that interaction order expectations are the same across Races. Essentially, White-dominated workplaces and other situations involving White authority (such as police and courts) enforce White interaction order expectations for Black citizens who do not know what these expectations are; and they are sanctioned for violations of White expectations without explanation. The assumption that White people make is that *any competent person* knows what the expectations are. This assumption is made even though White Americans don't know anything about Black American expectations and violate those expectations constantly. At least Black Americans know that there are two sets of expectations, whereas White Americans sanction Black Americans for not knowing White expectations without even being aware that they are White expectations.

CHAPTER FOUR

"A Man Is One Who Is Responsible for Others"

Achieving Black Masculinity in the Face of Institutionalized Stigma and Racism

[A] married man, in a family situation . . . should be responsible, or assume responsibility to be the provider of that family, if he's able. . . . But at the same time a man should be able to recognize that . . . if his wife makes more than him . . . a true man, in my definition, would recognize that they are a partnership, they are a team. —Single Black American man

In this chapter we present narratives of Black men talking about masculinity and health. We find that the way they talk about achieving masculinity illustrates various adaptations that enable Black men to achieve masculine role performances in spite of the institutionalized stigma and racism that confronts them every day in American society. The *adaptations* we document distinguish Black masculinity from the more familiar White American ideal and align with broad differences between Black and White interaction order expectations that were discussed in the first three chapters. For instance, we find that Black masculinity emphasizes equality and community over individual self-interest, and treats responsibility for others as more important than masculine self-reliance and control. However, while these egalitarian aspects of Black masculinity are strong preferences, it is important to note that most Black men still aspire to the conventional White male ideals of success (and its symbols) through jobs and education that would ensure personal and family stability. In this regard their *aspirations* align with those of White men, while the *adaptations* they have needed to make, and the egalitarian attitude that results, distinguish Black masculinity from the White ideal. Unlike popular misconceptions that treat the Black performance of masculinity as "deviant" behavior, springing from a "natural" (genetic) or "deficient" (culturally) form of masculinity, we treat it as a necessary and reasonable adaptation to blocked opportunities that is fundamentally democratic.

Achieving any social identity involves an interactional process through which a presentation of self is made in the presence of others, and then depends on those others for confirmation. An identity that is not confirmed is not achieved. In a context of stigma and racism, the stigmatized self is always at a disadvantage: presentations of identity, no matter how adequate, are likely to be disconfirmed any time an interaction involves Others who view the performance in stigmatized, or racialized, terms. Role performances need to be modified and defensive action taken to successfully achieve identity under these conditions. The stigmatized self will also need to distinguish between various audiences to their role performances: for instance, for a Black American man, a White audience always presents a danger of disconfirmation and "fractured reflections" of their role performances (see chapter 2).

Historic barriers to educational and employment attainment (Collins 2004), combined with the systematic mass incarceration (Alexander 2011) and negative stereotyping of Black men (Russell-Brown 1998), and the unwillingness of White Americans to employ them (Wise 2010) constitute significant barriers to the achievement of conventional masculine role performances for Black American men. In the face of barriers that prevent them from securing high-status jobs that would afford consistent support for their families, and the fractured reflections that disconfirm their role performances even when they do achieve success, Black men have needed to develop a way of securing confirmation of their masculinity that they can be confident of.

Our discussion of how Black American men perform their masculine roles is based on narrative accounts from three different research projects over a period of ten years. These narratives illustrate how these Black men understand and perform their gender identity. The first fourteen men participated in extended focus group interviews with Waverly in 1998 (Duck 2001). Sixty additional men were interviewed in 1999 for a broader study of the intersection between Black masculinity and health (Duck 2005, 2009). During this second round of interviews, participants were read key narratives from the first focus group study as probes and asked to respond. A third set of men were encountered while Waverly was doing fieldwork from 2005 to 2010 (Duck 2015). We present a selection from the narratives we collected from these men to illustrate aspects of the performance of Black masculinity as they describe it in detail. Most of the narratives we use come from the first set of extended focus group interviews with fourteen Black men. Two come from the fieldwork and are used to illustrate issues that the original fourteen men alluded to but were reluctant to describe in detail. When a narrative was used as a probe in the broader study done in 1999, we also indicate what proportion of the sixty men recognized the behavior described in the narrative.

The adaptations we describe, along with practices such as null-response, explain how Black American men have avoided developing what Fanon (1952) called the "colonial mentality." But we argue that the masculine conceptions and practices described in these narratives have become an interaction order "preference" only by necessity. Like White middle-class men, Black men would prefer to get a good education, secure good jobs, and be able to support their families, an ideal that Connell (2002) calls "hegemonic masculinity" because of its dominant and privileged character. Unfortunately, while expectations regarding women's contribution to family income are changing, it is still typical to view a man who *cannot* support his family, as many Black men cannot, as failing to achieve his masculine role. That women are often not able to support their families is not treated as a failure to achieve their gender role in the same way.

Instead of allowing the ideals associated with hegemonic masculinity to define them as "less than men" (Connell 1995; Gramsci 1971), the Black conception and performance of masculinity emphasize aspects of the conventional masculine role that Black men *do* have control over, including physical mastery, risky behavior, and sexuality. This pattern is similar to that of poor White men, but as a form of masculinity, it has become increasingly devalued among the general White population since WWII and is generally considered deviant. This makes it difficult to see that in adopting a performance of masculine selfhood that emphasizes what they *do* control, Black men have made a practical and rational adaptation (Jones 2018).

Popular misconceptions of Black masculinity that paint Black men in deviant and negative terms result from a strong tendency to treat differences between the way Black men perform masculinity and the White hegemonic ideal as invidious and indicative of inherent sexual promiscuity and criminal tendencies. We argue, instead, that the Black conception and performance of masculinity should be recognized as a largely positive adaptation to systematic racism and inequality. Because the racialized stigma and structural challenges Black men face are well-known within the Black community, the interaction order preferences of that community have for the most part accommodated the needs of Black men in this regard, such that this conception of masculinity harmonizes with other aspects of the Black interaction order. The White community, by contrast, treats the Black performance of masculinity as inferior.

The Black interaction order consists of many adaptations to the challenges facing Black Americans, which allow for the achievement of a degree of equality and success within the Black community that is denied African Americans by the broader society. Without such adaptations, Black Americans would not achieve any equality, and Black men would not achieve masculinity. Having blocked opportunities is bad enough. But any man who cannot meet the requirements of hegemonic masculinity may also personally consider himself a failure. According to Goffman (1963: 128), "Any male who fails to qualify in any of these ways will be likely to view himself—during moments at least—as unworthy, incomplete, and inferior; at times he is likely to pass and at times he is likely to find himself being apologetic or aggressive concerning known-about aspects of himself he knows are probably seen as undesirable."

This self-condemnation is as problematic for White men who do meet the criteria but somehow fail in their performance of it as it is for Black men who are prevented by social barriers from meeting the criteria. But their situations differ. Middle-class White men are socialized into an interaction order that expects them to meet these dominant White hegemonic male ideals. Black men grow up in an alternate interaction order that socializes them into a different masculine role performance. They are less likely to blame themselves entirely for their failures and more likely to find women and members of the broader community who accept their adaptations.

Furthermore, as Garfinkel (1967) observed in discussing "Agnes," a transgender person, for those who cannot meet the "standard" qualifications, achieving gender identity always requires extra effort, which generates self-awareness. Garfinkel (1967: 129, 133) described Agnes as 120% female in her performance of gender. Because she could not relax and take her identity for granted, she worked harder at it and was more aware of what she did to achieve female identity than other women. For Garfinkel, Agnes served as a window into how gender roles are achieved for everyone because she is hyperaware of what the rest of us take for granted. We argue that this is also true for Black men and explains many misconceptions. Just as Black Americans develop a double consciousness about Race, Black American men develop a double consciousness about gender that may explain some of the egalitarian characteristics they have been reported to exhibit, including a willingness to share power with women and to consider husband and wife a team (Intons-Peterson and Samuels 1978; Segal 1993). These are often misconstrued as "feminine" characteristics. Black men are not feminine. But they do have significant insight into sexism. In our research on fractured reflections (chapter 2), some high-status Black men made meaningful comparisons between their own experiences and those of women in positions of power. White men, who have had no such experiences, cannot do this.

This more egalitarian attitude toward sharing responsibilities with women, family, and community is consistent with the Black interaction order as a whole but is missing from the White hegemonic ideal. Evidence of the Black American ideal of a community of equals was on display at the March 24, 2018, March for Our Lives in Washington, DC. Alex King, a young Black self-identified "peace warrior" from Chicago, greeted the crowd with the words: "Good afternoon, family." Then he paused, looked around at the crowd and said, "Yes. I said family." He used the term "family" to refer explicitly to the shared pain he saw in the crowd, saying: "Us hurting together brings us closer together to fight for something better." D'Angelo McDade, another self-identified peace warrior from Chicago who spoke alongside King, declared:

> For we are survivors. Let me say that again for you. For we are survivors of a cruel and silent nation. A nation where freedom, justice, equality, and purpose are not upheld. A nation where we do not live out the true meanings of our creed. When will we as a nation understand that nonviolence is the way of life for a courageous people? When will we as a nation understand that we are not here to fight against one another? We are here to fight for life and peace.... For we are survivors. For I am a survivor. *For we are survivors* not only of gun violence, but *of silence*. For we are survivors of the erratic productions of poverty. But not only that, we are the survivors of unjust policies and practices upheld by our Senate. We are survivors of lack of resources within our schools. We are survivors of social, emotional, and physical harm....

Racism exacts a high price from Black men and their families, forcing men to perform masculinity in ways that are not ideal. The men in question have tried to turn this into an advantage. While Black men have succeeded in adopting standards and practices of masculinity that they can succeed in meeting, however, there are still significant negative consequences for the men and their families of the constraints under which Black masculinity must be achieved. Because achieving masculinity relies on resources Black men *do* have control over, risky behavior, physical mastery, and sexuality play an outsize role. Gains in equality between the sexes in the coordination of family life do not balance out the consequences in terms of health risks, blocked opportunities, and family instability.

The special challenges to the achievement of masculinity encountered by Black men in American society, and the ways Black men have adapted to those challenges, make it impossible to understand Black masculinity in terms of the hegemonic White ideal: the popular portrayal of Black masculinity as a dysfunctional combination of hypermasculine and feminine characteristics is a consequence of trying to do so. The achievement of Black masculinity should be considered, instead, in a broader context of both systematic and institutionalized stigma and racism, and the interaction order preferences of the Black community that mediate its effects.

The Black Interaction Order Taboo against Health Talk

In setting the Black presentation of masculinity in the broader context of Black interaction order preferences, we first consider a Black American taboo against health-related talk and how it intersects with the achievement of Black masculinity. In focus groups, seminars, community meetings, and alumni open forums, Black Americans consistently expressed a preference for not talking about personal health. By contrast, talk about health is so important for White Americans that White participants would ask openly how friendship obligations can be fulfilled if friends can't share their health problems. White participants told us stories about how they share health narratives with friends. They also told us about strong Black/White friendships that had fallen apart when the Black "best" friend got sick and wouldn't talk to their White friend about it. Because they didn't realize there was a taboo against health talk among Black Americans, they had been confused and hurt by their Black friend's refusal to discuss health problems, and now lamented the loss of these friendships. Even given this understanding of the problem, however, Black participants remained adamant that they would not engage in such "private" talk.

For White Americans, sharing stories about health and medical treatment is not only essential to friendship—it is also one of the main ways of learning about health and illness. Friends and family expect to discuss their experiences with symptoms, doctors, and treatments. The contrasting preference for treating health information as private restricts what and how Black Americans learn about health. A Black man in a focus group that took place in a graduate seminar told us that he and his twin brother, both suffering from stomach cancer, had not discussed their condition or exchanged information about symptoms or treatment. After the group discussion, however, he said he was going to call his brother and try to open a discussion of their shared condition. Another Black man in that group said that the only time health had *ever* been discussed in his family was when his mother told him not to get an STD (sexually transmitted disease) when he was twelve years old without telling him what that meant or how to avoid getting one. White participants expressed shock that this was the only health talk that had ever occurred in his family.

The way the taboo on health talk limits the access Black Americans have to information about health of necessity also affects their willingness to seek medical help and, consequently, impacts the amount and quality of care they receive from physicians. This, in turn, contributes to higher levels of health problems among Black Americans and accentuates the perception of risky behavior. The prominence of talk about STDs when other health information is taboo also means that the topic of health, when it is raised among Black Americans, often turns quickly to talk of sexuality, which seems strange from a White perspective. This tendency observes the Black taboo on health talk while also intersecting with the prominence of sexuality in conceptions of Black masculinity in a way that reinforces the tendency of White Americans to sexualize Black people.

In a mixed Black/White group discussion, the association of health with sexuality quickly became confusing. Talk about health among White Americans involves a lot of information about many different diseases. They might discuss STDs, but only as one of many health topics, and they freely share stories about diseases they have experienced and what they have learned about them. White American talk about health is an important part of being friends. This can involve detailed graphic descriptions of symptoms and bodily functions that Black Americans generally consider to be gross and rude. But it also means that White Americans are more likely to have *information* about many different disease conditions, their symptoms, the different treatment options available, and their side effects.

Information about health in the Black community, by contrast, tends to be more narrowly focused on STDs and on specific diseases, like diabetes and breast or prostate cancer, that have been the focus of sustained informational campaigns. This has serious consequences. While less is known about health in general, a lot is known about STDs and cancers that can interfere with sexual performance (and much of what is shared is misinformation). Men who depend on a performance of sexuality for the achievement of masculinity do not want to find out that they can't have sex. Because going to the doctor tends to be associated only with these diseases, and because prostate cancer and STDs can make it difficult to be sexually active, the Black American men we talked to described a general tendency to avoid going to the doctor, and to avoid tests for HIV/AIDS and prostate cancer in particular, as masculine behavior.

When sexual functioning and risky behaviors are considered an essential part of the masculinity tool kit, as they tend to be among Black men, anything that threatens to interfere with those practices will likely be avoided. Going to a doctor for help may be regarded not only as a general sign of weakness, but as compromising masculinity by threatening to limit sexual activity. Testing and medication related to diabetes, HIV/AIDS, heart disease, hypertension, and prostate cancer all have the potential to place restrictions on sexual practices. Popular treatments for high blood pressure and high cholesterol, such as statins and ACE inhibitors, can directly impair sexual function. If men view the diagnosis and treatment of these health conditions as a threat to their achievement of masculine social roles, they will be less likely to seek screening and/or treatment. Tacitly, they are acting on the premise that not going to the doctor will protect them from potential "bad health news" that could place restrictions on their sexuality.

Talking about the Performance of Black Masculinity

The initial inspiration for the idea that there is an intersection between Black masculinity and health behavior came from a focus group discussion in a seminar taught by Anne that included Waverly. That discussion focused on differences in the willingness to talk about health issues that correspond to Race. During the discussion, a young Black American man said the only reason he would go to the doctor was if he were "really sick" or had "caught VD" (venereal disease). His coupling of the idea of extreme illness with fear of sexually transmitted disease was strongly suggestive of a connection between sex, masculinity, and health-seeking behavior. He had no conception of preventive health care and said he considered going to the doctor unmanly. In the follow-up discussion, he said that he did not worry about serious diseases like cancer, heart disease, or diabetes. He actively worried only about sexually related diseases.

White participants in this seminar were shocked, both at his limited knowledge of health issues and at his limited opportunities for learning about health. White participants described frequent conversations they had about health, both at home and among friends. The fact that their Black classmate's primary worry was that medical problems might have an inhibitory effect on his sex life was revelatory: Black men do not describe themselves as opposed to getting medical screenings (although they rarely volunteer for them) if the screenings do not interfere with their current lifestyle behaviors and practices (Duck 2009; Cheatham, Barksdale, and Rodgers 2008). But in our data, they report that they actively avoid both knowledge and treatment of medical problems that could interfere with their sex lives, especially if those medical problems cannot be cured.

This initial discussion prompted a consideration of why sex was so important for Black men, while at the same time knowledge about sexually related diseases and diseases that might impair sexual function was in short supply. Waverly made this the focus of his MA thesis. Additional focus groups were organized to explore the achievement of Black masculinity and its relationship to health (Duck 2001). Participants were identified through a snowball sample, meaning that participants invited others who were known to them to participate. The subjects consisted of fourteen Black American Protestant men from the Midwest, ranging in age from twenty-two to fifty-six, all with a high school education or above, and all reporting that they were legally employed. Only one of these men said that he did not have medical insurance. Their incomes (in 2019 dollars) ranged from $44,000 to $156,000 (with an average of $64,000).

Given the sensitive nature of the topics of masculinity and health for Black American men, and the fact that these men were all known to each other, the focus groups were each held in a participant's home in the evening for greater privacy and comfort. Participants were asked not to identify other participants by name (because the discussion was being recorded), and not to discuss what others said in conversations outside the group. Participants sat around a table with an audio recorder in the center. Each session began with an explanation of the study, and the discussions were audio recorded and transcribed.

During focus group discussions, participants were asked open-ended questions by the researcher: How do you define masculinity? How often do you go to the doctor? What were the circumstances of your last doctor's visit? They were also asked to describe their conception of masculinity and its relationship to their health-seeking behavior (i.e., going to the doctor) and were encouraged to respond with complete narratives. The discussions ranged from one to two hours. The participants were surprisingly eager to offer information about their health experiences and their conceptions of masculinity. It seems that the focus group setting afforded a welcome opportunity to talk about issues they did not usually have an opportunity to discuss.

Two basic narrative themes emerged during these discussions. The first theme of marriage, family, and responsibility for others produced accounts of how these men achieve masculine identity through family and social responsibility, in a context of sexual promiscuity and less-than-ideal employment. The second theme of health care avoidance and sexually transmitted diseases (STDs) produced narratives focused on health care avoidance and in particular the idea that *men are raised to not go to the doctor*. These health narratives also distinguished between curable and incurable diseases, making the point that these men saw no point in getting treatment for incurable diseases, many of which have sexual implications.

"A man is one who assumes responsibility . . . not looking for praises . . . from anyone else"

While the difference between Black masculinity and White masculine ideals is often blamed for instability in the Black family, the narratives of the Black men we talked to suggest that for them masculinity involves a stronger focus on marriage, family, and responsibility for others than is typical of White men, even when Black men are single. None of these Black men talked about independence, self-reliance, or freeing themselves from constraint, all of which are important aspects of the White hegemonic masculine ideal. Instead, they emphasized their belief that for mature men the achievement of masculinity takes place within the family and involves taking responsibility for others, which as they tell it, replaces the self-interest of younger males. In other words, the independence and self-reliance that is so prized by White men, and so evident in conservative White political leaders, is a sign of immaturity from the perspective of these Black American men.

Greg, a twenty-four-year-old single Black man, initially said only that masculinity is "what makes a man." When asked to elaborate, however, he said that a man assumes responsibility, is a provider for his family, and accepts responsibility for his wife, as well as for society in general. Instead of emphasizing independence, he emphasized the need to *accept social responsibility*. This is particularly interesting given that Greg was single. When considering the possibility that a wife might make more money than a husband, a hypothetical situation that Greg himself proposed, he ended on an egalitarian note that emphasized partnership and responsibility:

Tape #1 (R is the researcher)
GREG: Masculinity is what makes a man. It's the definition of a man, to me.
R: What is your definition of a man or manhood?
GREG: Hmm (.) that's a good question. My definition of a man is one who assumes responsibility and knows his responsibilities, what he is supposed to be responsible for. I would just say assumes responsibility with no questions asked. Not looking for, you know, praises from anyone else, but know that this is who he (.) what he he's supposed to be.
R: Can you give me examples of some responsible roles that this person would assume?
GREG: Okay. An example is a married man, in a family situation. He knows or he should be responsible or assume responsibility to be the provider of that family if he's able. But at the same time a man should be able to recognize that if his wife makes more than him (.) A true man, in my definition, would recognize that they are a partnership, they are a team.

Greg's account focuses on the centrality of social and family responsibility to the achievement of masculinity. Although a man would like to make more money than his wife, it is common in Black families for a wife to earn more than a husband. Greg's point is that a man achieves his masculine role within the family, and therefore should accept his wife's salary for the good of the whole family, and not put a premium on his own ego. A true man achieves his masculinity through his service and responsibility to family and society, not by getting praise for himself.

Paul, a forty-six-year-old married man with children, connected the achievement of masculinity to family and marriage through the Bible. Masculinity, he said, is "a characteristic that a man possesses, in which he displays leadership to his family, strength to his family, being a support to people around him, and just overall being a leader in society." While Paul went on to acknowledge that "some people view the Bible as being chauvinistic or biased towards men," he maintained that "there is definitely a place in this world for men and for women, and the Bible clearly distinguishes the two." Paul interprets this biblical idea in terms of family relationships. For Paul, as for the other Black men, achieving masculinity centers on a man's leadership in the family and in society. Therefore, while Paul appears to give a more traditional definition and is aware that some might regard it as "chauvinistic," his narrative is similar to Greg's in emphasizing that mature masculinity can only be achieved in the context of family and community responsibility.

None of these men described masculinity in terms of the rugged individual who aspires to climb Mount Everest or to live alone at Walden Pond (Henry David Thoreau) that is so commonly revered among White men, and none put self-interest, personal achievement, or independence above responsibility to family and community. Instead, these Black men ascribe these characteristics to young immature males who have not yet become men. This view stands in stark contrast with the White hegemonic ideal, which elevates self-interested "strong men," who seek praise for personal accomplishments, wield power over others, and avoid social constraint. The Black men in our focus groups did not seek personal power or praise, but rather sought to *mature as men in service to family and community*.

When asked what it is to be a man, Alex, a thirty-five-year-old unmarried man with children, underscored the idea that a man is one who is not self-interested but rather "displays leadership characteristics to friends, family, and society as a whole." Alex went on to say, "A man is one who has values that are based on not just bringing himself up, but bringing up those around him. A man is one that takes responsibility for his actions. A man is a . . . person that takes responsibility for his family." Alex went further than the others in emphasizing that a man is responsible not just for his own personal growth, but for overseeing the growth of all those around him.

The conceptions of masculinity expressed by the Black men in our focus groups are consistent with Du Bois's argument that Black men prioritize a democratic commitment to the good of the whole, that we call "Submissive Civility," whereas the White masculine ideal emphasizes the individual self-interest of the individual "Strong Man." It was Du Bois's (1890) position that the Black American ideal/practice supports democracy, whereas the White ideal is a threat to democracy and is responsible for division and infighting—and in particular for the Civil War (also discussed in chapter 5). As the men in our focus groups tell it, concern for the community is a necessary foundation for the Black American achievement of masculinity.

"I would have sex with a lot of women. . . . Now as a man my priorities have changed"

While there is ample evidence that Black men, like White men, value being sexually active, they contrast a younger phase in which having sex with lots of women was desirable with a mature phase in which they realize that they cannot fulfill their functions as men unless they are in committed relationships with women. (Observations from college students suggest that White men value this immature stage longer than Black men.) Although all the men we interviewed alluded to this, in our focus groups only one man, James, talked openly about his own sexual promiscuity and specifically connected it with his conception of masculinity. Therefore, in order to explore the relationship between sexual promiscuity and masculinity, Waverly took James's narrative and used it as a probe in the larger study of Black men, asking them whether they identified with James's narrative. Of the sixty men interviewed, thirty said that they strongly identified with James.

In the original narrative, James, a single thirty-four-year-old Black man, had explained that the number of his sexual liaisons used to be extremely important to him. He said, "I would get respect for having sex with a lot of fine women. Some of my boys wanted to be me, but now it's different. Now as a man my priorities have changed. I know who and what I am responsible for. I am not looking for, you know, praises from anyone else." Maturity and responsibility for others runs through these discussions of sexuality and relationships.

"It's like men got more choices than females, you know?"

To illustrate in more detail the attitudes of these men toward the interplay between sexuality, on the one hand, and family and social relationships, on the other, we present the narratives of two men Waverly encountered during fieldwork between 2005 and 2010. Dave, a drug dealer, and Fred, an infrequent drug user, were willing to talk openly about their sexual relationships and to explain how they managed to juggle sex with more than one partner with committed relationships and a meaningful level of social responsibility. They represent a different demographic from the men in the initial focus group interviews, who all claimed to be legally employed.

But their descriptions of how they see themselves as responsible men in sexual relationships are similar in essential respects.

Fred, who was fifty-two and unmarried, had been consistently involved with two women for many years. Waverly once joked with him that he was incapable of being single, while at the same time incapable of maintaining a relationship. Fred quickly pointed out that his two sexual relationships had both started as casual dating. But he did not brag about having more than one sex partner. Instead he emphasized that both women represented long-term relationships. Fred had lived with each of the women at some point in the past and continued to spend several days with each of them during different parts of the month. He even had tattoos of both women's names, one on his arm and the other on his shoulder.

It seemed important to Fred that we understand that these relationships were both relatively stable and that he fulfilled important responsibilities in each. He described how these relationships had developed into understandings based on what he and his partners could realistically achieve. In his involvement with these two women, he was very much aware that he could not place any demands on them concerning their personal lives. But neither could they place any such demands on him. Each relationship was in a sense a failed monogamy. The two women became part of a network of lovers and friends who built a trusting and reciprocal, although limited, relationship with him based on the likelihood that Fred would do what they asked of him. The network benefited Fred as well as the women and their children, adding some stability and normality to all of their lives. The dynamics of these associations grew out of the fact that none of the parties was able to satisfy the demands of a traditional monogamous relationship. After the relationships had ceased to be monogamous, they became and remained more fluid, with less stringent requirements with regard to both commitment and time.

One of Fred's partners worked as a bus driver. She was three years older than Fred with three adult children, two daughters and a son. Her son, in his early twenties, his girlfriend, and their two-year-old child lived with her in a house that she owned. Fred complained that he felt uncomfortable living in "her" house, where he was not able to dictate who came and went. The only serious complaint he made to us was that he did not have a home of his own.

Fred's other partner, who was in her mid-forties, lived in a housing project and worked as a hairstylist and beautician. Fred had been involved with her for over eight years. She had two adult daughters and a sixteen-year-old son living with her. Fred had initially dated her exclusively for more than a year, but she ended the exclusive relationship when a man she had dated before Fred was released from prison and she took up with him again. After that her relationship with Fred continued on a more casual basis. Fred often said that his relationship with her was purely sexual. But he also complained about her inability to commit to him, which indicates deeper feelings. He showed us text exchanges in which she said that she had no desire to be in a relationship with him, but nevertheless appreciated the time they spent together.

Although both relationships had transitioned to more casual sexual attachments after the failure of the initial committed partnership, both remained meaningful and long term. Fred spent birthdays with both women, took them to casinos for long weekends, provided transportation, performed odd jobs, and mentored their children. He finally admitted that he sincerely loved both women. But he still had a tendency to stress the sexual nature of these relationships in a way that was inconsistent with these claims.

It became clear after meeting both of his partners that these relationships were much more than sexual, each having become a type of alternative long-term intimate friendship that came with a certain level of autonomy that limited the demands placed on all involved. Although sex was important, the companionship, free room and board, small loans extended to Fred, and his assistance with their household and family needs turned the two relationships into stable, dependable, mutually responsible networks for both Fred and his partners.

Dave, who was twenty-seven and a part-time drug dealer but who also has what he calls "an aboveground job,"[1] discussed his relationships with women and offered the wisdom of an experienced man. The implication of his narrative is that, as in James's initial narrative, a young man could choose to have a lot of sex with a lot of women. But through experience, a "man" learns that having sex with every woman who is willing is not to his advantage.

DAVE: Well, I ain't gonna say it's easy to cheat. Temptation is what you make it. Like, you can do a lot of things. Females always gonna talk to you. Anytime a girl asks you, "You want some ass?" "No, I'm good." It's a whole thing that when you stop thinking about what you got to gain, and worry about what you got to lose, it's kind of easy to fall back, relax. 'Cause ain't no such thing as free pussy, and the minute you hit it, you don't know her psychological makeup. You know what I'm saying? You could fuck her, and she might chill, and y'all might be cool. You call every now and then; do what y'all do or whatever. Or she could just be crazy, fuck around and say that you got her pregnant, or you know what I mean? Just any silly stunt she could pull. But you bring that to the table every time you randomly fuck somebody else. Now, [when] you young, you gonna do what you gonna do, but after a while, it gets old. Like, you get tired. It's too many different personalities to deal with. It's too much sometimes. It ain't even worth it 'cause at the end of the day, you end up losing.

Like James, Dave maintains that when a man is young, he may take all the opportunities he can get for sex. But as he gets older, he realizes that this is not to his advantage. When dealing with women, a man learns over time that having sex "randomly" is only asking for trouble. The strong implication is that *the person who has not learned that yet is not a man.*

A month after our initial conversation, Dave broke up with his girlfriend of eight years, and when we saw him again, he was already with another woman. When asked how he found a new committed relationship so quickly, Dave answered in terms one would associate with the stock market, saying, "Haven't you been listening to *Marketplace* [a show on NPR that was often playing when Waverly picked him up for interviews]? *Pussy is at an all-time low.*" Dave's point about the availability of women to a man like himself echoes William Julius Wilson's argument in *The Truly Disadvantaged* (1987) that because of mass incarceration and unemployment, there were seventy Black women for every eligible Black man in Chicago. The ratio is even worse today. This gives Black men an advantage in the relationship market that White men do not have. As Dave explained: "It's like men got more choices than females, you know? It's like you get a girl, she got a college degree, and she's all that. But socially, she messed up 'cause she don't know how to treat a man, or know what a man's supposed to do." Dave emphasized that although he was a drug dealer, he had a loyal clientele. That meant that he was a single man with a good job with benefits, and he considers himself to be a good man. Plenty of women were looking for a man like him, and he was able to find a new relationship quickly.

As for why he was in a committed relationship if women were so easy to find, Dave explained that experimenting with lots of women is not desirable.

DAVE: Like, if he go out, you'll call him and stalk him every five, ten minutes 'cause you so scared that somebody gonna take him from you. You know what I'm saying? But you not secure in your womanhood. But that comes from making bad decisions. Like, you constantly make a bad decision fucking all these terrible n****s. You know what I'm saying? I mean, there's good women out there. A lot of girls have been through shit, and those are the type that, at the end of the day when they get a little older, they realize, they settle down, and then they find a man. "He trying to get shit together and whatever." They work with you. If you ever notice older females only mess with guys they call "fixer-uppers" or whatever. 'Cause it's like she see through the bullshit 'cause she done been through enough of it. She thirty-five, forty. She done went through all the ballers that sell drugs and all that shit. She know that shit ain't gonna last for so long, and she realize she want [to] work with the working man. You know what I'm saying? Slow and steady, you know what I'm saying? The fast grind, you burn out fast. Slow and steady win the race, man.

As a man gets older, according to Dave, he realizes that if he can find a good, reliable woman, he is better off sticking with her than taking the chance he will cross paths with a crazy woman who will make him miserable. A mature man learns he is better off with one experienced woman at a time—an older woman who has settled down herself and is dependable: "Slow and steady win the race, man."

"Two of the guys at the party contracted gonorrhea and chlamydia"

Len, a single thirty-five-year-old focus group participant, told us about a bachelor party he hosted that illustrates the connection between casual sexual activity and health-seeking behavior for Black men. Len's narrative about when he would go to the doctor begins in a way that does not appear to involve sex ("noticing changes in my body"), but it quickly became clear that the physical changes he is talking about that would take him to the doctor concern STDs rather than health issues more generally. Len describes having unprotected sex with "strippers" with a group of other men. He describes this as a "bachelor's party," but it had rather open boundaries and was obviously not a safe place for sex.

Tape #2 (R is the researcher)

R: I mean, like, under what circumstances would you go to the doctor for, um, problems with physical health?

LEN: Oh, okay. Physical health. Okay. Um [*laughs*], noticing changes in my body. Like, discovering something that's on my body that shouldn't be there, or feeling down, unlike I usually feel. Especially if I am out here doing something I am not supposed to be doing.

R: Like what?

LEN: I hosted a bachelor's party and had the invitation flyers printed at Kinko's. The guy from Kinko's shows up to the party. I was cool and let him stay, but several guys including "Kinko's" had sex with the strippers—raw. The girls were upset because they weren't making no money. Two of the guys at the party contracted gonorrhea and chlamydia.

R: Wait, they contracted both?

LEN: Yeah, nowadays you get both.

R: How did you find out?

LEN: Because I hosted the party and people complained. But again, they needed to make extra money.

While Len hosted the party, he did not expect uninvited guests like the guy from Kinko's. Nor did he expect that the women who danced at the party would have sex with partygoers. Operating without status filters, however, he let it happen. He wasn't expecting two of the men who attended to complain later that they had contracted STDs, but it should have been obvious that under those conditions they were likely to.

Chris, a twenty-four-year-old single Black man, also said that he and his friends engage in unprotected sex. A first-year medical school student at the time of the interview, Chris must understand the risks involved in unprotected sex, especially with women he perceives as promiscuous. And he indicated that fear of AIDS is ever present. Yet he and his male friends continue to engage in unprotected sex and do not want to find out whether they are HIV positive. In fact, Chris said, if his friends were infected, they would want to keep on having sex until they died from AIDS.

CHRIS: Some friends and I were having a discussion about getting HIV exams. You might hear a guy saying that they know they had unsafe sex and sometimes even with a girl that would be considered to be promiscuous. The fear of AIDS or whatever STDs would definitely be there, and a lot of other STDs are pretty detectable whether it's different forms: Crabs there's the itching, gonorrhea there is the burning, but HIV its undetectable and so deadly, and I heard the young men say if they had it they wouldn't want to know. You know they would just want to live their life until they die. You know. So they don't want to know.

When questioned, Chris pointed out that these men *would go* to the doctor *only* if they had an STD that can be cured. Gonorrhea and crabs are curable, while at that time effective treatments for HIV were not available.[2] Once the symptoms of AIDS occurred, they thought, it was too late to do something about it anyway, so in their view there was no point in going to the doctor.

In other narrative accounts, Black men said they would not go to the doctor for cancer, heart problems, hypertension, diabetes, and other conditions that can't be "cured" but only managed through drugs that can impair sexual functioning. Cory, a twenty-three-year-old graduate student, confirmed Chris's assertion that his Black male friends would not seek treatment for incurable diseases. Cory said, "The only reason I would go to the doctor was if I was really sick or caught VD [indicating curable forms of STDs]. I simply don't want to know if something is going to kill me." The distinction between seeking help for curable conditions and those that are likely to be terminal is an important one that impacts the health-seeking behavior of these men.

In the second phase of the research, when these stories from the initial focus groups were used as probes in interviews with an additional sixty men who were asked if they knew someone like the character in the narrative who avoids going to the physician, 63.3% of the men said yes. When asked if they had personally behaved in a similar manner, a third said they had. Furthermore, most said they would wait until a medical condition became extreme before seeking medical care. When they were asked about their last visit with a physician, half reported that they had gone to a hospital emergency room for an acute condition, rather than seeing a physician for routine care, even though they all had health insurance.

Over and over again in these focus group discussions, questions about going to the doctor were responded to with answers about sex and STDs. Not only did these men focus on STDs, but they often distinguished between curable and incurable diseases, indicating they would go to the doctor only for curable ones. These accounts often focused on HIV/AIDS, which they perceived to be incurable, and occasionally on hypertension and other conditions which are treated with drugs that could impair sexual performance. It was clear that for these men, "doing masculinity" by engaging in sex outweighs the risk of either getting or dying from disease. They do not want to find out if they have an incurable illness that could interfere with sexuality.

"I've been raised to . . . not want to go to the doctor unless it is . . . absolutely crucial"

Participants directly attributed their avoidance of doctors to their masculine gender identity. Brian, a thirty-one-year-old married man with children, said that he was raised not to go to the doctor unless it is "absolutely crucial" to his life. He considers this avoidance to be manly, whereas he considers going to the doctor a sign of weakness.

BRIAN: I think I was, I've been raised to believe, or it's embedded in me that, you know, or I have a desire not to want to go to the doctor unless it is something absolutely crucial. If my wrist was cut, I was bleeding profusely, you know, that would be a cause or means to go to the doctor. So I think it's your upbringing and the way you were raised, you know, in whether or not you go to the doctor to seek physical help. But for me, I think that it would not, unless it's something dire or crucial to my life, I don't think I would run to the doctor as quickly as some people.

Because Brian was brought up to think it is unmanly to go to the doctor, poor health-seeking behavior seems normal to him. He does not view this as a problem that could interfere with his health or see his ambivalence about going to the doctor as a risky behavior. It is simple: men do not go to the doctor for preventive care.

Dean, a twenty-four-year-old single man, agreed with Brian. He exhibited a tough persona and expressed ambivalence about going to the doctor, saying that he would only seek health care services "if I'm just not looking well. If I feel like my health is just failing, and I'm coughing all over the place and I'm falling down and I can't move around freely." Like the other men, he has no conception of routine preventive health care as a benefit. Later in the discussion, when asked if he would go to the doctor when he was sick, he referred explicitly to Brian's account of being brought up to think it's not manly, saying: "Ninety percent of the time I'm healthy. You know what I'm saying? Aside from colds, and I only had the flu like twice in my life, so you know what I mean? I don't have to be on my deathbed, but only, only if I feel that it is something, basically the same thing that [Brian] said. If I, I need to go." While he would see a doctor if he were too ill to go on with normal life, he indicates a belief that if he did go to the doctor, his masculinity and his pattern of perceived good health might be damaged.

Doug, who was fifty-six years old and single, echoed the sentiment that he would see a physician only if he was "really sick." To emphasize his resolve to avoid going to the doctor and his desire not to elaborate on his health problems, Doug stated flatly that "health is something we don't talk about in my family." He recounted: "My brother did not go to the doctor until he was really sick. By that time it was really too late. We knew about it, I knew he had cancer. I have it too, but we did not discuss it much." Doug and his twin brother had done no more than acknowledge to each other that they both had cancer when it became obvious and it was too late to do much about it. For these men, waiting until they were "really sick" before seeking medical care had serious consequences. But in their eyes, this behavior is "manly." Moreover, it is reinforced by the general Black interaction order taboo against health talk.

Conclusion

There is a long history behind the Black American avoidance of talk about health that relates to high levels of surveillance of health and family behavior by various social welfare agents of the state, charitable associations, and the private sector. The racial exclusion and segregation that was characteristic of the White-controlled health care system until very recently resulted in a general neglect of the health of Black Americans. However, when their health did attract attention, Black people were subject to heightened intervention, supervision, and even unethical and dangerous experimentation. Most African Americans are well aware of welfare programs that separate a high proportion of Black children from their families. They are also well aware of the Tuskegee experiment and programs of forced sterilization of women of color. Harmful health-related experiments continue today in American prisons and jails, in which African Americans are vastly overrepresented. All of this has led to a widespread mistrust of health professionals within the Black community.

Conventional explanations of the health-avoidance behaviors of Black American men tend to focus on lack of access to health care and what is described as a kind of "abnormal" or "hyper-" masculinity that values risky and deviant behavior (Mosher 2001). Such explanations overlook the complex sexual and social politics that have shaped the lives of Black men in the United States for centuries. Nor do they consider the possibility that Black interaction order ideals of masculinity and health differ from the hegemonic ideal for good reasons.

The health-seeking and health-promoting behaviors of men in general are shaped by cultural norms about health talk and appropriate male behavior in their communities (Pleck 1981; Connell 1995, 1998, 2005; Anderson, 1998, 2009; Duck 2009). When practices and beliefs about health intersect with those involving masculinity and manhood, as in our narratives, men may favor practices for achieving manhood even though they have negative implications for their physical health (Duck 2009; Eisler et al. 1998; Sabo and Jansen 1992).

We suggest that with regard to Black American men, these differences involve a family- and community-oriented sense of responsibility that differs from the White male ideal of self-reliant individualism (sometimes characterized in terms of "strong men," "strong man religion," and "lions vs. lambs"), which depicts idealized male figures as a type of Robinson Crusoe or Tarzan, as if they did not live in, and benefit from, both state and society—a social contract that they betray whenever they take advantage of those they depict as weaker than themselves or claim that their accomplishments are theirs alone.

The Black American conception of masculinity differs from this White hegemonic ideal, as with other interaction order differences, in being less individualistic and more egalitarian, as well as being protective of information that could be detrimental to the community and/or its members. Black masculinity also involves a more flexible notion of who counts as family that one is responsible for—it is a broader conception than the middle-class nuclear family.

This divergence in the practices of Black and White men accords with Du Bois's (1890) argument that awareness of difference and discrimination led African Americans to develop a double consciousness that orients them toward the general interests of the community and away from personal self-interest. Conceptions of Black masculinity should be understood in this context. Black masculinity is usually evaluated on the basis of surveys that compare Black American men to the "norm" for White American men. Such research predictably finds variously that Black men are *less* masculine, *equally* masculine, or *more* masculine than White men, depending on the context of the research. Black American men are alternately described as "hypermasculine," "androgynous," or "effeminate" when compared to the hegemonic White ideal. They are labeled "hypermasculine" in comparison with White American men to explain their role in crime and sexuality. But they are conceptually castrated and labeled "androgynous" or "effeminate" to explain the finding that Black American men are more egalitarian as husbands/partners than men of other ethnic and racial groups (Bem 1976, 1985; Mosher and Tomkins 1988; Bruce 2004), an approach that weirdly treats equality as unmasculine.

If we follow Collins's (2004) advice and examine conceptions of masculinity as an outgrowth of the social and economic realities of American society, in which masculine hegemony is equated with aspirations for and achievement of wealth and social status through physical or business dominance and ownership of property, then it becomes clear that most Black American men are at a profound disadvantage. Few Black families are members of the propertied class, and unemployment rates are much higher for Black men than for White men (Wilson 1987; Williams and Collins 1995). Black American educational achievement is limited by an unequal distribution of wealth that results in poorly funded schools that offer an inferior education (Lemelle 1995; Massey 2002; Anderson 1990, 1996, 2009). Mass incarceration and the school-to-prison pipeline make it even more difficult for Black men to pursue the educational opportunities that do exist. Not being educated affects employment, and being unemployed or underemployed makes it difficult to buy a home and remain married (Hamer 2001); the primary way of achieving hegemonic White masculinity.

These disadvantages have necessitated the development of an alternate set of ideals and practices for achieving masculinity in the Black community, although the aspirations of hegemonic masculinity remain a goal. As a consequence, the achievement of Black masculinity has centered on aspects of self that Black men do have control over, with an emphasis on sexuality and emotional and physical control—what some of our participants called "acting like a man." The resulting emphasis on sexuality and physicality could explain why the Black men in our research associated talk about "health" with losing control over their masculinity in their narratives and evaluated medical treatment in terms of its potential effect on their sex lives, rather than considering knowledge about health to be beneficial. The general taboo against health talk also meant that they did not have much valid information to start with.

As with other interaction order differences that we consider in this book, we treat these adaptations as a protective reaction to oppression: to the fact that traditional masculine roles have been blocked. The way these Black men describe achieving masculinity does not represent a preference but rather an alternative to blocked aspirations. The Black interaction order preferences that result intersect with blocked opportunities, discrimination by the criminal justice system, and hyper-surveillance by social services and schools to produce outcomes for Black men and women that seem deviant from a White perspective but that are normal in the context of the Black interaction order. While these preferences are responses to oppression, we also argue that aspects of them, and in particular the focus on equality and responsibility to the community, are improvements on the hegemonic ideals that they replace.

The practice of "submissive civility" that we discuss in chapter 5, for instance, and the finding that Black men are more willing to do tasks that are considered "feminine" in the home, like washing dishes and taking care of children, are important improvements on White masculinity. Unfortunately, the way this "submission" alternates with a forceful and physical portrayal of masculinity, and with the risks to both health and family that are involved, confuses things, leading to the impression that the Black conception of masculinity is conflicted in serious ways, swinging from hypermasculinity to effeminacy, and that these conflicts are to blame for the "failure" of Black men to achieve the traditional markers of masculine success to which White men aspire.

We argue, by contrast, that this is an *illusion* which results from comparing Black masculinity to conceptions of masculinity that belong in the White interaction order. The Black conception of masculinity is a Black interaction order preference that has developed as a reasonable response to racism, oppression, and blocked opportunities. In the Black interaction order, it is considered "normal" for a man to be both very masculine and very helpful around the home. It is considered "normal" for a strong man to submit to the democratic needs of the group and therefore to be less individualistic. It is also considered "normal" to reject inquiries about health whether they come from friends, coworkers, or agents of the state.

In any case, it is way past time to stop considering it feminine and dysfunctional for men to help around the house. The question should be why are White men who refuse to help their wives still considered "normal"? From a Black interaction order perspective, the men who are considered deviant are those who do *not* help their wives in the home, who believe that they *are* superior to women, and who think they do not need to bow to the needs of the group or family (all typical White male norms). The Black male norm accords better with modern conceptions of equality and democracy. It is also more consistent with Du Bois's insistence on the importance of submitting to democracy, which we explore in the next chapter. Aspects of the achievement of Black masculinity have the character of egalitarian civility.

CHAPTER FIVE

The White Self-Interested "Strong Man" Ideal vs. the Black Practice of "Submissive Civility"

In a Black/White Police Encounter

with Jason Turowetz

Yes sir. Yes sir. Yes sir. I've been living here for *ten* years.　　　　　—Dejuan Yourse

This chapter introduces a Black interaction order practice we call "submissive civility," arguing that this practice of civil politeness and cooperation, which developed as a response to racial domination and threat, is better suited to democratic public life than the White American "Strong Man" ideal. In 1890 W. E. B. Du Bois introduced his conception of the "Submissive Man" as a Black American ideal/practice that acts as a counterbalance to the "strong man" ideal. The White ideal places the highest value on the independence and self-interest of the individual, while the White interaction order reproduces a hierarchy of categories (Race, gender, status) that are consistent with self-interested individuals. By contrast, Black Americans adopt a form of practice that resists hierarchy, emphasizing civility, respect for uncategorized personhood, and submission to mutual responsibility. Du Bois proposed that the Black American grasp of democracy is stronger than that of White Americans, precisely because the experience of racial oppression, in the context of a strong Black/White binary categorization system, led to the development of a double consciousness about that oppression that, in turn, encouraged the development of a preference for equality and democracy that is evident in Black interaction order expectations.

Building on Du Bois, we introduce our conception of submissive civility in the context of video from two Black/White citizen/police encounters that went viral on the internet. While we consider the practice more cooperative than submissive,[1] we call it "submissive" in Du Bois's sense of "submit to the good of the whole" and in deference to his conception of the Black American response to racism as a necessary counterbalance to the individualism of the dominant "American dream" narrative, which, as he argued, elevates the self-interests of "Strong Men" like Jefferson Davis (and Donald Trump)[2] at the expense of the community, stripping society of its democratic moral core and ultimately of its humanity.

The first incident we consider occurred at a Starbucks in Philadelphia, on April 12, 2018; the second, in a Greensboro, North Carolina, neighborhood, on June 17, 2016. In both cases, the public quickly got involved as the videos went viral, and there were widespread expressions of public outrage. The police can be seen in these videos enforcing White interaction order expectations, including the perception that Black citizens don't belong in a place and the failure of White Americans to recognize the legitimacy of their calm, reasonable, and submissively civil responses to racialized violence and threat. In the Greensboro case, our analysis of a transcription from the video also shows how submissive civility was explicitly treated as evidence of guilt.

In both incidents, citizen callers played an important role in directing the police to the scene—a problem that is becoming more public as more and more incidents surface on video. It seems that White citizens are very quick to call the police when they see a Black citizen who looks "out of place" to them. It has even been reported that before the April 22, 2018, arrest of Chikesia Clemons at a Waffle House in Saraland, Alabama, the employee who called the police told Clemons that she should "know her place" (Chikesia had asked for contact information so that she could complain about being charged for plastic utensils for her take-out order).[3] In other cases, when the police arrive and discover that a caller has exaggerated the "police worthiness" of a complaint, they often decide to take no action; sometimes even warning the citizen about the caller (calling them "dime droppers"—a reference to old-style pay phones) and telling the caller that if they keep doing it, they will be in trouble. However, in these incidents involving Race, we see police doing the opposite, using the *fact* of the citizen call as sufficient warrant to treat an otherwise ordinary situation as an occasion for police action: even as requiring their action.[4]

The Black citizens in these videos tend to be cooperative and civil when confronted by police. Unlike most White Americans, they are well aware of the dangers that racism, and police authority in particular, poses to them, even though they are not doing anything wrong. But White Americans lack such awareness. A survey done after the Starbucks incident found that 48% of White Americans thought it was an isolated incident, while only 33% realized that it is a pervasive pattern. By contrast, only 10% of Black Americans thought it was an isolated incident. Most are aware of many similar incidents and worry about them.[5] This is consistent with the findings of other recent polls about Black and White Americans' experiences with the police, indicating that such experience differs widely by Race. In a 2016 PEW poll, 70–75% White Americans approved of the police, while only 30% of Black Americans approved. A 2017 Marshall Project Poll shows that White confidence in the police has been increasing: they record 61% of White Americans as being "Very Confident" in the police (up from 57%), while only 30% of Black Americans said they were confident in the police (Ramsey 2017).

The Black American experience with the police has not been positive, and many Black Americans live in fear of the police. As Rashon Nelson said of his police encounter at Starbucks, he thought he "might die." In the face of racialized domination and threat, Black citizens attempt to minimize danger by being civil and submissive. The constant awareness of danger that this involves is not unlike living in a war zone. But the experience is invisible to most White Americans, and the police do not seem to take it into consideration. We believe that had the two Black men at Starbucks not remained submissively civil, White customers would likely not have perceived the injustice of the incident—blaming them instead for "acting out"—something that only White patrons in the Starbucks incident actually did.

In a democratic society, access to situated identities—like "neighborhood resident" and "coffee shop guest"—should be equally distributed by Race. But after four hundred years of oppression and exclusion, and the "White racial framing" of situations that has resulted, Black citizens are not expected to hold legitimate and/or high-status identities in most public places in the US (Feagin 2009). This makes it difficult for Black Americans to get their identities recognized by White Others, even when they occupy high-status positions (see chapter 2).

The problem is not entirely tacit either: there is often open resentment expressed by White Americans that Black Americans are trying to occupy these spaces. But the fact that Black interaction order preferences are not recognizable to most White Americans makes things worse. In both incidents, we examine Black citizens adopting a preference for submissive civility in combination with other Black American interactional preferences, such as a preference for "volunteering" information rather than asking and being asked (Rawls 2000); null-response to fractured reflections of identity (Rawls and Duck 2017); and forthright "honesty" (Rawls 2000).

The meaning and legitimacy of such practices are not recognized by White Americans. Acting without the self-awareness of double consciousness, those White Americans who aspire to the strong man ideal put the highest value on an idealized dominant self-reliant man, while also claiming to be democratic. In doing so, they undervalue equality, mutual responsibility, and caring for others, which may explain the upsurge of what is being called "White male rage." Not only is the ideal of White masculinity nearly impossible to achieve; it is not conducive to developing a modern democratic form of self that can accommodate diversity.

The strong man ideal embeds a number of contradictions that are damaging to those who follow it, which includes White men. An essential function of democracy is to protect the weak from the strong, whereas the strong man ideal is to make the strong stronger at the expense of everyone else. When people are starved, harassed, arrested, and killed because they are women, minorities, poor, or immigrants, by those posing as strong men, there is a cost: both to those who are directly harmed and to those who tacitly act out the practices of inequality. The strong man role undermines the ideal democratic selves of those who enact it—leading to a social and moral emptiness. In spite of these contradictions, however, White social practices are enforced by citizens, authorities, and the police, *as if they were superior*; the problem, we are falsely told, is that Black culture is inferior. It is not.[6]

By contrast, with the strong man ideal and its contradictions, Du Bois argued that the Black American practice of submission is a much undervalued strength, usually considered a weakness—he called it a strength. We argue that the practice of submissive civility for the good of the whole community *should* be preferred by all who value democracy. By contrast, the strong man ideal aligns with the racist/sexist/classist belief that those who can't "pull themselves up by their own bootstraps" don't deserve voting rights, health care, education, food, or shelter; and that government should let the strong do what they choose to everyone else. This ideal relegates to second-class status work that is essential to society, like caring for others, educating the next generation, supporting the vulnerable, manual and farm labor, and even thoughtful and compassionate leadership: both in terms of pay and prestige. It equates contributions to society with strong White men (even though the contribution of those who pursue only their own self-interest is questionable at best), not with women or minorities; calls emotion irrational and feminine; equates freedom with the unrestricted right to dominate others; refers to social security benefits that working people have earned as *entitlements*; and considers the poor and the weak unimportant except insofar as they can be forced to make profits for the rich/strong (Mayer 2016).

We follow Du Bois in proposing the interactional practice of submissive civility as a counterbalance to the individualism of the White interaction order and its "American dream," "bootstraps," "self-reliance," and "free-market" narratives. Black interaction order practices elevate submission to democratic principles of civility above individual self-interest and treat adherence to those principles as manly (chapter 4), equating strength with mutual responsibility rather than with individual dominance. This is a more egalitarian vision of manhood. The well-being of both individual and community depend on a broad commitment to equality and mutual cooperation: the strong man ideal erodes this commitment, while the Black American practice of submissive civility strengthens it.

Progressive and liberal White Americans who retain the strong man ideal while at the same time believing in democratic equality are unwittingly and uncomfortably living a contradiction: their tacit interactional practices contradict their beliefs. For democracy to work in diverse modern societies, for America to finally become "the land of the free and home of the brave," each individual must not only commit to the principle that equality and democracy are more important than individual self-interest; they must also commit to being aware of whether, and how, their tacit social practices support or undermine that commitment in everyday interaction.

Because it differs from the dominant White ideal, the practice of submissive civility, which relies on heightened cooperation and formal respect ("sir/ma'am") by otherwise strong men (and women), is generally misunderstood by White Americans,[7] who tend to act as if White interaction order preferences are the only legitimate practices. Our analysis shows how tacit racism in the failure to recognize the legitimacy of Black identity and Black interaction order practices can lead to serious legal consequences that ultimately undermine American democracy for *everyone*. The civility of public spaces is shattered and the fairness of our democratic ideals and practices are undermined when police action (and citizen callers) are driven by tacit racism: tacit racism thus imperils not only the Black citizens it targets, but also others in the situation, as well as the community at large. We see in the videos how tacit racism leads to the enforcement of White interactional preferences by citizens and the police, as if they were legal requirements.

The Two Incidents

Video of the first incident, at a Starbucks in Philadelphia, was recorded on the cell phones of two patrons and lasts about eight minutes. Video of the second incident in Greensboro, North Carolina, was recorded by two police body cameras and lasts over sixteen minutes. We chose these incidents for analysis because in both cases there are interaction order problems, the video is publicly available and widely disseminated, the outcomes were publicized, the legitimate identities of the Black citizens involved were publicly verified, and there were widespread expressions of citizen outrage. In the Greensboro incident, there was a press conference that made it clear that the Black citizen had claimed a valid identity, and that both police officers lost their jobs as a result of their actions. In the Starbucks incident, the manager who called the police is no longer with the company, store policies and training have been changed to prevent future incidents, and the Philadelphia police commissioner has set new guidelines for how the police will handle such calls in the future.

Both incidents are good illustrations of submissive civility because the Black citizens involved were able to maintain a submissively civil stance during threatening police confrontations. The Greensboro incident is particularly salient because the Black citizen resident was able to remain submissively civil during extreme provocation for over nine minutes before the White male police officer grabbed his phone and initiated violence. It also matters that the latter encounter was long enough to track the progress of turn pairs across interactional sequences. Unfortunately, the video from Starbucks is not the same quality and did not last long enough for this to be possible. To support our use of conversation analysis (CA) to track troubles with reciprocity and mutual alignment across an encounter, sound quality and length of interaction are crucial, and consequently our turn-by-turn analysis focuses on the Greensboro incident.

Overview of the 2018 Starbucks Incident

The Starbucks incident occurred in Philadelphia, Pennsylvania, on April 12, 2018, and within days video of the incident had been viewed over 11 million times. It was referred to as a case of "retail racism" and "shopping while Black." The public expressed outrage over the way the two Black men were treated in Starbucks, being arrested within minutes of their arrival because they were "waiting" for a friend without making a purchase. The story quickly went viral. Kevin Johnson, current CEO of the Seattle-based company, flew to Philadelphia to meet with the two men, Rashon Nelson and Donte Robinson, and apologize to them. Johnson called the arrests "reprehensible" and ordered more than eight thousand Starbucks locations closed on the afternoon of May 29 so that nearly 175,000 employees could receive training on unconscious racial bias.

In a televised interview with the Associated Press, Nelson, one of the Black men arrested, said he was worried during the incident that the situation would spin out of control and he might die: "Anytime I'm encountered by cops, I can honestly say it's a thought that runs through my mind." He continued, "When you know that you did nothing wrong, how do you really react to it? . . . You can either be ignorant, or you can show some type of sophistication and act like you have class. That was the choice we had." They close sophistication and class—which we identify as submissive civility.

Another disturbing aspect of the call to the police is that the description changed from the initial call from the Starbucks manager (about "two gentlemen" in the café refusing to buy anything or leave), to the police dispatcher's report of a "group" causing a disturbance, to allegations of a police report that claimed the two men were swearing at the café manager. We have seen this kind of "enhancement" of a complaint to the police in other incidents. According to Nelson and Robinson, the manager came over and asked if she could help them but did not ask them to leave. It is possible that due to tacit racial bias she was afraid to ask the men to leave and called the police instead. Calling police to handle small problems with Black citizens is common and appears in reports of other incidents, like the arrest of Chikesia Clemons at a Waffle House on April 22, 2018, where the staff seems to have called the police because a Black customer asked for the number of the head office to make a complaint. A number of such calls have gone viral on the internet, and the callers have been given names: "Barbeque Becky," "Corner Store Caroline," and "Sidewalk Susan" among them. This marks a disturbing and dangerous trend (Guynn 2018). The fact that police dispatchers may be "enhancing" such calls, as the Starbucks incidents suggests, increases the danger and injustice. In the Starbucks case, the initial 911 call did not mention swearing, a group, or a disturbance. The police dispatcher and subsequent reports appear to have enhanced the call.

After the incident it was also discovered that most Starbucks do not have the policy this location claimed to have, that a person needs to buy something to sit in the café or use the bathroom. The manager of this Starbucks, located in a newly gentrified area of Philadelphia called Rittenhouse Square, likely adopted this policy to keep Black people—the original residents of the neighborhood—out of the café: a frequent consequence of gentrification (although Starbucks officially says that this location did not have such a policy [see Duck 2019 on gentrification]).

It was not only the store manager who treated Nelson and Robinson differently from other customers, however; the police also treated the two Black men differently from the way they treated the White friend the two men had been waiting for and other White patrons of the café, who began yelling at the police about the incident and creating an actual (though justified) disturbance. When the police arrived, Nelson and Robinson followed the Black preference for volunteering information and gave a reasonable explanation for their presence in Starbucks. The police were not responsive to what the two men said, merely repeating their "order" for the two men to leave. Officers moved chairs out of the way in preparation for the arrest as if they expected a physical confrontation from two men in a coffee shop who remained quiet, civil, and polite throughout. By contrast, the police did not seem to worry about the White friend who was literally in their faces. And while they did not respond to what the two Black men said, ignoring their speech, the officers did respond at length to their White friend, refusing his request to let the three of them go elsewhere, which would have deescalated the incident, but nevertheless answering his questions, saying, "We are way past that," indicating that their decision to arrest the men would not change. That decision must have been made before they entered the café, since nothing happened after they entered that would have warranted arrest.

While the police were themselves making a scene, moving chairs and tables and disrupting the entire café, they kept telling the two Black men, who were still sitting calmly, "Okay, let's not make a scene" and "Let's not get into a fight here." The two men later said they were scared for their lives.

In addition to interaction order issues about volunteering information and submissive civility, the incident involves identity issues with regard to where Black citizens belong, the perception of Black men as scary and violent, the role of citizen callers in accomplishing racism by calling the police, and police officers at the scene not being responsive to Black citizens.

The mistreatment of Nelson and Robinson eventually resulted in television appearances, a negotiated settlement between Starbucks and the two men, the retraining of all Starbucks managers worldwide, and an apology from the Philadelphia police commissioner announcing new policies for the police handling of such calls. The mayor of Philadelphia also got involved, saying that the incident reflected the deplorable state of racial injustice in 2018.

Overview of the Greensboro, North Carolina, Incident

The second incident occurred in Greensboro, North Carolina, on June 17, 2016, while police body camera footage became publicly available that September.[8] The incident involved the violent arrest of a Black resident who was sitting on his own/mother's front porch after a citizen caller reported him to the police. The public was outraged by the incident as video became widely available on the internet, on various news sites, and on YouTube. The city council held a public meeting to discuss the event. According to WREG Channel 3 in Greensboro (Tribune Media Wire 2016), the White female officer was fired, while the White male officer (Cole) resigned from the Greensboro Police Department in light of the investigation, and because he had resigned, charges against him were dropped. To stop him from working in law enforcement elsewhere, Mayor Nancy Vaughan read a resolution at a public press conference, calling for permanent suspension of his law enforcement certification. The resolution passed the council by an 8–0 vote. Greensboro City Councilman Mike Barber said, "Well, it's horrible! And I say this as a white male representative."[9] During that press conference, Mayor Nancy Vaughan apologized to Dejuan Yourse (the citizen), who was in attendance, calling the incident "ugly."

The data we analyze consists of a sixteen-minute video (available on the internet) spliced together from the two police body cameras, from which we compiled a transcript (of 648 lines), only portions of which are reproduced in this chapter. We use conversation analysis (CA) to analyze the various troubles and misalignments in the interaction (see chapter 1, note 3). This allows us to identify sequences where failures of reciprocity and recipient design indicate that tacit racism is present. We reproduce lines 1–182 and lines 364–369 of our transcript in this chapter, stopping well before the physical altercation and formal arrest initiated by the police officer, and then reproducing only five lines after that point, our purpose being to focus on how tacit racism escalated the encounter and not on the excessive force itself (for the rest, see Rawls, Duck, and Turowetz 2018). The sixteen-minute length of the video was of particular interest. Most police/citizen encounters that end badly, for which video exists, are so short, and the video so poor, as in the Starbucks incident, that interactional misalignments are impossible to track across the encounter.

Although we refer to the Black citizen as the citizen/resident (CR) for the remainder of the chapter, because *it is his legitimate legal identity*, we want to note that in this interaction his functional status is "Black male" about whom there has been a citizen call/complaint, an all too frequent occurrence. He is not yet a "suspect" because the police keep saying he isn't. He is a Black American citizen standing on the porch of his own/mother's house—where his ID says he resides—who cannot get his identity recognized; a frequent problem for Black men in America.

The officers tell him they have a call about "somebody walking around with a shovel" (line 7), and that "neighbors" are worried about recent "break-ins" (lines 24–25). The official accounts mention a "possible breaking and entering" call to which the officers were responding. But in a part of the video where the officers talked to each other in private (time code 0:47–1:29), we hear the female officer tell the male officer that the computer shows only old calls about break-ins, "nothing recent," and that the old calls involved "Asian peoples." So while it is possible that the computer is wrong, the officers at the scene have no evidence of recent break-ins. What they have is a citizen call about a Black man walking in his yard with a shovel.

This is a type of citizen call many officers have told us about ("six Black teenagers just went into the sub shop"). The police must respond. But what they do when they get there is a matter of judgment. There is no police-relevant problem involved. Although some officers treat these as serious calls, many officers recognize these calls as racial profiling by citizens (the kids probably went in to buy subs) and try to do the minimum when they arrive. But even if they just take a look and don't ask any questions, the "kids" will notice the police walking through and looking at them. In the Greensboro case, the citizen's ID should have settled the identity question and told them the citizen call was racist. Instead, the officers kept questioning CR and then held him in physical custody, refusing to let him leave his porch, after they had verified his residency from his ID and assured him repeatedly that there was no problem. Technically, he had been under arrest for many minutes while the police were still telling him there was no problem. But there was no crime, although the male officer (PO2) kept fishing for one. When CR finally becomes agitated, PO2 asks (in dialect), "What going on?" (line 285—not reproduced in this chapter), as if CR has nothing to be upset about. Later, after he has punched CR in the face several times and has him on the ground in handcuffs, PO2 says, "YOU GAVE ME A PROBLEM" (time code 11:35) and "I'm gonna figure out why" (time code 11:37—not reproduced in this chapter). Although the officer is punching CR in the face, he still has not identified a problem he can arrest him for.

The incident is instructive on several levels. In particular, it facilitates an examination, in real time and on a turn-by-turn basis, of how an interaction between two White police officers (one male/one female) and a Black male citizen ended in the use of excessive force by the police and the assault and arrest of an innocent citizen. We argue that in addition to problems stemming from how the officers initially fail to recognize CR's identity as legitimate, the misalignments escalate because the officers and CR are acting in different interaction orders: they are literally making sense in different social forms of life. Furthermore, while CR tries hard to bridge these differences, the officers do not try—rather, they continue to judge CR according to their own preconceptions and are not interactionally responsive to him.[10]

Double consciousness gives this Black citizen an ironic advantage: whereas he understands that he is in trouble, even though both officers tell him he is not, they do not try to see his perspective, instead treating his claims of innocence as evidence that he is up to "something" and his increasing agitation, which given the situation is more than reasonable, also as evidence of "something." Respect for the legitimate cultural status of Black interactional preferences, combined with respect for a Black citizen's identity, would have been helpful to the police and might have saved their jobs. Failing such respect and understanding, CR's attempts to get his "normal" behavior recognized as ordinary and legitimate were treated by the police as evidence of guilt.

Interaction with the White Female Officer PO1

The Greensboro video opens with a White female officer (PO1), who is answering the call for service, approaching a Black male citizen (CR), who is standing in front of a large house in a well-kept neighborhood. For the first 46 seconds, the video we see is from the female officer's body camera. As she approaches, she asks, "is everything okay?" (line 1). The question is built to elicit a yes or no answer. But CR says, "Yeah," and then volunteers: "I live here" (line 3). This is an important claim of *resident identity*. After PO1 explains that they got a call "about somebody walking around with a <u>shovel</u>" (line 7), CR volunteers more information (lines 9, 12, 15, 16). "Yeah I␣was- gettin' the shovel (.) out in the yard (there)" (line 9). He responds by "answering with more than the question asked for—it only required a yes-no response" (Raymond 2003). His response, however, exhibits a Black interaction order preference for volunteering information about the immediate situation rather than asking and being asked, and for being submissively civil.

#1: Greensboro, Part 1 (PO1 body-cam starting time code: 00:10)

```
1.   PO1:   Hey (.) is everything okay?
2.          (.)
3.   CR:    Yeah. (.) I live here.
4.          (.)
5.   PO1:   Okay.
6.          (.)
7.   PO1:   We got a call about somebody walking around with a shovel.
8.          (.)
9.   CR:    Yeah I was- getting' the shovel (.) out in the yard (there).
10.         (.)
11.  PO1:   Yeah o kuh(h)- .h(h) [okay(h) (h).h [Good deal.
12.  CR:                         [Uh(h) huh    [This is my mom's house.
13.         (.)
14.  PO1:   Oh okay. O[kay.
15.  CR:              [Yeah. Yeah that's- my name is (.) Dejua:n ((pointing at
16.         the house)) This is my mom hou[se.
17.  PO1:                                  [Okay.=What's your mamma's name?
18.  CR:    Livia. [((Nods))
19.  PO1:          [I'll- I'll check the [(    ) real [quick just to make sure.=
20.  CR:                                 [Livia-      [Livia
21.  CR:    =L:ivia >('s j's)<- (.) [Livia Sue Yours.
22.  PO1:                           [Okay.
```

23.		(.)
24.	PO1:	O:kay. One of the neighbors was con<u>cer</u>:n:ed they've- (.) they've had
25.		some break-ins over here, >I [guess< they didn't recognize you or=
26.	CR:	[Oh nah not <u>me</u>.
27.	PO1:	=somethin' like tha:t [I don't know.]
28.	CR:	[No. Not me.] I come here every day.
29.	PO1:	.hh O:kay. O↓[kay,
30.	CR:	[Yes ma'am.=
31.	PO1:	=Good deal.
32.		(.)
33.	PO1:	Have a good one. ((PO1 starts walking away))
34.	CR:	You too.

CR's first response, "I live here" (line 3), to PO1's first question, "Hey (.) is everything okay?" (line 1), indicates that he treats the question as implying that he should not be there. He recognizes immediately that he is having an identity recognition problem. The officer's sequence-closing third turn (Schegloff 2007), "Okay" (line 5), appears to indicate that she accepts his response (we see later that she does not). But then instead of verifying his residency by asking for ID, she continues her account: "We got a call about somebody walking around with a <u>shovel</u>" (line 7). Besides accounting for her presence on the scene, the officer's response marks a specific action as police-worthy. There was a "call" to the police about "somebody" with a shovel (even though walking around with a shovel is normal for a resident). Most police work involves responding to citizen calls. The reported "somebody" is vague and does not directly implicate CR (although the caller likely described him as Black).

Immediately following PO1's account of why the police are there (line 7), CR again volunteers information, explaining that he was walking around with a shovel before she drove up: "Yeah I was- getting' the shovel (.) out in the yard (there)" (line 9). This combines the Black preferences for volunteering and forthright honesty. CR is confirming that he is the "somebody" reported to the police in the call the officers are responding to. He lives here and he had a shovel. This occasions a laugh-punctuated response from PO1 (line 11). CR joins in the laughter (line 12) and, in overlap with PO1's assessment of "Good deal" (line 11), he again asserts his resident identity saying that the house is his mom's. At this point CR and PO1 are in mutual alignment, something CR and the White male officer (PO2) do not achieve.

CR then volunteers his name "Dejuan" (line 15) and repeats his residency claim for the third time, "This is my mom's house" (line 16). In response to PO1's query, "Okay.=What's your mamma's name?" (line 17), CR says, "<u>Li</u>via Sue Yours" (lines 18, 21). After three claims of residency, the officer has finally asked for residency information. However, she still does not ask for ID, and the sequence results in a problem, as we see when PO1 reports (lines 217–218) that she can't find CR in the computer. She has not asked him for ID, or how to spell his or his mother's name, so she can't find him in the computer. Her use of "mamma" to refer to the mother of a grown man may also be a tacit indicator of the troubles to come. PO1 acknowledges CR's response, "Okay" (line 22), and then, following a silence (line 23), restates her reason for being there, again citing a neighbor's concern: "O:kay. One of the neighbors was con<u>cer:n</u>ed they've- (.) they've had some break-ins over here, >I guess< they didn't recognize you or= somethin' like tha:t I don't know" (lines 24–27).

PO1's account supplies a candidate reason for the call to the police: "they didn't recognize you" (line 25), which the officer hedges with uncertainty markers: "I guess," "I don't know" (lines 25, 27). In response, CR offers a denial, "oh nah not <u>me</u>" (line 26), indicating that he heard the prior turn as suggesting that he is an unknown person in this neighborhood. He then repeats his denial (line 28), and volunteers a report of his habitual behavior: "I come here every day" (line 28). The adverbial phrase "every day" is an *extreme case formulation*. It suggests that it is impossible for the neighbors not to know him. As Pomerantz (1986: 227) observes, such formulations are often used "to assert the strongest case in anticipation of a non-sympathetic hearing" and are typically employed in environments where "accusing, justifying, and defending" are relevant.

Thus, in response to the suggestion that he is not recognizable in the neighborhood, CR emphasizes how frequently he comes to the house. PO1 appears to accept his response, as indicated by her acknowledgment tokens, "Okay. Okay" (line 29), and assessment, "Good deal" (line 31). This is punctuated by CR's use of formal polite language: "Yes, ma'am" (line 30). PO1 then initiates an ordinary closing (Schegloff and Sacks 1973), "Have a good one" (line 33), as if they were done, to which CR responds with an equally ordinary return closing, "You too" (line 34).

It would appear that PO1 and CR have concluded a successful interaction. The White female officer appears to have accepted CR's responses, has managed a series of turn alignments with him, and the two have engaged in shared laughter. CR has been cooperative. They also appear to have understood each other throughout. These elements of the interaction appear to reflect the presence of what Garfinkel (1963) calls "Trust Conditions": a condition of mutual reciprocity necessary for the achievement of mutual understanding. However, that is illusory.

Even during the first 46 seconds, it turns out that PO1 was not being entirely honest with CR—which she reveals backstage to the White male officer, PO2 (time code 0:47–1:29). This part of the video was recorded on PO1's body camera after she left CR and returned to her patrol car, where PO2 (who had joined her on the call for an unknown reason) was waiting for her. She says to him, "I'm just gonna check him real quick. He says it's his mother's house" (0:34). She continues, "Um, I was gonna . . . we don't have anything . . . recent. It's got like stuff from 2015 but it's all like- Asian peoples" (0:34). There are no recent reports of criminal activity, and not even old ones for anyone fitting CR's description; that is, anyone Black. This also means "no recent break-ins," which means there is no evidence to support PO1's account to CR about recent break-ins. PO1 nevertheless does further background checks on CR. In this backstage setting (Goffman 1959), PO1 expresses sentiments that contradict those she displayed front stage with CR.

That PO1's assurances that she is satisfied are not to be taken at face value becomes clear to CR when the White male officer PO2 approaches him. While PO1 starts her computer check, PO2 leaves the patrol car and approaches CR on the porch, where he is still standing. At this point, the video has switched from PO1's body camera to PO2's body camera. This part of the recording lasts approximately five minutes (time code 1:34–6:40). CR and PO2 are misaligned from the outset of their interaction. Unlike the first 46-second interaction between PO1 and CR, which at least achieved the appearance of mutuality, PO2 and CR obviously fail to achieve a mutual understanding: a sign that trust conditions (Garfinkel 1963) are not being met and that what Goffman (1959) called the "working consensus" is not in force.

Beginning of Interaction with White Male Officer PO2

From the very beginning (lines 35–37), this interaction involved misalignment. PO2 opens with an apparent attempt at humor: "What are you doing breaking into your mom's house?" (line 35). But CR does not laugh, instead treating it as an accusation and giving a serious answer (line 36). Then PO2 laughs (line 37), a further invitation for CR to laugh with him (Jefferson

1979). The problem is that CR is a Black male citizen, a population that has constant problems getting their identity recognized and is also subjected to excessive surveillance by the police. We also discover later in the interaction that CR has been arrested before and has been to prison. He is being accused of breaking into his mother's house by a White police officer. He does not see anything funny about it. Not affiliating with laughter is always a problem. But PO2 does not attempt *repair* to fix the problem, even though he is the one who initiates the problem. In addition, whereas PO1 offered several accounts of why the police were there, PO2 has not done so, opening immediately with this failed "joke" at the expense of CR's identity.

#2: Greensboro, Part 2 (PO2 body-cam starting time code: 01:34)

35.	PO2:	What are you doing breaking into your mom's house?
36.	CR:	I'm not breaking in here.
37.	PO2:	Uh(h) heh huh heh
38.		(.)
39.	PO2:	What's with the shovel?
40.	CR:	The shovel was here before.=I just picked it up off the yard when I
41.		got here sir.
42.		(.)
43.	PO2:	Yeah they said you tried to open the garage door with it.
44.		(.)
45.	CR:	No I didn't.=I want- all- this is what I did.=This is what I did.
46.		(.)
47.	CR:	This is what I did ((walks over to garage door and demonstrates))
48.		(.)
49.	CR:	I got to <u>make sure</u> the dog wasn't in the- uh: garage. That's all I tried
50.		to do.
51.		(.)
52.	CR:	That's all I tried to do.
53.		(.)
54.	PO2:	<u>A</u>lright.
55.		(.)
56.	CR:	That's it. Nothin' [more nothing less.
57.	PO2:	⠀⠀⠀⠀⠀⠀⠀⠀⠀⠀⠀⠀⠀[But you can understand what it looks like.
58.	CR:	>Yes sir. Yes sir. Yes sir.<=I've been living here for <u>ten</u> years.
59.		(.)

STRONG MAN IDEAL VS. THE PRACTICE OF SUBMISSIVE CIVILITY   145

If PO2 had wanted to produce a problem in the interaction, he has been effective. If, however, he was hoping to communicate, then he has made the interaction more problematic. To PO2 it is apparently humorous that he has accused a Black man of breaking into his mother's house, and that when the police got there, that man was still sitting on the porch (or maybe he was trying to provoke CR). As PO2 says several times over the course of the interaction, it is a very unlikely scenario. Nevertheless, he continues to question CR. The situation does not seem funny to CR. It is in fact happening to him. He already told the first officer who he was, identifying himself as a resident of the house. She indicated that she was satisfied. But after the officers conferred at the police car, PO2 walked up and initiated a "joke" that CR treats as an accusation. His responses indicate that he treats the encounter as having immediately become much more serious.

There have now been two instances of laughter (lines 11–12 and 35–37) that are quite different. In the first encounter with PO1, CR laughed first, followed by PO1, who demonstrated reciprocity by receipting CR's laughter with a positive assessment, "Good deal" (line 11). She also receipts his claim that the house is his mother's with a token of recognition ("oh") plus acknowledgment ("okay"), which indicates that the response is satisfactory (line 14). At this point, CR and PO1 were collaboratively completing sequences of talk in overlap. Each question-answer pair is acknowledged and, to all appearances, treated as sufficient by both. This suggests they were achieving some degree of mutuality (Rawls 1987), as does the occurrence of shared laughter (Glenn 2003; Jefferson 1979). None of this happens in the interaction with PO2.

Following a pause in which CR does not respond to his laughter, PO2 asks another question that is hearable as an accusation—"What's with the shovel?" (line 39)—and CR treats it as such. In asking for an account here, PO2 implies that CR's possession of a shovel is problematic and requires justification. The female officer had introduced the shovel in the context of her description of the call to the police. However, PO2 asks a direct question: "What's with the shovel?" (line 39). As Bolden and Robinson (2011: 96) observe, questions that solicit accounts and/or justifications embody "a type of suspension of Trust conditions by claiming that [the speaker] cannot make 'typical' sense of the causes of, or motives for, the event."

If the police were accepting CR's identity as a resident of the house, then his possession of the shovel would not require an explanation. Residents can carry shovels in their yards. CR responds with an account of what he did with the shovel (lines 40–41). PO2 follows this with a more explicit accusation—the third from CR's perspective: "Yeah they said you tried to open the garage door with it" (line 43). But this time he does so indirectly, reporting the speech of an absent third party, likely a reference to the call to the police: "they said . . ." In response, CR makes an explicit denial, "No I didn't" (line 45), followed by a physical reenactment of "what I did" (line 47), during which he gets off the porch, walks to the garage, and then returns to the porch. The reenactment is accompanied by an account: "I got to make sure . . ." (line 49), which refers to his concern about whether his dog was locked in the garage. CR's turn-final "That's all I tried to do" (lines 49–50), which he repeats (line 52), is another extreme case formulation (Pomerantz 1986): "all" places a maximal boundary around his actions and the intent behind them, as does his subsequent turn, "That's it" (line 56).

As a resident of the house, CR could have used the shovel to try opening the door. And he could have said this to PO2. Instead of asserting his right to do so as a resident, however, he show/says what he did. We refer to this reenactment as a sequence of submissive civility, in the face of a series of what CR treats as accusations—all following a serious initial misalignment occasioned by PO2's "joke." Because CR has told the police officers many times that he is a resident of the house and they are still questioning him as if he were not a resident, CR knows that they don't accept his identity claim. In not arguing that as a resident he has a right to do the things the caller reported to the police, he is being smart, polite, civil, and trying to avoid trouble. For Black men, particularly in talking to other men (and a White police officer at that), this can be a challenge. CR needs to cooperate to the maximum, while still making it clear that he is a man who is not afraid, and that he doesn't think it's funny to be accused of breaking into his mother's house. He will not laugh at a joke that demeans his identity, and it is unreasonable to expect him to.

After the exchange about the shovel and the dog, and in overlap, PO2 responds with another implied accusation, this time imputing to CR the ability to understand what it "looks like" to the police: "But you can understand what it looks like" (line 57). Instead of asserting his residency, CR is again submissively civil, responding with a "multiple saying" (Stivers 2004), which suggests that yes, he does indeed understand what PO2 means, and that it is not necessary for PO2 to give a further explanation of "what it looks like" to the police. In fact, one could argue that CR's acute awareness of what it looks like to the police has informed his responses from the beginning. He knows that the situation is not funny and that they are not accepting his identity claim.

CR then volunteers that he has lived in the house for "<u>ten</u> years" (line 58). This is not only hearable as a further identity claim—resident—and a profession of innocence (his being at the house is normal), but is also further evidence of submissive civility: he is being cooperative and volunteering more information. In this response, CR also selects a polite form of address (*sir*) which he had not used previously, and repeats it three times: "Yes sir. Yes sir. Yes sir. I've been living here for <u>ten</u> years" (line 58). This displays not only respect and compliance with PO2 (submissive civility and volunteering), but also marks this point in the interaction as one in which things are becoming more serious from CR's perspective. CR is displaying his willingness to go above and beyond what is normally expected to clear up this serious misunderstanding. He will continue using this form of address with PO2 at intervals through the rest of the interaction.

Following this exchange, in which the questions from the police indicate that they have not accepted his identity claim, PO2 again implicitly challenges CR's identity claim, while using informal language and mimicking Black speech, "Where's yer key brah?" (line 60). His question treats the fact that CR doesn't have a key to the house as accountable. But the reason CR is waiting for his mother to come home is because he doesn't have a key. The use of exaggerated speech, coupled with the term "brah" to sound Black, could be taken either as an attempt at alignment or as mocking CR. A recent study by Eberhardt (2016) suggests that this sort of informal address by the police is used overwhelmingly with Black citizens, whereas police officers are much more likely to use terms like "mister" and last names with White citizens. Eberhardt considers this disrespectful. As with the joke the officer opened with, CR does not treat the turn as affiliative and refuses to align with the slang. Instead, he answers with an open-class repair initiator, "Huh?" (line 61), which signals that he is having a problem responding to the prior turn (Drew 1997). Then ignoring PO2's use of slang, CR follows this problematic turn with an account for not having a key, thus treating the question as another accusation: "I don't have the key. That's why I'm waiting on my mom. She's coming from . . ." (lines 61–62).

This account performs a null-response to PO2's use of Black slang, and what it implies about CR's identity (see chapter 2). Then PO2 follows up with a direct accusation, phrased as a question, "Do you <u>actually</u> live here?" (line 64): "<u>actually</u>" proposes a contrast (Clift 2001) between CR's version of events and "reality." While PO2's subsequent repair—"I mean <u>still</u>?"—downgrades the challenge (allowing that CR may have lived there at one point), it nonetheless preserves its accusatory edge. CR responds with a defensive "I mean"–prefaced utterance (Maynard 2013), clarifying that he is "in and out" of the house: "I mean: I'm in and <u>out</u>" (line 67).

#3: Greensboro, Part 2 (PO2 body-cam starting time code: 02:07)

60.	PO2:	Where's yer key brah?
61.	CR:	Huh? =I don't have the key. That's why I'm waiting on my mom. She's
62.		coming from ( ).
63.		(.)
64.	PO2:	>Have yuh-< Do you <u>actually</u> live here? [I mean <u>still</u>?
65.	CR:	[Yeah.
66.		(.)
67.	CR:	I mean: I'm in and <u>out</u>.
68.		(.)
69.	CR:	[Yeah but she told me to wait right- wait <u>here</u> for <u>her</u> until she get
70.		off the=
71.	PO2:	[Mm hmm.
72.	CR:	=highway 'cos she was gonna give me some <u>money</u>. (.) And I just
73.		wanted to make sure the dog wasn't in the garage. That's all. That's <u>it</u>.=
74.		Nothing more, nothing less.
75.		(.)
76.	CR:	I know who lives <u>there</u>, I know who lives <u>there</u>, I know who °lives
77.		there.° ((Points to houses on "there")).
78.		(.)
79.	PO2:	((Turns to look in direction CR pointed, then turns back to CR)).
80.	PO2:	Now I dunno who called but it must've been someone you don't know.
81.		(.)
82.	CR:	Okay but I ain't- I ain't tryin' to break- break in here sir.=I wouldn't
83.		(.) park my car, (.) do all that. (.) I'm not trying to °break in here sir.°
84.	PO2	Well- we usually don't have somebody:: (.) try: and then sit on the front
85.		[porch]
86.	CR	[I gonna try] and get my mama on [the phone for you]=
87.	PO2:	[Uh(h) heh heh heh]=

88. CR: =(.) just to let you know I'm not lying.
89. PO2: Okay

Following PO2's accusation and clarification, "Do you actually live here? [I mean still?" (line 64), CR explains why he's waiting at the house: "she told me to wait right- wait here for her . . ." (line 69). CR then repeats his earlier account of what he was doing with the shovel (lines 72–73). When he volunteers this information, he is again volunteering *more* than he was asked for.

CR again follows these accounts with extreme case formulations: "That's all. That's it" (line 73). Such formulations attempt to place a maximal boundary, or upward limit, on what was intended by an action. Then, following a silence (line 75), in which PO2 does not respond to CR's attempt to place a boundary on the interpretation of his actions, CR treats the lack of response as significant and volunteers still more information, pointing to some of the surrounding homes and saying that he knows who lives in them. In so doing, he is exhibiting himself as a bona fide member of the neighborhood, as non-members would not possess such knowledge (Sacks 1992). However, PO2 responds (as PO1 did earlier) by suggesting that the caller who reported CR "must've been someone" he doesn't know (line 80): thereby challenging the claim that CR knows all of the people in the neighborhood.

CR acknowledges this, "Okay" (line 82), but immediately reasserts his resident identity and his innocence: "but I ain't- I ain't tryin' to break- break in here sir" (line 82). The "sir" is again both respectful and submissive. CR is demonstrating his cooperation. Moreover, he cites the same behavior (parking his car in the driveway and sitting on the porch) that PO2 "joked" earlier is inconsistent with criminality. Here, CR appeals to PO2's commonsense grasp of what a "reasonable person" *would* do under such circumstances, *if they were* trying to break in (see Edwards 2006). PO2 agrees, saying people "usually don't" attempt to break in and then "sit on the front porch" (lines 84–85).

Here CR's appeal to common sense echoes PO2's failed opening "joke" in which he described this same behavior as "breaking into your mom's house." PO2 then recycles that failed attempt at humor: "Well- we usually don't have somebody:: (.) try: and then sit on the front porch" (lines 84–85) and laughs again (line 87), as CR tries to call his mother on the phone. Because this second iteration of the "joke" begins after CR says, "get my mama on the phone for you" (line 86), it's not clear whether PO2 is still laughing at CR's identity problem (the recycling of the initial joke), or at his reference to his "mama" (PO1 had previously referred to her as "mamma," whereas CR had previously called her "mom"). In either case, PO2's laughter is post-turn completion laughter—a post-turn-completion stance marker—which proposes that the prior turn should be understood as humorous and ironic (Schegloff 1996). It may also be inviting reciprocal laughter and alignment from CR (Jefferson 1979).

Again, CR does not laugh: another null-response and misalignment with no repair.

We don't know whether PO2 actually sees the situation as funny at this point in a way that affiliates with CR, or whether he is laughing *at* CR. What we *do* know is that, once again, CR does not join in the laughter. What we *can* say is that telling a joke more than once that the other person clearly does not think is funny would ordinarily be considered rude—even bullying. CR does not see the humor, and PO2 doesn't perform a repair. Instead, CR remains focused on validating his identity, offering to call his mother so that she can confirm his story (lines 86, 88).

As the interaction continues, PO2 asks for CR's mother's name (line 91), which CR again provides (line 94). This becomes a problem later (lines 254–264, not reproduced here), because CR has said his Hispanic origin name in a "proper" (Anglicized) way, not as it spelled. PO2 asks if CR "grew up in this house" (line 100), and they establish that CR did grow up in the house (line 101), but currently lives in an apartment nearby (lines 111–114). This is more forthright honesty, which we discussed in chapter 3. CR does not need to say any of this. His ID (which he has not yet been asked for) shows the address of the house he is standing in front of. Following this disclosure, CR produces the first of a series of "asides" that are hearable as complaints. While continuing to be overly cooperative, he addresses an aside to be overheard by PO2: "it's a shame I can't even sit on my own mother's porch without somebody calling the police on me" (lines 118–119). The complaint/aside at this point is not yet about PO2 per se, but about the anonymous citizen caller. Coming after the three-minute mark, it is the first of CR's oscillations from submissive civility to expression/complaint.

#4: Greensboro, Part 2 (PO2 body-cam starting time code: 02:53)

90. CR: and I'm gonna try to [get ( )-
91. PO2:   [What's your mom's name?

92.	CR:	Li̲via. The woman ((pointing to the right)) [uh:
93.	PO2:	[Livia what,
94.	CR:	Yours.
95.		(.)
96.	CR:	Yours?
97.	PO2:	Yours?
98.	CR:	Yes sir.
99.		(.)
100.	PO2:	>So what< y:ou:- (.) grew u̲p in this house? Or[::,
101.	CR:	[Yes. ((nods)) (.) Yeah.
102.	PO2:	°Yeah.°
103.		(.)
104.	PO2:	So you li:ve- el̲sewhere but this [is the house you grew up in.
105.	CR:	[Yeah.=I live down (victory) road.
106.		(.)
107.	PO2:	Okay.
108.	CR:	Yeah (right there) on (victory) road.
109.		(.)
110.	CR:	((Looking down at phone, talking softly))
111.	PO2:	YOU GOT AN APARTMENT OVER THE:RE::
112.		or [a house er what
113.	CR:	[((Nods "yes")) Yes sir.
114.		I stay in the:: (Hunter Straits) apart[ment(s)
115.	PO2:	[Yeah. Okay.
116.	CR:	°Okay.° ((looks back down at phone))
117.		(.)
118.	CR:	It's a shame that I can't even sit on my own mother's porch without
119.		somebody calling the police on me.
120.		(.)
121.	CR:	°That's crazy.° ((Dialing number on phone))
122.		(.)
123.	PO2:	You can just put it on speaker and talk to her.
124.	CR:	Okay.
125.	PO2:	Tell her what's goin' on.
126.		(.) ((Phone starts ringing))
127.	PO2:	°What's yer name (man),°
128.		(.)
129.	CR:	Hm ((Looks up from phone))
130.	PO2:	I didn't get yer- uh- she has your ID=What's yer name?

131. CR: Oh. Dejuan.
132. PO2: Dejuan?
133. CR: °Yes sir.°
134. (.)
135. CR: ((Hands phone to PO2)) And that's her number right there. (.) If- if
136. she don't answer the phone. °(Or something like that).°
137. (.)
138. ((Phone message: Your call has been forward to an automatic voice
139. messaging system . . .))

CR's expression/complaint is an "aside" that is obviously designed to be overheard by PO2, marking the fact that "*even*" an obviously innocent behavior, like sitting on his "*own*" mother's porch, is being construed as evidence of wrongdoing. He thereby openly displays his understanding of the situation as one in which he is being unjustly interrogated for something he is *clearly* innocent of, while remaining submissive and cooperative in his direct speech to PO2.

Partway through his "aside" (lines 118–121), CR directs his gaze away from PO2 and again dials his mother's number on his cell phone. While CR is dialing the phone, PO2 asks for his name (line 127). Then as the call to his mother is being completed and ringing can be heard on his phone, PO2 gives an account for asking for his name, telling CR that PO1 has CR's ID: "I didn't get yer- uh- she has your ID=What's yer name?" (line 130). PO2 is wrong about this—PO1 did not ask for CR's ID (which is why she is not able to find him in the computer). CR says his name is "Dejuan." When CR's mother doesn't answer (the phone goes to voicemail), PO2 says, "(Don't) bother to leave a message=We'll just see" (line 140). Without aligning with PO2's inclusive "we" pronoun, CR offers to call his mother again—"(I can- try to call her again)" (line 142)—and projects an account for doing so: "I'm trying to see . . ." (line 144); but before he completes the account, he cuts himself off and says to PO2, "you do believe me right?" (lines 144–145).

#5: Greensboro, Part 2 (PO2 body-cam starting time code: 04:16)

140. PO2: (Don't) bother to leave a message=We'll just see.
141. (.)
142. CR: °(I can- try to call her again).°

143.		(.)
144.	CR:	I'm trying to see if anybody in the- (.) uh- I mean (d'yuh)- yuh- you
145.		<u>do</u> believe me right?
146.		(.)
147.	CR:	That- (.) <u>oh</u> okay [I mean ih- if- if I need] to go: (.) keep=
148.	PO2:	[Well <u>no</u> that's what I'm <u>say</u>ing like-]
149.	CR:	=callin' people [I will.
150.	PO2:	[Well if people- no because [it's- like I said it's- (.)=
151.	CR:	[Uh(h) huh huh.
152.	PO2:	=usually if some[one's gonna-
153.	CR:	[Uh you can go ask [Charlie over there ((pointing))
154.	PO2:	[try to break into a house they're
155.		not gonna- (.) sit on the front porch and huh(h)!
156.	CR:	Yeah you can- I mean [you can ask Charlie over there ((points))
157.	PO2:	[you're so busy
158.		(.)
159.	CR:	I mean Charlie knows me very well.=eh I'm pretty sure he's home.
160.		(.)

This is a significant point in the interaction. CR's direct question "you <u>do</u> believe me right?" (lines 144–145), at around the five-minute mark, is the first of its kind. PO2 responds with silence (line 146), which confirms to CR that there is a problem. This has been a problematic sequence of turns. PO2 said "we" (line 140), projecting that his interests and CR's are the same. But CR's response in the following lines (142–149) used "I/ me" seven times, signaling that he does not treat their interests as the same. Then CR asks directly if PO2 believes him. This question ("you <u>do</u> believe me right?" lines 144–145), particularly with its turn-final tag ("right"), strongly prefers a "yes" response (Schegloff 2007). When PO2 doesn't answer (line 146), CR treats the silence as a "no" and registers this with a marked change-of-state token ("<u>oh</u>") (see Heritage 1984) plus an acknowledgment ("okay"), followed by an upshot: "If I need" to keep calling people . . . (lines 147, 149). CR is orienting toward "calling people" as a course of action that is required to establish his identity. PO2, however, says that he does not require this course of action and will later say that he considered it suspicious activity.

There is significant disfluency at this point in PO2's answers (lines 148–150). The disfluency continues, displaying the problematic character of their misalignment. In overlap with CR's turn, and immediately following his change-of-state token, "okay" (line 147), PO2 initiates a repair of CR's understanding of the situation: "Well, <u>no</u> . . ." (line 148). PO2 then cuts himself off after the initiated repair and restarts, "Well, if people-" (line 150), then cuts himself off again and restarts again: "no, because it's-" (line 150). That's a lot of trouble: four restarts.

When PO2 doesn't say he believes him, CR recycles his suggestion that they ask a neighbor to vouch for him. By naming someone ("Charlie," lines 153, 156, 159) and pointing to where Charlie lives "over there" (line 153), CR is again providing deictic (situationally embedded) evidence (his knowledge of local residents) that he is known in the neighborhood and therefore innocent (on formulations of place and person, see Schegloff 1972).

PO2 then reformulates his earlier "joke" (for the third time) about the incongruity between CR's behavior and what "someone" trying to break into a house would do (lines 152, 154–155), and then laughs again (line 155). This is the same identity issue PO2 has already laughed at twice (lines 37 and 87) without uptake from CR. At this third try, PO2 is still laughing. *CR is still not laughing.* PO2 could be suggesting that CR is innocent, or he could mean that there is something not normal about somebody who sits on the porch of a house he is robbing after parking in the driveway. The ambiguity sits heavily over the interaction. What this turn does not do is answer CR's question about whether PO2 believes him. It is non-responsive.

Nor does the turn display any sensitivity to the fact that CR doesn't think it's funny. By recycling the "humor" at these critical points, PO2 is giving an "answer" to CR's question (about whether he believes him or not) that does not give CR any information. That this continues to be a problem is demonstrated by the fact that PO2 does not get alignment from CR at any of these points. The repeated attempts at "humor" could have been taken as an indication that PO2 recognizes CR's innocence. But PO2 does not stop questioning CR and does not say whether he believes him. If PO2 believes CR is innocent, why doesn't he answer CR'S question? Why does he continue interrogating him? PO2's failures to confirm CR's attempts to prove his identity/residence prompt CR to persist in trying to verify his identity. However, as we see later, CR's continued professions of identity/innocence are being interpreted by PO2 as indications of guilt. He is volunteering too much.

The occurrence and placement of laughter in this exchange is significant. Both CR and PO2 laugh but not together, and they do so for different reasons. This displays serious misalignment. CR's post-turn-completion laughter at line 151 is performing troubles-resistance (Jefferson 1984). Such laughter does not invite co-parties to join in, but instead displays the speaker's ability to take the trouble in stride. By contrast, PO2's single laugh token (line 155) is doing the same thing it did earlier (e.g., at lines 37 and 87), projecting an ironic stance toward his accusations and inviting CR to join in the laughter, which he again does not do.

#6 Greensboro, Part 2 (PO2 body-cam starting time code: 4:46)

161.	PO2:	Now what is- Dewan what's your <u>last</u> name?
162.	CR:	Your say.
163.	PO2:	Your say?
164.	CR:	Yes sir.
165.		(.)
166.	PO2:	And your mom's last name's <u>Yours</u>.
167.		(.)
168.	CR:	Yer- j's- (.) ((gesticulates)) that's how you <u>say</u> it. Our last name is
169.		p- pronounced your say [but °we just say yours.°
170.	PO2:	[Okay.
171.	PO2:	So it's the ex[act same name (and//as)-
172.	CR:	[Yeah.
173.	CR:	Yeah. I'm just [(I use it)- proper.]
174.	PO2:	[That makes sense. Yeah.]
175.		(.)
176.	CR:	(Ay//Uh) ((smiling)) the proper uh::: (.) correction.
177.		(.) ((M waiting on phone))
178.	PO2:	No warrants on file for you or anything [like that?
179.	CR:	[No. ↑No man I'm ↓chillin',
180.		alright-=
181.	PO2:	=I'm just- [I'm just <u>ask</u>ing.]
182.	CR:	[(I'm jus)- I'm] <u>chillin</u>' bro. I'm <u>wait</u>in' [here for my mom.

PO2, in turn, does not respond to CR's proposals to "go ask Charlie" (lines 153, 156, 159), instead asking CR for his last name again (line 161). Following a brief exchange in which PO2 asks how the surname is pronounced (lines 163–176), PO2 asks, "No warrants on file or anything like that?" (line 178), to which CR responds, "No. No man, I'm just chillin'...

I'm waiting here for my mom" (line 182). CR's answer again gives back "more than the question projected" (Raymond 2003). Treating PO2's question as an accusation, he not only answers in the negative ("No"), but offers another account for his presence ("just chillin'... waiting"; line 182). In addition to addressing PO2's implicit accusation, CR's response again exhibits the Black interaction order preference for volunteering information, rather than being asked for it.

The questioning continues for approximately five more minutes with the female officer returning to join them and *finally asking for CR's ID*, then going back to the patrol car to make another search with information from the ID, including the correct spelling of his name, which she had not asked for before. While she is gone, CR's attempts to confirm his identity become increasingly desperate, culminating in a phone call for "help," to which PO2 responds by grabbing CR's phone and then throwing him to the ground and punching him.

At this point, the excessive force begins, with PO2 wrestling CR to the ground on the front porch, punching him several times in the eye, and then dragging him onto the lawn. Meanwhile, CR loudly demands that PO2 stop "punching" him and explain what he did wrong and, by way of a report about what PO2 is doing to him, yells, "AHH YOU PUNCHED ME ..." (line 364), which can also be seen on the video. Then, as PO2 directs him to put his hands behind his back, CR says, "I'm not resisting" (line 366), to which PO2 responds loudly: "YES YOU ARE! YOU WERE RESISTING THE WHOLE TIME!" (lines 367, 369).

#10: Greensboro, Part 3 (PO2 body-cam starting time code: 10:19)

364. CR: AHH YOU PUNCHED ME IN MY FUCKING EYE.
365. PO2: [YOU ( ) PUT YER (ARMS [DOWN). BEHIND YER] BACK.=
366. CR: [( )   [I'm not resisting.]
367. PO2: =YES YOU ARE!
368. CR: =I am not resis[ting
369. PO2:   [YOU WERE RESISTING THE WHOLE TIME!

CR's response, "I'm not resisting" (line 366), treats PO2's actions as unwarranted. He is not resisting. He has not been resisting. He has been cooperative the whole time. Given that he has given the officers proof of residency, there is no legal reason for PO2 to have physically restrained him on the porch for several minutes prior to this altercation, either. However, PO2 counters: "YES YOU ARE!" (line 367), and, when CR recycles his denial: "I am not resisting" (line 368), PO2 asserts loudly in overlap, "YOU WERE RESISTING THE WHOLE TIME!" (line 369). Given CR's overly cooperative and submissive stance throughout the first nine minutes of the encounter, it is significant that PO2 should accuse him of resisting.

While it is a common police practice to push a "suspect" until they react, so that their reaction can be used as a pretext to arrest them for "resisting" (and PO2 is likely engaging in this practice), CR, who is not a suspect, was technically under arrest on his own porch for many minutes before PO2 initiated the use of force. Even if we understand that PO2 was looking for a pretext for arrest on the basis of resistance, it is significant that PO2 managed to construe nine minutes of cooperation and submissive civility, from a person PO2 told repeatedly he did not suspect of anything, as resistance.

Conclusion

Our analysis of the Greensboro video shows how tacit elements of racism in the interaction—involving failures of reciprocity, misaligned turns, and the failure to recognize a Black citizen's legitimate identity—were used by the officers to sustain, justify, and amplify the overt racism in the encounter, which began with a tacitly racist and unwarranted citizen call for service.[11] CR's heightened cooperation, his repeated attempts to establish his identity by getting the officers to talk to the neighbors, and his refusal to align with PO2's repeated attempts to "joke" at the expense of his legitimate identity resulted in interactional misalignments that became part of the police reasoning about him.

Both White officers responded to CR's identity claims as if they were accepting them, but then continued to question him in a way that only makes sense if they thought his residency claims were false, and they did so even after they had seen CR's ID with that address on it. They treated submissive civility and other Black interaction order preferences (like volunteering and honesty) as unusual, deviant, and suspicious.

Black men worry when they are questioned by the police, even before any problems arise. But these officers treated CR's expressive responses as suspicious and unwarranted. They also treated his attempts to verify his identity by talking to neighbors as suspicious. When you explain too much, you look guilty to the police. If we follow it through, this means that the officers embedded White interaction order expectations and a White attitude of trust toward the police into their reasoning about what CR's behavior told them about his guilt or innocence—treating his uneasiness, his submissive civility, and other Black interactional preferences as evidence of guilt, such that they were effectively enforcing White interactional preferences.

That is a problem.

There are several identity issues at work in the encounter that have particular relevance to how the tacit racism develops into a problem across the encounter. CR can't get the officers to recognize him as a person who belongs at his own/mother's house: a common problem for Black men that we call a fractured reflection of identity (chapter 2). CR projects a competent and legitimate self, but the officers don't recognize that self. Instead they orient toward a criminal and illegitimate self, which is a racial stereotype that CR refuses to accept. There is a second identity issue that leads to trouble at a deeper level of reciprocity. The officers don't see the "ordinary reasonableness" of CR's actions. Or they don't try. If he does live here and is waiting for his mom, his actions are *all* reasonable, and due to the public nature of the case, we know that they were. However, because PO2 and PO1 don't see CR's perspective (in Mead's [1934] sense of "taking the role of the other towards the self"), and PO2 doesn't engage in reciprocity with him (his turns are fundamentally unresponsive to CR), the officers miss the possibility that CR has a legitimate identity in this situation. If they had considered this, they might have seen the implications of questioning a resident for sixteen minutes because he had carried a shovel in his own/mother's yard, and holding him in physical custody while they carry out computer searches after being shown an ID that establishes his residency at that address. They lack the double consciousness about Race that CR, as a Black American, possesses: which would tell them he could be a legitimate citizen and still have different responses and interaction order preferences.

We see from PO2's initial attempt at "humor" that from his perspective this Black guy, this "brah," was acting in a way he didn't consider "normal" from the beginning. But he can't arrest him without a reason: a pretext. Resisting is a preferred pretext (Bittner 1967, 1970; Chevigny 1969). While the opening joke may initially have been intended as an "icebreaker," it positions CR as a deviant, and PO2 told the "joke" and laughed at it (by himself) four times (the fourth time is in a part of the transcript that is not shown in this chapter). This failure of reciprocity indicates that PO2 is not engaged in mutuality with CR: he is being disrespectful and not responsive to how CR feels about it—not a good icebreaker.

In the end, PO2 asserts his legal right to punch CR repeatedly in the face, wrestle him to the ground, and arrest him, loudly yelling that he has been "resisting" him "the whole time"—a "pretext" for arrest that is contradicted by CR's submissive cooperation. Any resistance offered by CR was interactional, reasonable, and constituted a civil, submissive, and legal exercise of his rights, his legitimate identity, and his Black American interaction order preferences.

On top of the overt racism and racial profiling in this incident, for which there is strong evidence, tacit racism leads the officers to impute actions, motives, and identities to CR that he does not have (such as "resisting"), based on his "deviation" from their White interaction order expectations. CR finds himself in a kind of double bind: if he asserts his rights as a resident—as one would expect a White resident to do—he risks being seen as uncooperative; but in his efforts to be cooperative, he risks being seen as resistive and deviant, and he is arrested anyway. *The way the officers are able to formulate submissive civility as resistance matters.*

According to PO2's White interaction order expectations, the "Black male" he is questioning is volunteering too much information, and he says so several times. In the Black interaction order, volunteering is preferred. However, the White preference is to ask and be asked. From the perspective of a White officer, it is suspicious to volunteer so much ("I said even . . . We didn't have to keep callin' people and go door to door"; lines 300–301). As CR's attempts to establish his identity fail and the encounter escalates, from the 3:25 minute mark on, he is no longer able to maintain a consistently submissive posture. He begins alternating between submissive civility and expression/complaint—a manifestation of the Black preference for honesty (chapter 3). This alternation is also treated by PO2 as suspicious. As the officer eventually put it, "You are hot and cold" (lines 605–606), implying that this alternation is suspicious and that CR is trying to hide something: "You gave me a problem . . . I'm gonna figure out why" (line 425; transcript for these lines not shown in this chapter).

As with other aspects of cross-Race interaction that we have documented in this book, where interaction order differences by Race are mirror opposites (e.g., volunteering vs. being asked in greetings; being confronted with interaction that misrepresents your identity and performing a null-response; taking a "joke" about identity failure literally and not laughing; and, in the Starbucks case, staying calm and civil): the mirror-opposite interaction order expectation we find here is that the Black interaction order preference for being extra-cooperative is interpreted as resistance: which is convenient for the police as a pretext for arrest. Without an understanding of interaction order differences, a recognition of Black men and women as citizens, and recognition by police and other authorities of the legitimacy and widespread character of Black Americans' fear of the police, such injustices will continue.

There were similar problems with both overt and tacit racism in the Starbucks incident. The Philadelphia police chief initially made the public statement that the mere fact that there had been a citizen call for service gave the police legal standing to make the arrest. However, police are required to assess a situation once they arrive. When the police arrived at the Starbucks, the two Black citizens that the officers arrested remained calm and civil while explaining that they had a right to be there doing what they were doing: sitting quietly at a table waiting for a friend to meet them. The men volunteered that "we didn't do anything illegal," and one of the two men said, "Some people are prejudiced," referring to the Starbucks manager who had called the police. The police could have saved themselves, the public, and the community they serve a great deal of trouble by listening to these two Black citizens. But the officers were also non-responsive.

Both overt and tacit racism prevented the police from hearing Black citizens in both incidents. The officers remained non-responsive to Black citizens whom it is their job to protect and serve, even while, in the Starbucks incident, explaining what was going on to their White friend. Black men are perceived as dangerous and suspicious even when they are being civil and polite: in fact, because they are being civil and polite. Du Bois maintained that being submissive is an important strength we need more of in a democracy. However, in these incidents, the submissive civility of Black citizens was not interpreted favorably. Nor was their legitimate fear of the police recognized. There was no empathy. The Black citizens caught up in these two encounters are strong men. But in attempting to establish their identities as legitimate occupiers of the spaces they are in when the police approached them, they adopted submissive and cooperative postures: which is particularly important given the willingness of the police to shoot Black men at the slightest provocation.

We find that this submissive civility—which is necessary and valuable—is held against these Black citizens. It is a practice that should be valued in a democracy. In keeping with the strong man ideal, it is not what police officers expect "innocent" men to do. The police confront these Black citizens as if they had no rights, with PO2 even loudly shouting at CR (after the 10-minute mark) that he has no rights, while at the same time treating racist citizen calls to the police as if they were a legal mandate for arrest. As a consequence, the police officers in both cases can be seen aiding and abetting citizen racism and enforcing White interaction order practices as if they were legal requirements.

CHAPTER SIX

"Do You Eat Cats and Dogs?"

Student Observations of Racism in Their Everyday Lives

It's not racist. . . . Back home whenever we don't like anything, we call it the N-word. Like when something breaks at home, we call it the N-word. —White college student

The narratives we discuss in this chapter are drawn from the observations of college students—Black, White, and Other (Asian, Latinx/Hispanic, and West Indian/African)—of the racism they experience in their everyday lives. Their observations—made over two decades on several college campuses in the Midwest and on the East Coast—show how the interaction orders of Race and tacit racism that we discussed in the first five chapters manifest in the ordinary things people say and do on a daily basis. Because in the US the Black/White binary structures how we perceive Race, those who are located in the various Other categories find themselves positioned against the American Black/White binary in unfamiliar and unwelcome ways. Some (like Asian Americans) are positioned as permanent outsiders when they are insiders, some (like "Black" Latinx/Hispanic and West Indian/African) are positioned as Black insiders when they are outsiders, who often self-identify as White. We present the narratives roughly as they were given to us, editing for narrative flow, and changing names and other details when necessary to make them anonymous. These narratives show that in relation to the Black/White binary that characterizes American society and structures tacit relationships between Races, to be seen as Asian is to be permanently Other, foreign or not American, while for "Black" Latinx/Hispanic or West Indian/African, it typically means being treated as a Black American insider and expected to adhere to unfamiliar Black interaction order expectations. Because Latinx/Hispanic and West Indian/African are not Race categories in the American sense, however, a "White" Latinx/Hispanic can find instant acceptance as a White insider.

In spite of the complications, the racism these students describe has no gray areas: students are assigned to categories that distinguish privileged White from oppressed Black "insiders" and separate both from foreign "outsiders"; it is about how being White makes one acceptable, even "hot," while being Black is considered bad, broken, stupid, inferior, less than.

The racism students report in these narratives is sometimes tacit, sometimes overt, and often has elements of both. It comes from strangers and roommates, as well as from close friends, teachers, and family members and often involves stereotypes and expectations that the student who is being targeted is not aware of. For all students, White, Black, and Other, the instances of racism they describe are often unexpected and catch them off guard. For Black/Other students, however, even though individual incidents can pop up when they least expect it, the problem itself is a long-term and ever-present reality in their lives. When these incidents happen, they know what they are up against. Most White students, by contrast, had not noticed the racism in their lives before they started paying attention for our classes and were surprised by the extent of it when they began making observations of it. Like many White Americans, some had not even believed that there was any racism. When similar things had happened in the past, they had not been aware of it. When they did start "looking," however, they found racism everywhere, including in their own behavior, and realized that it must have been going on all along without their even noticing.

The big news is not that there is racism on college campuses. There have been reports of many serious incidents of racism at American universities for decades. There have even been stories of public school teachers in grade school and junior high teaching their students to "stay away from Black kids" and that they will not be safe "until we kill every Muslim." Unfortunately this is not the big news, either. The big news is that White students are inundated by racist statements, observations, and jokes from their friends, roommates, and family members that *they* cannot escape from. This is serious because it is where the racism of tomorrow will come from. These narratives suggest that we have greatly underestimated the amount of racism that all college students—Black, White, and Other—are forced to endure. We are not talking about an occasional incident, but rather a *constant daily downpour* of racism. Unless White students start paying attention to the racism around them—and take action to stop it—they will absorb this racism and participate in it, becoming in many ways both overtly and tacitly more racist themselves by going to college.

When White students do start to really listen to what is being said around them, they are horrified. Unfortunately, their efforts to censure that racism often immediately rebound on them in ways that make interaction difficult. When White students object to what their White friends are saying, those friends push back and become more overtly racist: "Oh, come on, you know that Black people are stupid" or that "Black people stink," and contend that it's not racist for them to say so because it's a "fact." Their White friends expect—insist—that their racist beliefs be ratified as common knowledge, and they do not respond well to being called out for their racism.

Through these narratives we learned that calling out a friend for saying racist things often results in the White student who objects being called a racist for objecting. This, we argue, represents a form of defensive "circular racist thinking" that we associate with racism (and the denial of racism) that makes reasonable discussion impossible. It works as a "racial boomerang" against anyone who tries to object to racism. How does it work? It silences the person who objects and changes the course of the conversation by projecting racism back onto the person who called out the racism. In one of the narratives below in which a White girl said, "Black people stink and their houses stink," the White student making the observation tried to rebuff this comment by saying that she is "not aware that Black people's houses smell bad." The response she gets for trying to resist a racist comment is that if she doesn't know that Black people stink, it must be because she doesn't have any Black friends. She is told that she is objecting to the comments not because they are racist, but because she herself has a "diversity problem."

This is the circular reasoning: you disagree with someone who is saying something racist, who then says basically, "If you really knew what I know about Black people (or any other category), then you would know that they are stupid, or stink, or whatever the racist belief in question is; so, it's not me who is being racist, it's you." They often complain that "you are making me sound racist," as if the problem is with the person who is objecting to their racism and not with what they themselves have just said or done.

We refer to the omnipresent character of such racist talk and the assumptions behind it as "Race pollution" and to the assumption that such racism is factually based as "fantasy." Wherever these fantasy beliefs originally come from—and they have many origins—they are sustained both by the limited number of interactions across Race that the average White student has and by the kinds of racist interactions between White Americans that promote the racist beliefs and actions that we present in this chapter. The self-referential character of the thinking involved (when there is any thinking) is circular racist thinking. Another form of racist reasoning is the "exception," which allows for the exclusion of facts that contradict the argument, as in "I don't mean you" or "that" school, person, time, place, et cetera. In one observation, a Black student we call Charles discovered that another White student he had considered a friend was a self-professed racist, who said he hated Black people. Charles asked him how that was possible given that they had been friends. The White "friend" told Charles "You're not Black," by which he explained that meant Charles was not "a ghetto, lazy, stupid Black person." In other words, because Charles didn't fit his White friend's racist stereotype of Black people, he was not Black. Charles was an exception. The exception can be made to cover any facts that might challenge circular thinking, such that unwelcome facts can always be dismissed. In fact, they can be made to reinforce the circularity in weird ways.

Racist talk and action are so ever present, performed by friends, roommates, teachers, and passersby, that it becomes as taken for granted as the air students breathe. On the campuses we studied, all White students are living in the midst of and generating such Race pollution, while Black/Other students are the constant targets of it—and we expect that this is the case everywhere. Once White students learn to actually *hear* what they have been listening to, they are shocked. But unless they continue to talk about Race, this awareness will not grow as it needs to.

What we ask our students to do is simple: When they think they have heard something racist, they should ask, "What do you mean?" Unless the racism is direct and overt, we don't advise them to accuse the person of being racist, although sometimes they do. Often with tacit racism, they are not even sure that what they heard is racist. When they ask, "What do you mean?" the answers they get back clarify what was going on. Tacit racism becomes more explicitly racist as the question is answered. A person who does not believe they are being racist—which is how tacit racism works—will not edit the racism out of their response. In these narratives, the racism becomes progressively more explicit as they explain, until the person speaking begins to become alerted to the racial implications of what they are saying and then starts trying to justify their position. This usually makes the racism clearer.

Take, for instance, the following observation: A Black student named Tracy was in her dorm suite with several White friends. One of them said the N-word. Tracy said, "Did you just say the N-word?" Her friend replied: "Yes, but it's not racist. It doesn't mean anything." When Tracy asked her what she meant by that, she explained: "Back home whenever we don't like anything, we call it the N-word. Like when something breaks at home, we call it the N-word." This is supposed to explain how using the N-word has nothing to do with Race. In this case, an overt form of racism is being sheltered by a "family practice" such that this White student feels comfortable using the N-word in front of Black friends. She grew up in a home where using this word in a mundane way was a common practice—therefore, it can't be racist. She is sufficiently unaware of how racist the practice is to give this account to a Black friend and even to complain that Tracy is *making a big deal out of "nothing"* when she persists in questioning her use of the N-word. Black students report that they frequently run into this complaint when White friends are called out for being racist.

What does an examination of her family practice show that she is really saying? As she said, in her family they all call *things they don't like the N-word:* When something is *bad, broken*, it is an *inferior* product that *doesn't work* and makes them very angry—all stereotypes for Black Americans: *Therefore, it is the N-word*. How is this not racist?

The objective is to get White students to hear themselves—to become self-aware.

The Narratives about Racism

We present and discuss a selection of the observations we have collected from students over many years, on a number of different college campuses. In some observations, the racism reported is subtle, and sometimes the students asked the person, "What do you mean?" In other observations, the racism is more obvious and there is no need to ask. The public nature of some observations did not afford the possibility of asking because students are reporting what they overheard.

We selected the twenty-five observations in this chapter (from over seven hundred) to illustrate the various kinds of racism that are characteristic of college campuses, from the unconscious and tacit, to more overt expressions of explicit racism. When we say that expressions of racism are "tacit," we mean that they come from deep-seated racist assumptions and practices that nevertheless come out without conscious intent. The observations are loosely grouped, beginning with racist assumptions about Black Americans that are a commonplace on college campuses, to give a sense of what we mean by "Race pollution." These are followed by observations illustrating racist assumptions about Asians/Asian Americans that show how they are positioned as outsiders against the Black/White binary. Then we try for rough groupings on racist rudeness and ignorance, racism in college classes, and a selection of quite overt racist incidents, all of which target Black, Asian, Latinx/Hispanic, and West Indian/African students.

As the observations make clear, tacit expressions of racism are no less racist than intentional and overt racist expressions: they may be even more so since the students making these comments are so sure they are not being racist in expressing their deeply held beliefs—often shared by their families—that they are not at all careful when and how they say these things. It is the tacit character of racism that allows it to become so public and to be so openly defended. It matters that these are expressions of deeply held, often unconscious, and taken-for-granted beliefs, because if this is where racism lives, we can't get at it by changing "attitudes" or teaching people to be more racially "sensitive."

Trying to produce tolerance by exposing White Americans to the culture and life stories of minorities will not work either, if they are operating on the basis of tacit racist beliefs about the superiority of their own culture and the inferiority of the culture they are being exposed to. In fact, as some of the observations show, class exercises that were intended to increase familiarity between students of different cultures became exercises in racism when the White American students involved took them as an opportunity to ask rude questions and flaunt the supposed superiority of their own way of life. As long as our students view their own experiences as superior and believe they are speaking and acting on the basis of "facts," they will not be aware that they are being racist, and Black/Other students will continue to suffer from these classroom exercises in "cultural sensitivity." Professors are no less guilty of this than students.

We hope that these narrative observations will enable readers to better *hear* the tacit Race pollution in their own lives—and that when they begin to develop an awareness of this racism, they will do something about it. We encourage everyone to stop laughing at racist talk, stop going along with it, and call people out, or at the very least ask them, "What does that mean?" and change the world by changing themselves.

Commonplace Expressions of Tacit Racism on College Campuses

"Black kids in general are given special treatment at all schools"

This observation was made by a White female college student we call Amy. She was in the Student Center doing homework on a Tuesday night around nine p.m. Two White boys came and sat at the table next to Amy and started talking about their grades on an exam. What started out as a discussion about an exam, however, quickly turned into a discussion of Race. The first boy asked, "How did you do on the exam?" The second boy answered, "Oh, I did okay . . . I mean honestly I could have done so much better, but I had midterms all week. I just didn't have enough time." The first boy nodded in agreement and then said, "Did you hear what that Black athlete got?" The second boy said, "No. I know he was bugging about it though." The first boy said, "Yeah. He told me last night he failed the exam and that his professor had no sympathy about it." The second boy said, "Finally he doesn't get away with something."

After the second boy said "finally" there was something the Black athlete wasn't getting away with, the first boy looked confused and asked, "What do you mean 'get away with'?" The second boy said, "Well, you know why he got into this school, right?" The first boy said, "Yeah, he was recruited just like all the other athletes." The second boy said, "Yeah, but because he's Black, and because of that they lowered their standards and expectations for him." The first boy said, "Oh. I mean that's true with any of the Black kids here. None of them had to work as hard as the rest of us to get in here." The second boy said, "It's ridiculous! And then he goes to office hours for his professors and because he's Black and an athlete they just boost his grade." The first boy said, "I just think the *Black kids in general are given special treatment at all schools* and it's not fair to the rest of us." They nodded in agreement.

This narrative illustrates several racist beliefs: that Black students are given special treatment and that they are not as smart as White students or as well prepared. It also illustrates the resentment against Black classmates that White students feel justified in openly expressing on the basis of these beliefs. Finally, the narrative illustrates what we call "circular racist reasoning." If the Black student athlete was actually getting the special treatment these White students believe he is getting, his professor would have given him the break they say he did not get. The very premise of the discussion is contradicted by the outcome for the Black athlete: "Finally, he doesn't get away with something." However, the evidence that he does not get special treatment does nothing to change their beliefs—in fact, it acts as an exception that seems to reinforce their assumption.

This Black student has obviously been confiding in these two White students—presumably because he considers them to be his friends. Friends empathize with and help each other. But this Black student is not going to get any help from these White students. When he expresses his anxiety and fears, they are glad he is afraid and they celebrate his failure, a common problem in cross-Race friendships that is discussed by Picca and Feagin (2007).

"Do you know why there are so few Black students at the university?"

This is a question that many White students report overhearing as they move around college campuses. One or more White students who are casually walking across campus will ask this question and say related things about affirmative action loudly enough for bystanders to hear them. Who knows why they do this. But they do. Many different answers to the question have been reported to us. They are all racist, such as the statements: "Because they are too stupid to get in," "Because they have criminal records," "Because you have to work hard here and they are lazy," and "Because they can't afford the tuition." Sometimes those who overhear such conversations know the students who are talking, and sometimes they don't. Black students don't report overhearing this stuff, although they know their classmates think this way. So it seems to be something White students may not be consciously aware is racist, but they also know enough to be careful who is around when they say it, and they don't often say it casually around Black students, although they will make arguments about it in class (Warikoo 2016).

These beliefs are troubling for many reasons—not least of which is that they are factually incorrect. What concerns us in particular is how these beliefs contradict other racist assumptions held by the same students. For instance, these students are likely to believe that Black students can always get into college because of affirmative action and that Black students get all of the scholarships. But if they can always get in because of affirmative action, then there would be more Black students at this college; and if Black students get all the scholarships, then tuition would not be a problem for them. This is more circular racist thinking. Why do White students say these things? Why do they believe them? How can they so easily hold contradictory beliefs without noticing the contradictions? Why do they think that other White students will not be offended by hearing what they say?

Given that Harvard is able, year after year, to achieve a ratio of 10% African American students—not just Black, but American Black—and that other top universities are able to come close to this ratio, the very low ratio of Black students at a more modestly rated university cannot be explained as a result of there being no Black students smart enough to be accepted by that university (especially since we know that in an effort to keep the numbers of White men up, some colleges need to drop their requirements, with the result that many White male students with C averages are admitted). It may be that the university these White students are going to is just not good enough to attract large numbers of the best Black students—who are in high demand at places like Harvard and Princeton, which place a premium on diversity because they know it adds value to the overall educational experience. But that has not occurred to these White students.

It is also the case that Black students may choose not to apply to a university for a variety of reasons—one of which could be that if there are very few minorities there, it probably means that the social climate is unfriendly to minorities. Why don't White students worry that Black students are likely avoiding their university? This is a real reason that they don't consider. It has nothing to do with being stupid. In fact, it is very smart to avoid a university where you will be subjected to high levels of racism every day both inside and outside the classroom. Because of these White students' racist attitudes, their university is forced to spend a lot of time and money trying to attract the very same minority students that these White students are assuming are not good enough to get in. Thus their racist thinking is adding to the cost of their own tuition, as well as detracting from the ability of their university to offer them an experience that is diverse enough to prepare them for the real world of work in which they are hoping to succeed.

Black students typically make up between 2% and 6% of the overall student body in American colleges and universities. The percentage of Black students is almost never equal to their percentage in the population except at historically Black institutions. But people still believe that they are getting an affirmative action boost. Harvard—which does achieve a

10% Black student ratio—routinely graduates a higher percentage of its Black students than its White students (between 96% and 98%). This suggests that the Black students at Harvard are more than equal to their White counterparts.

The fact is that it is twice as hard for Black students to get a scholarship than it is for White students (Wise 2010). But White students still believe that Black students are getting all the scholarships. This is similar to the beliefs White people have about Black people and jobs. White men with no college education and a felony arrest record are twice as likely to be offered a job as a Black college graduate with no criminal record (Wise 2010). However, many White students still believe that affirmative action gives Black job applicants the advantage. *These beliefs are false*. In fact, it turns out to be the case that White men still have by far the easiest time both getting into college and finding jobs.

Black students realize that their White classmates think they don't deserve to be in college. But there is nothing they can do about that racist belief. It is in their face every single day, and they just have to live with it. It is what we call a fractured reflection of who they are that makes them very uncomfortable. It is one of the things White students (and some faculty) consider a "fact" and have little hesitation saying out loud. They seem to feel entitled and not at all apologetic about this.

"I am not getting callbacks. . . . I even checked off the box for Black"

The belief among White college students that Black people have an advantage over them getting jobs just because they are Black is so deeply embedded that in one of our observations a Black student we call Jermaine reported that one of his White friends told him he had checked off the box for Black when he applied for a job, hoping to increase his chances of getting a callback.

The observation began with three friends sitting at a table together on campus: Jermaine, another Black friend, and the White friend, who was trying to find a job. The White friend said that he was bummed out and complained to his two Black friends that he had sent out lots of résumés but had gotten no responses. They said that was strange because the university had a great record for placing its students. They told him they were surprised that he hadn't gotten any callbacks. Then their White friend said that he had "even" checked off the box to indicate that he is Black and had still not gotten any callbacks. At this point his two Black friends could have told him that being Black makes a person *less* likely to get a callback—not more likely. But, according to Jermaine, they just didn't know what to say. Their White friend believed so profoundly that they had the advantage over him—that it was an advantage to be Black—that he was pretending to be Black to get a job. Then when he didn't get any callbacks, it still *never occurred to him* that it might have been because he said he was Black.

There is a lot of circular reasoning involved here. First, there is the belief that Black people have an advantage in getting jobs—which is false. Then there is the belief that if a White job applicant pretends to be Black, they should be able to get this advantage for themselves (how was he planning to get through the job interview?). However, when the White person with these beliefs gets no callbacks after claiming to be Black, it doesn't make him question his original premise. Instead he still believes that it is an advantage to be Black—but he now has an additional complaint: *he doesn't think it is "fair" that this advantage is not working for him*. The facts haven't changed his belief. He is just trying to figure out *what* has gone wrong with the application process. His beliefs appear to be so deeply embedded that he would likely not have believed his friends if they had figured out how to tell him that being Black is not an advantage and that he had reduced his chances of an interview by checking off the box that indicates he is Black.

"I'm sure you're supporting Ben Carson"—because you're Black

This observation was made by a White male college student we call Andy. His observation took place in his own dorm room while Andy was socializing with three of his friends. Two of them were White males like himself and his other friend was a Black male. They were talking about the usual stuff, such as the game last night, weekend plans, classes, and all that. At some point, however, they stumbled onto the topic of politics.

Andy's two White friends are conservatives and were talking up Donald Trump big-time, showing their support for him (in early 2016, before he was nominated for president). While they were doing that, they were also criticizing the other candidates, especially Ben Carson. What caught Andy's eye was that it seemed to him that they were "dancing around the fact that Carson is Black." At some point, after being very critical of Carson, they looked over at Andy's Black friend and said, "What do you have to say about Carson? I'm sure you're supporting him."

The thing that really bothered Andy about this is that their Black friend had already told them all earlier that he was a Bernie Sanders supporter—so Andy and his friends knew that he would not be supporting Carson. But Andy's Black friend just shrugged when they asked him about Carson and said, "I have no opinion" (which Andy knew wasn't true), and awkwardly laughed. Then Andy said that everyone laughed, including himself. Looking back on it, he realized that he should not have laughed. Not only did they all know that their Black friend supported Bernie Sanders; the only reason they were assuming he would vote for Carson is because they're both Black. Although everyone laughed, it wasn't funny. Andy's Black friend definitely felt awkward and insulted by the comment, but in a room surrounded by only White people, he just "lay low" and pretended he had no opinion. According to Andy, if he could go back in time, he would call out his friends and say, "We know he is supporting Bernie. Why do you assume he'll vote for Carson just because they are both Black? And you did it right after being very critical of Carson. Not cool."

Positioning Asians and Asian Americans as Permanent Outsiders

To start with, just as there is no such thing as Black and White Races, except as social categories, there is no such thing as Asian. The category itself is an offensive catch-all that collects people from many different countries on more than two continents who have nothing in common. Yet, in the United States they are all identified as Asian. If the category worked as a collector to gather all these people into one group, it might have the potential to work the way "Black" did to transcend historical national/cultural divisions. But, for the most part, those categorized as Asian in the US do not identify strongly with this collector term, tending to self-identify instead by nationality or culture. Asians/Asian Americans tend to emulate the White American ideal, in the hope that working hard to become model citizens, to be what Chou and Feagin (2014) call "Model Minorities," they will achieve acceptance. No matter how hard they work or how much they achieve, however, the Black/White binary positions them as outsiders whom most Americans tend not only to see as foreign, but also as privileged in ways that they resent.

In positioning Asians as outsiders—as foreign—Americans do not expect Asians to be able to speak "good" English, to be able to drive, talk, or even to walk competently; they don't expect to be able to distinguish one Asian from another and consequently don't try; and they don't expect people they identify as Asian to be American or to have American names. When Asians do have names that are Chinese or from another Asian country of origin, Americans often consider their names "strange" and hard to pronounce. This leads to trouble in college classrooms. Asian students report that their professors sometimes openly demand that they invent American names for themselves before the next class to make calling attendance easier. White students also report hearing these requests. But when Asian students do have American-sounding names, they are often asked for their "real" names—because the presumption is that they are not American.

An Asian American is still positioned as an outsider—rather than being recognized as an American—no matter how many generations their family has lived in the United States. The stereotypes about Asians are consistent with the perception that they are foreign, exotic, and impossible to understand. Driving is very American. We love our cars. In the student observations that follow, White students were heard stating without qualification—as if it were a fact—that Asians cannot drive. There are jokes about this. Those identified as Asian sometimes even participate in such jokes as way of fitting in. Even crossing streets properly is something students report hearing White Americans saying that Asians cannot do, even complaining that there is a lot of "jaywalking" in China, when they know nothing about China. When Americans who are engaging in such stereotyping realize the Asian person they are talking to is American, or the wrong kind of Asian, or that they may have offended in some other way, they become embarrassed and end the interaction quickly instead of apologizing.

"My name is Maggie." "Maggie, yeah, but what is your real name?"

An Asian American student, whom we call Maggie, talked about her struggles with racism and stereotyping on her college campus. In a story she rarely tells, Maggie explained that she was raised in an all-White community in Oklahoma, by White American parents, and that there were only three other Asian girls in her school district. She describes her upbringing as "American as apple pie" and was surprised when she faced what she described as "an immediate sense of Otherness" in college that she had never felt in Oklahoma. One of the questions Maggie finds the most invasive and inadvertently racist that she is asked all the time by other students, professors, and administration is "*Maggie*, yeah, but what's your real name?" She then assures them that her name is Maggie. But she says that they usually press on, "Yeah, but actually, legally, what's your name on paper?" She always replies, "Maggie, that's what's on my birth certificate." This is offensive in many ways. First and foremost, it implies that because she is Asian, she must have an "Asian-sounding" name and that Maggie couldn't possibly be her "real" name. It assumes that she is not American. She recalled a conversation that occurred her first semester of freshman year in an introductory course while attendance was being taken by a professor:

PROFESSOR: Maggie?
MAGGIE: Here.
PROFESSOR: So you want to go by Maggie?

There was a pause while the professor looked at Maggie expectantly, but she could not figure out what he wanted, so she just answered "Yes?" with a bit of hesitation.

PROFESSOR: . . . and your real name is?
MAGGIE: Maggie [Last Name].
PROFESSOR: Oh, okay . . . can I just have your real name for the roster purposes?
    It's not listed here where it should be.

At this point, in her first week at college, Maggie explains she was "red-hot with embarrassment" that the professor was taking such a long time pursuing her name when other students had been marked present with no hesitation. She said, "It felt awful to be seen as different already by the professor." She repeated that her name was, in fact, Maggie [Last Name], and finally the professor nodded and accepted her response. She was grateful that the subject seemed to be dropped. But then at the end of the class, the professor pulled her aside and asked her again what her real birth name was. She again said "Maggie," this time volunteering to the professor that she had grown up in rural Oklahoma on a farm her entire life. According to Maggie:

> He didn't really seem convinced, but he let me leave that class, which I was grateful for—it was one of the most awkward experiences I'd ever had with

a teacher before. What I didn't know was that that question and conversation would become pretty standard here. It gets boring and offensive pretty fast. I'm tired of defending that I grew up in America all the time.

Teachers often ask Asian American students what their legal, birth, or "real" name is, assuming that all students who are Asian are international students and not American. Many Asian students are, however, just as Maggie said, as "American as apple pie." But they are seen as different and not American because of their Race by peers and professors alike. Some will never actually believe that Maggie's name is, in fact, *Maggie*. This is just another example of the tacit and overt racism that is prevalent every day on American college campuses; it really is not surprising that Maggie rarely chooses to share her story; it is both mentally and emotionally exhausting to tell and is a constant reminder of her Otherness at college.

"How did you learn to speak English so well?"

Another Asian American college student we call Jill was being interviewed for a job. The interview was long and involved many questions about her training and background. At the end of the interview, the interviewer complimented Jill on her command of English. Jill thought it had been clear from the discussion of her background that she was American and had grown up in this country. But when she explained that to the interviewer, she was asked where her parents were from. This is an all too frequent experience for Americans who are categorized as Asian. Because they are perceived as foreign, they are not expected to speak English well. They are not expected to be American. White Americans pursue the question until they can locate a country of origin other than America as if it made a difference—and will do this in spite of the fact that their own parents may be immigrants. Because Black Americans do not typically ask "nosey" questions, they are not as likely to engage in this kind of questioning.

"Have you ever seen an Asian? They can't see, dude."

That Asians cannot drive is another prevalent stereotype. In doing research with the police, we have observed that many police officers hold this stereotype and have heard them invoke it to explain traffic accidents.

This could be working like stereotypes about Black people and crime to raise the likelihood that Asian drivers will be found at fault in accidents: a circular and self-fulfilling prophecy. The student who reported this observation, whom we call Paul, was in his car driving along with a friend when they approached a traffic jam on one of the main streets near their college. They decided to take a back road to avoid the traffic. As they were making a right turn onto the back road, a car cut in front of them, making Paul slam on his brakes and honk the horn in frustration. Paul was very irritated with the driver who had just cut in front of him and perplexed as to why they thought it was safe to do so.

The other passengers in the car wanted to see who the driver was, meaning according to Paul that they were interested in the gender and Race of the driver who had cut them off. When they got close to the other car, the front seat passenger said, "Oh, of course she is a woman, they are the worst drivers on the planet." Shortly after that he said, "And she is Asian! This lady has two strikes against her. Imagine if she was Jewish? Then she would be driving a BMW instead of a slant box." The comments that this individual made were highly offensive and blatantly racist.

When the passenger was finished commenting on the Race, gender, and hypothetical religion of the other driver, the driver asked, "What do you mean by that?" He reported that his passenger "looked at him like he was crazy and had two heads" and proceeded to say, "I can't believe that you don't know what I am talking about. Have you ever seen an Asian? They can't see, dude." He went on to add, "Women are the most indecisive and dangerous drivers out there. They can't get out of their own way." After hearing his response, Paul asked him if he thought his comment was racist and sexist. Like other situations we had discussed in class, the passenger went on to say that Paul was making him sound racist and sexist, insisting that he was stating a fact rather than judging or jumping to conclusions.

"Why do Asians always travel in packs?"

This observation was reported to us by a White male college student we call Jim. When Jim was inside one of the classroom buildings, he observed a group of White students coming out of a classroom and talking in an open area on the Wednesday just before spring break.

STUDENT #1: So can any of you guys meet before break? I've been ready to go home for days now.

STUDENT #2: I could probably do like Thursday morning. My first class is at twelve thirty.

[*Three Asian students got up from couches they were sitting on nearby and left the building.*]

STUDENT #3: Dude, why do "they" always travel in packs!? I never see a Chinese kid just walking by himself; they're just together all the time.

STUDENT #1: They're gonna take over the campus next week. I bet by Wednesday night they're gonna be the only ones still here, slowly taking over the library even more.

[*They all laughed at this as if it were a really good joke.*]

STUDENT #3: They just form these groups that other kids can't get into and they take over all the study rooms. Between them and the groups of Black kids that you randomly see in the library, you can never get a study room.

STUDENT #2: Yeah, all the five Black kids that go to this school. I mean it's true, I'm pretty sure all of my major classes are 99% white.

STUDENT #3: Well, it's not an easy school to get into—obviously it's mostly white kids. Not many Black students are smart enough to get in.

STUDENT #1: [*Now looking uneasy with the conversation.*] "Okay, I have to get my work done, can we just figure out when we can meet?

What seemed strange to Jim as he listened to them talking is that there are groups of White kids walking around all the time (including the group he was listening to) and more often than not they are all-White groupings that "other people can't get into." But these White students don't see that. What they see is minorities walking around in "packs." They don't see or hear themselves.

"I think you have the wrong Asian"

This observation was reported to us by a White female college student we call Judy. On a Thursday night Judy went to the dining hall for dinner with her roommate who is half Japanese. As the cashier was cashing the two students out, he asked, "Are you two related?" They said "no" that they were just roommates. He replied, "Oh, I thought you were sisters or something." After walking out of earshot, Judy's roommate said to her, "Usually people think I am some other Asian they know." Her comment reminded Judy of a recent Facebook post by another Asian friend of hers. Her friend had posted: "I went to order food the other day and the cashier asked me, 'Aren't you that guy who had his food stolen the other day? By that girl?' I told her 'no.' Then she asked me if I was sure my food had not been stolen. I told her, 'Yes, I am pretty sure.' Later a stranger with cash in his hand taped the same guy on the shoulder and asked, 'Hey, did I owe you the $15?" He said: 'No, you don't. Do I look like every Asian person?"

According to Judy, the semester before this happened she was taking a class with another of her roommates who is not Asian. The class included a group project that required that a team contract be signed by every member of the group. Judy and her roommate arrived to class early and began to get their contracts signed by their group members. There was an Asian student in her roommate's group. The roommate proceeded to walk up to an Asian student in the classroom and ask him to sign her contract. He said: "I think you have the wrong Asian." Judy says that the other students sitting around them quickly turned their heads away and began focusing on their cell phones and computers. Some students laughed. But the Asian kid just continued making his way to his seat as if this were just a normal occurrence for him. Judy said that her roommate blushed and then turned away and tried to pretend it didn't happen.

General Racial Rudeness and Ignorance

"Well, I, like, consider you a White guy"

The student who reported this observation is a male Black student athlete, whom we call Steven. He was observing a White girl talking to a Black guy she obviously liked at a party on campus. Steven explained that because he had a Race observation due for class, he was looking around to see if any interesting racial things were happening and "keeping his ears open." Near him at the party, he saw a light-skinned Black guy talking with a White girl. While he was listening, he heard her say, "This party was crazy in here tonight. I had so much fun."

To which the Black guy responded: "Yeah, you aren't lying there. This place was lit."

Then the White girl moved closer and asked, "So are you going to 'late night' to get some food?"

The Black guy said, "I'll probably leave here to pick something up before I head back to my room. Why do you ask?"

She then said, "Oh, I was just wondering. I might actually do the same. I'm just glad I got to chat with you a little before I headed out of here."

The Black guy laughed at this and said, "Oh yeah, why's that?"

White girl: "Well, I, like, *consider you a White guy* and think you're the hottest guy in the school."

At this point the Black guy gave her a perplexed look and said, "*Wait, what?* Why do you see me as a White guy? As you can see, I'm far from that."

The white girl answered, "I don't know why I do. I just do. *Just accept the compliment:* I just said you're hot!"

The Black guy laughed and said, "I mean the second part is straight. But I'm really confused as to why you consider me a White guy." Then he pointed to a darker-skinned guy in the room and asked, "Do you consider him a White guy?" (Both were dressed preppy—the only difference being skin tone.)

She said, "Oh no, not at all. *Stop making such a big deal!!* I'm saying you're hot. Accept my compliment!"

The Black guy said, "UHHHH, I still don't get it. But thanks, *I guess*."

The White girl smiled and hugged him. "Finally you accept that I think you're hot."

Steven saw the Black guy roll his eyes, pretending to accept the "compliment" and letting the White girl hug him. However, he didn't leave with her like she wanted.

What makes this observation so interesting is that it is obvious that the White girl liked this Black guy and wanted to leave with him after the party. She was trying to compliment him, not offend him. But what she said was that she considered him White, implying that being White made it possible for her to think he was "hot" and leave with him. When the Black guy told her he was having trouble with what she said, she did not apologize, instead she put it on him—the racial boomerang—saying: "*Stop making such a big deal!! I'm saying you're hot. Accept the compliment!*" *But it is a big deal.* He doesn't consider it a compliment to be considered White, and he doesn't want to be hugged by someone who would say that to him. She, on the other hand, hasn't got a clue.

"Interrogating the Mexican"

This observation was made by a female college student we call Ruth, who had recently relocated with her family to the US from Mexico. When White students hear that Ruth is from Mexico, she says they launch into a series of questions based on assumptions they make about Mexicans. She calls this "Interrogating the Mexican." They say things like "You must find life too fast here, right? In Mexico everyone's lax and all," implying that Mexicans are lazy and operate on what is often disparagingly called "colored people time." They also assume that all Mexican families are very large and very poor, which leads to questions about how Ruth's family managed to afford the "expense" of moving such a large family to the US. Ruth wonders why they assume that her family isn't rich. When she tells them that she is an only child, they refer to her as a "unique" Mexican. While Ruth has a broad musical training, they assume that she only likes Mexican music and ask her about "mariachi and ranchera." They even comment on her clothing, saying that she must have changed her wardrobe when she moved to the US because she doesn't wear sombreros and pointy shoes. Then after all this, they say: "Okay. Welcome to America." Needless to say, they do not make Ruth feel welcome.

The university Ruth attends understands that the success of both students and the country as a whole depends on the ability of Americans to get along with people from other countries and cultures in a global economy. Many university programs are aimed at increasing cultural tolerance. Americans should be very worried about the abject ignorance displayed in such "interrogations." We are not winning any awards for achieving cultural tolerance.

"Do you eat cats and dogs?"

The student who reported this observation is an Asian American female college student we call Alice. She was born in the US. But, like many Asian Americans, Alice is constantly confronted by White students who assume that she was not born in this country. For her Race observation, she decided to interview her roommate who is from China and find out what her experiences with racism in the US have been. Her roommate said, "Well, yeah, I mean there is racism. I mean, I don't think people do it intentionally. But, like, I think they are curious about other cultures. But the questions they ask are like . . ." Then, according to Alice, her roommate made a face like there was a bad smell. Alice asked if her roommate could give an example of the kind of questions she is asked that she considers racist. Her Chinese roommate said, "Like 'Do you eat cats and dogs?' and I'm, like, 'really'?" Alice asked, "How do you respond to that?" Her roommate said, "Well, I was, like, I cannot represent everyone in China. But in my area, I really don't know anyone who does that." Then she said that White

Americans are surprised by her answer. "I mean they didn't say, 'Oh, I am surprised,' but their facial expressions definitely showed that they were surprised. I don't know where people get these ideas."

Alice asked her Chinese roommate how these questions made her feel about the person who asked them. Her roommate said, "Well, I didn't think they were stupid or whatever. But I was surprised because more than one person has asked me this. So it was definitely not just a one-time thing. I just don't know where they get this impression of us. But it's kind of weird. I don't think they said it to offend me." Then Alice asked her what she does when she is offended by questions like this, or when she thinks that someone tried to offend her on purpose. Her roommate said, "Sometimes I walk away or prepare answers in case I meet someone." Alice asked her for an example. Her roommate said, "I would say, 'Um . . . like, I know you want to know more. But next time when you ask that question, some other person might get offended.'" Then she said, "But I don't even want to spend the time with them. . . . I don't have the time."

It was generous of her Chinese roommate to say she didn't think the people asking these questions were "stupid or whatever." But they were being stupid, displaying an amazing level of ignorance. It is embarrassing to be an American when you realize how frequently White Americans say stuff like this and apparently have no idea at all that they are being offensive. If nothing else, it should be a simple issue of manners. Students who feel comfortable saying things like this are not going to do well in diverse integrated workplaces.

"Why don't you identify as Black, instead of Jamaican?"

The next observation was made by a college student from Jamaica we call Chantal. She was sitting in a multicultural student meeting at her college. The students were sitting together in a room and in order to get to know each other better were asked take turns saying their names, preferred pronouns, and how they identify themselves. Chantal said that this was her first time having people ask her what she identified as, so she said she "was very thrown off." When it was her turn, she said, "My name is Chantal. I go by *she* and *her*. And I identify as Jamaican." Then, according to Chantal, "This one girl laughs and so I asked her what was funny. She goes on about how 'People from the Caribbean never want to admit that they're Black. Why don't you identify as Black, instead of Jamaican?'" According to Chantal she just said, "I don't know," and let it go on to the next person to do their introduction. But later she said that she had realized that it's only Americans who don't really identify as their nationality first. For most other people in the world, Race is not the primary identifier, but Americans take it for granted that their way of identifying is correct—and that a Jamaican who does not identify as Black is wrong—and can be publicly corrected.

"Why do I need to defend who I am?"

The student reporting this observation is a Black Latinx/Hispanic female college student we call Cheryl whose family is originally from the Dominican Republic. Her observation took place in a course she took that was supposed to increase cultural understanding. For one of the class exercises, the students were told to pair up and discuss their personal lives: how they came to choose this college, their home life, and their community involvement. Cheryl said she paired up with the student who happened to be sitting next to her—a White boy. They began to work their way down the list of things they were supposed to discuss, and her observation begins at the point where it was her turn to discuss her home life.

Cheryl said, "Well, I moved to Lawrence around the time I was five years old with my mom and my sister. At the beginning it wasn't easy, because we had to move from shelter to shelter. But it got better. In the course of about eleven years, we moved seven different times. Which *I think* is kind of fun. But now we are settled and everything is good." While an expression of empathy might have been appropriate, instead Cheryl's White male classmate, who appeared to be confused about what she had described, asked, "Where was your dad?" Cheryl said, "He didn't live with us. It has always been just me, my mom, and my sister."

Her White classmate then asked (seeming intrigued): "So, did he, like, leave when you were born? Like, do you and your sister have the same father?" Cheryl said, "No, he didn't leave when I was born because he is my sister's father too." Then her White classmate asked, "Then why doesn't he live with you? Where is he?" Cheryl answered, "I don't know where he is. My mom left him and I haven't heard from him since."

At this point Cheryl said she was getting a little frustrated with this questioning and wondered: "Why do I need to defend who I am?" But her White classmate continued asking questions that indicated a lack of awareness about why women end up in shelters or even that families often live without fathers in the home. He asked, "So, like, you grew up without a dad? Or did your mom have a lot of boyfriends?" Insulted by the implication that her mom was sleeping around, Cheryl said, "No. My mother has not been with anyone since my father." Her White classmate said, "How was that for you? Living without your dad?" Cheryl said, "It wasn't that big a deal. I didn't really miss him because my mom gave me everything I needed."

Then Cheryl's White classmate said, "Really? Didn't you say you lived in a shelter? Like I know for sure my dad would never let that happen to me. That must have been rough. But I guess that's normal in 'YOUR' community. You said you're from Lawrence, right? Well, I'm from a small town and it's really nice and everything and *I honestly never heard of anyone living without their dad.* Like my dad would coach all my teams and even taught me to play piano. But I guess that's normal for 'US.'"

Getting a little more agitated, Cheryl said, "My life was perfectly fine without my father." Her White classmate said, "Sure. Okay. How did you get to college? I thought Lawrence was like really bad with like drugs and gangs and stuff." Thankfully, at this point the teacher told them it was time to end their discussion. With this huge level of ignorance, this White student was nevertheless convinced of his own superiority.

The Limited Viewpoint That "Whiteness" Sustains

"We were the only White ones there"

The student making this observation, whom we call Daniel, is a White male college student. He noted that White people never seem to worry when there is only one Black person in a room or in a class. But when they are the only White people somewhere, they don't like it. Daniel called this "funny." He had invited some of his White female friends to a dance party on his college campus. There was an even ratio of boys to girls at the party (about twenty-five total). However, most of the partygoers were Black or Latinx, except for Daniel. When the White girls he invited arrived at the party, they greeted him and then stood there looking very uncomfortable. He introduced them to two of his friends, both Black, and tried to make conversation over the sound of the music. His White friends made very subdued greetings to his Black friends and then continued to stand there looking uncomfortable. Another of his White female friends, arriving later than the others, walked in, looked around, and then came over to the group and said, "Let's go," ushering the group of White girls out.

Daniel was a little confused as to why they left so abruptly. He got a text message from the girls a few minutes later that read: "We were the only White ones there."

"Don't sell yourself short—there's no way he's smarter than you"

The student making this observation is a White female college student named Jane. Her observation occurred over spring break while she was at home. Various friends and family were visiting her house. Jane's aunt said, "Sweetie, come sit next to me and tell me how school's going." Jane moved over next to her aunt and said, "Really good. I like it more than I thought I would." Jane began scrolling through Instagram while sitting next to her aunt, who was looking at the pictures as they scrolled by on Jane's phone. She asked, "Are those some of the people you know at school?" Jane answered, "Yeah, well, it's both my high school friends and my college friends. Here I'll show you some of my friends at school." Jane spent the next few minutes showing pictures of her college friends to her aunt, and explaining her relationship to the people in the pictures. Then a picture with a Black male student came up.

AUNT: Oh. Are you friends with him too?
JANE: Yeah, we had a few classes together last semester, and he's hilarious and really smart. He's probably the reason I passed those classes.
AUNT: Oh, honey, don't sell yourself short—there's no way he's smarter than you.
JANE: I have my strengths. But he has his too.
AUNT: Well, it's a shame he has such nice characteristics.
JANE: What do you mean?
AUNT: What do you kids call it? Friending. No, that's not it. Friend zone! Yes. That's it. It must stink for him to be friend zoned by you.

According to Jane, she was a bit perplexed by what her aunt said, and she started to say: "Well, I wouldn't say—" Her aunt cut her off and said, "Well, *I'm not being racist or anything*. Don't get me wrong. But it's no surprise that you're friends with him. *You have always been a little wild* with who you befriend. It's like you're *trying to give your father a heart attack.*"

JANE: Are you saying it's wild that I am friends with people who are not White?
AUNT: Don't be silly. *You're making me sound like a racist.* Well, I suppose it's time for you to go set the table.

Jane was surprised. She is a freshman. Her parents have paid a lot of money for her to go to a good college, and the college she attends emphasizes diversity. She has tried to share her college experience with her aunt. But because she has *one picture* of a Black male student among the many pictures she has been scrolling through, her aunt calls her wild and suggests she is trying to give her father a heart attack. Jane explains that this is a classmate who has helped her with assignments. The aunt refuses to believe this is possible. This Black student cannot be smarter than Jane, and she chides Jane for suggesting the possibility: "Don't sell yourself short."

The way the aunt is able to turn Jane's questions about what she means back on Jane at the end is an illustration of the racial boomerang. If you question someone about something racist they have said, they will often accuse you of *making them sound racist*, just like Jane's aunt did in this narrative.

"What's up, dog"; "Hi, N-word"

Several White male college students have reported realizing that in their dorm rooms and suites their White roommates are constantly using the N-word. This had been going on all along, but they had not noticed it until they started observing racism. They had been taking it for granted as normal. They report that their White male friends are using the term as a way of affiliating. In other words, they are using it the way they think Black people use it as a test of friendship: "What's up, dog"; "Hi, N-word." And if they are using the word with a person, it means that they trust them. When they were questioned about their use of the N-word, they said that using it was an important step in developing friend relationships with other White men. When the White male students making these observations told them they should not be using the N-word, their friends and dorm-mates protested that it is okay to use it that way in their dorm rooms because they do not mean anything racist by it and there are no Black people in the room (or anywhere nearby where they could overhear). Some even said that Black friends had given them a "pass" to use the word. When our students told them none of that makes it okay to use the N-word, they complained that they are being held to unreasonable standards of "political correctness," asking: "What are you the PC police?"

There is a big problem with this use. If White men on college campuses are developing ways of making and testing friendships that depend on using the N-word, but they will not use it around Black people, the effect will be to exclude Black men from their friendships. If the word becomes an important part of making trusted friends, while they are also careful never to use that word around Black people, then either they will not be able to make Black friends at all, or a Black person who does overhear their use of the term can choose to ignore it, and by allowing them to use the word around them can become friends. But this requires the Black person to demean themselves. We have many reports of such complicity by Black friends, which is part of the colonial mentality—taking the attitude of the colonial oppressor toward yourself—and involves self-hatred. These are not the kind of cross-Race friendships that anyone with a commitment to racial equality wants students making.

Racism in the College Classroom and in Assigned Group Projects

"I just redid them because they looked wrong"

The student making this observation is a Black Latinx/Hispanic female college student we call Ann, whose family is originally from the Dominican Republic. Her observation took place in a café on campus during a group meeting. She was in a class that had been divided into groups for a group project. The group she had been assigned to was meeting to review their work. As Ann put it, she is the only person of color in the group.

GIRL 1: Well, I was looking over everything and I changed a few little things. *I just redid them because they looked wrong.*

Realizing that Girl 1 was referring to *her* work, Ann asked, "What was wrong with them?"

GIRL 1: They just didn't look right, and I didn't like how they were formatted. So I changed them. They look better now.
GIRL 2: Okay. Well, besides that what is there to fix and change?
ANN: From what I saw everything looks okay. I double-checked my answers with one of my friends, and I am sure there was nothing wrong with them. The answers Girl 1 has produced are very different from mine, so we definitely need to go over those.
GIRL 1: Yeah, I know which ones you are talking about, and those are the ones that I fixed. I looked them over *with my friends* and *we did it right*. The answers now *are the right answers*.

[*Pause while nobody said anything.*]

BOY 1: This is by far a better group than last semester. We're all on track and know what we need to do.

Ann wondered what was so good about it since they were changing her work without explanation and not listening to her when she said they should double-check the changes Girl 1 had made to her answers. In response to the comment that it was a good group, Girl 1 said, "Yeah, for the most part we are on track [*glancing sideways at Ann*]." The implication was that Ann was the problem with the group. Girl 1 then said, "Well, I need to go. I have another meeting I need to go to. But I'll look over everything again just to double-check." Ann decided to let it ride, which is what people usually do, and said, "Sounds like a plan. I gotta go to class, so I'll see you guys at the next meeting."

The next meeting was a week later, and the same questions were still a problem *of course* because Ann's correct answers had been replaced by incorrect answers. At that meeting Girl 1 said, "So, I looked over everything again, and some of the answers were way off."

ANN: Which ones? Maybe I can look them over and redo them?
GIRL 1: That doesn't matter. I already started working on them and should have them done by tonight.
GIRL 2: Well, I can look them over too. Is there anything else that needs to be done?
GIRL 1: Yeah, there are only problems with one question—which I am sure you can understand [*again looking sideways at Ann*].
ANN: Anything I can do?
GIRL 1: Nah, it's okay. I can do it.

They didn't change anybody else's answers. Only Ann's. Girl 1 substituted incorrect answers for Ann's correct ones. But she still blames the problem on Ann and will not let her help fix the problem—even though Ann had the right answers and they didn't.

This particular observation is interesting for several reasons. Ann is a straight-A student, the best in almost any class she is in. Therefore, the attitude of the other students toward her is particularly striking. Because they assume that they are smarter than she is, they have changed her answers. Now those answers are wrong, and the whole group is likely to get a lower grade. But they still will not listen to Ann or use her answers. Not only is Ann being blamed for this, but she will end up with a lower grade herself, even though the problem is the result of racist assumptions being made about her competence by the group, and not a result of her own work. This is something that many Black students have reported in their observations. Their White classmates offer to do their work for them on group projects because they want to get a good grade and assume that their Black classmates will do the work incorrectly.

The reverse often happens with Asian students, whom White students assume are smarter than they are, particularly at math, and consequently assign them to the most difficult parts of group assignments. Many Asian students have told us that this has happened to them in courses in which they had no idea how to do the work. It does not occur to these White students that acting on their racist assumption about Race and intelligence, like changing Ann's answers because they assume she is not as smart as they are, could be lowering their own grades.

"You didn't raise your hand high enough"

The student making this observation is a Black West Indian female college student we call Lisa. The experience she describes took place in a math classroom in which she was the only student of color. The math professor was an older White male. Students 2 and 3 are White male students, and Student 4 is a White female. Lisa entered the classroom, greeted the professor, and took her seat.

The professor asked, "What's your name?" Lisa told him her name. The professor marked it down in his attendance book and began to teach.

The professor asked: "What is the derivative of ln(x)?" Lisa raised her hand and so did two White students—Student 2 and Student 4. The professor called on one of the White males: "Yes, Student 2." He gave the answer: "1 over X." The professor said, "Correct," and continued to teach. This happened several times. Then he asked another question. Several hands were raised including Lisa's. Without raising his hand, Student 3 answered the question. The professor said, "Correct," and continued to teach the class. Then the professor asked the class another question: "How do you find C after you take the integral?"

Lisa raised her hand again and so did Student 4. The professor called on Student 4, who gave the wrong answer. The professor explained what was wrong with the answer and then asked if anyone else had the answer to the problem. Without raising her hand again, Lisa began to give the correct answer to the question. The professor cut her off and said, "If you have the answer, please raise your hand," and then called on Student 4 again. This time Student 4 got the answer right.

Lisa never did get called on during the class. After class she went up to the professor and asked if she could ask a "quick question." The professor said, "Sure, what is it?" Deciding to push things further than she usually would, to see if she was really confronting a Race issue, Lisa asked, "Why didn't you call on me to answer any of the questions in class?"

The professor said, "Because you didn't raise your hand high enough." Lisa was really shocked by this answer and decided to continue asking questions. She said, "So you saw that I was raising my hand, but it just wasn't raised as high as the other students?" The professor then said, "No, it's not that. I can tell that you came from a good school and you would know a majority of these answers. I'm just trying to give the other students a chance to participate." Lisa said, "Okay, thank you," and exited the classroom.

Not getting called on in class can happen for many reasons. That's why Lisa decided to ask some additional questions to find out what was going on. But the professor's answers give the Race aspect of the problem away: they make no sense. First, he said that her hand was not raised high enough. Then he said that he was just trying to give the "other students" a chance because he can tell from her educational background that she will know the answers. This is a big tell. The professor has no idea what school Lisa went to—he does *not* have that information. And because it is the beginning of the semester and he has never called on her before, he doesn't know whether or not she knows the answers. He is calling on the others without knowing whether or not they know the answers, either. But in her case, he feels he needs to know before he can call on her?

Lisa is the only Black student in the class. But the professor says he feels the need to give the other students "a chance," as if she might otherwise monopolize the classroom? Student 3 answered without being called on, and the professor did not object. Then when Lisa finally tried that, after not being called on over and over again, the professor chastised her for not following the rule. This differential use of authority to keep Black people "in their place" is widespread: it happens with traffic laws, drug laws, and voting laws, to mention just a few. But it is still shocking to see it in a college classroom, and we have many reports like this (from both Black and White students—who become upset when they see Black students in their classes being treated this way). For anyone who teaches college, the professor's answers to Lisa's questions do not ring true. This is not how it works. It sounds like he was making up answers as he went along, having been caught out in a bit of tacit racism that he could see in retrospect was not cool, he did not tell the truth or apologize.

"I can't understand you—you need learn to speak better English"

Many students report problems with teachers not listening to Asian students in class or complaining about how they talk in their college classes. They describe Asian students who try to contribute to class discussion and are told that they need to speak English, or that they are not speaking English well enough, and should not try to participate in class again until they get some help with how to speak English. Asians often find that Americans claim to have difficulty understanding them—even when they speak perfect English. A friend of one of the authors, who has a high-level position at a university and speaks English better than most Americans, says that this is a constant problem he encounters in speaking with White Americans. They constantly tell him that they don't understand him. His English is perfect and clearly enunciated. He has no accent, having grown up in the United States. He speaks "normal" American English. Nevertheless, many Americans say they don't understand him—and interrupt him to say so. What he says he believes is that they do not expect to understand him, so they don't even try. It is hard to see how that could work since his English is so perfect. Americans must not be listening to him *at all* once they see that he is Asian, which is very rude.

The authors have had several Asian students with quite heavy accents in our classes, but we find that even with heavy accents, it is still possible to understand them. Their English is very good: they have had to pass examinations that many American students could not pass in order to get into the class. The problem is not with their English. *What they need is to be listened to carefully by Americans who will assume that they are making sense.* But this is what their professors are not willing to give them: experience with the process of interacting in an American classroom with a teacher and other students who are willing to treat them with enough respect to listen carefully to what they are saying. Is it too much trouble to listen carefully?

"Here we go. Another minority presenting for affirmative action."

The student making this observation is a Black male college student we call George. His observation took place in one of his classes during his first semester in college. It started when his professor assigned a project, and George chose the topic of affirmative action. Although he knew that his professor had very conservative views and had plenty to say without much filter, George chose affirmative action as a topic because he felt that he didn't really know enough about it. According to George, he was getting sick and tired of hearing from White students and friends that "you only got into college because you have 'minority points'" or "your brother got into college because he is a minority."

Even George's best friend, who was the valedictorian of his high school class, when George teased him about not getting into the top Ivy League schools, said, "Well, sorry. I'm the basic White student. Your cousins only got into the University of Pennsylvania and Harvard because they are Hispanic." George said that "all [he] really knew about affirmative action at that point was that if two people had the same qualifications, the minority was supposed to get the advantage." Eventually, George had started to believe that affirmative action was a form of reverse discrimination, because of all the complaints he was hearing from his White friends.

However, after doing the research for his class project, he realized that this was not the case, and that affirmative action is just meant to help disadvantaged people to compete. George was eager to present his findings because he thought that the professor and many of the students "honestly" believed that he had been "given" a seat in the class over a much more qualified White student. George, by the way, is another straight-A student. As he stood up to give his presentation, the professor said, "Here we go. Another minority presenting for affirmative action." Then, after his presentation, the professor asked him, "Do you think it is fair that you get to be here because of affirmative action over a White kid who was more qualified?"

George couldn't believe what the professor had just asked him. He had decided to ignore the rudeness. But then before he could answer, George said that "it hit [him]": he realized what his White classmates have in common is that they don't see him as a student who worked hard enough in high school to get where he is today. No, George said, "instead they see me as a PRODUCT OF AFFIRMATIVE ACTION, who does not deserve to be where he is." Not only that, according to George: "The people I am supposed to look up to and learn from, the professors, see me this way." George asks how society is supposed to work if people cling to this stupid idea that minorities in universities are less qualified and do not deserve to be there.

George says that he cannot achieve anything no matter how well he does, because nobody will give him credit for his achievements. He is sick and

"DO YOU EAT CATS AND DOGS?" 193

tired of being looked at as the *product* of an unfair advantage instead of as a *successful student* on campus. All of George's hard work is reflected back to him from his White classmates as if he had not done it: this is a fractured reflection of his hardworking student identity that he does not recognize.

Overt Racism—Including the "N-Word"—but Still Sometimes with Tacit Elements

"You make the whole room smell like a Black 'people' house"

Julia, who recorded this observation, is a White girl who is a junior in college and an athlete. Julia is constantly trying to balance her workout schedule with her studies, which she does not find easy. One day, as she finished her workout, Julia realized she was going to be late for a meeting with several classmates to work on a group project for class. Julia was really sweaty from the workout, but because she was running late, there was no time to take a shower. So she just put on her clothes and ran back to the dorm room where they were meeting. When she arrived, she rushed in and apologized for being late. Three White female classmates were waiting for her.

One of the three said, "Oh my g-d you're sweaty—you make the whole room smell like a Black 'people' house." No one else said anything. Julia asked her what she meant by that. She knew she was sweaty. But she was very surprised to hear her classmate say that smelling bad was a characteristic of Black people and their houses. Her classmate said, "You know, Black people stink and their houses stink." In an effort to be diplomatic, while also letting her classmate know that she didn't appreciate her comment, Julia said, "I am not aware that Black people's houses smell bad."

Julia's intent was to challenge her classmate's statement. But her classmate's response was that Julia must have grown up in an all-White town and gone to an all-White school if she didn't know that Black people stink. This response really surprised Julia. But it got worse. Her classmate then said that if Julia didn't understand this, she must have a "diversity problem" and that she needed to get some Black friends so that she could learn that they stink. Julia then asked her whether if she was blindfolded and people of different Races were standing next to her, she could identify their Race by their smell. The classmate said she could get "really close."

Julia said, "Can you believe that? She says Black people stink, but I'm the one with a diversity problem?" Because she knows the girl's background, Julia knows that this girl came from an even Whiter town than Julia did, and that she does *not* have Black friends, whereas Julia actually does. Given the degree of racism in her comments, this is not surprising.

Racism often takes this form—coming back at the person who questions it like a boomerang. It's probably one of the reasons we are so reluctant to question racism, but also why it is so important to do so. Otherwise the racial boomerangs will keep flying, good people will duck—and racism will win.

Another student, Beth, who has an internship off campus in a day care center, reported a similar experience that involved children who are only three years old. One child—a White girl—refused to lie down on her mat at nap time. When asked why, she pointed to Black children lying on their mats nearby and said that she could not sleep near them because "Black people stink." This girl had been playing with these same Black children all morning with no problem. But when nap time came, for some reason the racist lessons she had learned at home kicked in. Beth realized that if no one teaches her to think differently, this three-year-old will be telling someone else what Julia's classmate told her—that Black people stink—when she grows up. Obviously no three-year-old can intend to be racist. But acting in racist ways does not require intent—or even conscious awareness. All it requires is that racism is coded into our thoughts and actions in ways that produce racist outcomes.

"It's just a joke . . . can you CALM DOWN?"

An Asian male college student whom we call David reported a conversation that he overheard on a weekday night, around 9:30 p.m. in a college dorm. The conversation was between two third-year students, one female and the other male, and several other friends or acquaintances of the participants who were bystanders. The first participant is a White male we call Jeff, and the second participant is an Asian female of Thai descent we call Mimi. The participants, the observer, and bystanders were all talking in a dorm room. The conversation was about weekend plans.

JEFF: If we are trying to go into Boston for dinner tomorrow night, I can drive some of us, but my car won't fit everyone. Who else can drive?

MIMI: I finally have my car back on campus, so I can drive! I can probably fit four people so whoever wants to come . . .

JEFF: [*scoffs, makes a judgmental face, and turns to the rest of the bystanders to see if his reaction will garner any reactions from them*]

BYSTANDERS: [*all laugh, with a judgmental tone*]

MIMI: What? Am I missing something?

JEFF: Ohhh . . . it's just that . . . I mean [*seems a bit uncomfortable to say what he was about to say, but decides to do so anyway*]

BYSTANDERS: [*all laugh, excited to hear what Jeff is about to say*]

JEFF: [*laughs, and proceeds to talk in a joking manner*] Why would anyone want to get in a car with you? Not only are you Asian, but you're also a woman. That's like a two-for-one death wish waiting to happen.

BYSTANDERS: [*all laugh, some look confused, no one says anything*]

BYSTANDER: Ummm . . . you can't say that . . .

MIMI: No, its fine! It's a joke, okay?

JEFF: Yeah, it's a JOKE! [*says this in a mocking manner*]

JEFF: Hmmm . . . let me guess? You want to eat dog for dinner too! Sorry the restaurant we're going to doesn't offer that . . . are you sure you'll be fine?

MIMI: LOL, yeah, my favorite type of dog to eat is Vietnamese dingo, but don't worry I called the chef and he said I could bring my own.

BYSTANDERS: [*all laugh*]

BYSTANDER: What's wrong with you guys? Mimi, why aren't you defending yourself?

JEFF: It's just a joke . . . chill . . .

MIMI: Yeah, it's just a joke . . . can you CALM DOWN?

David reported that his immediate reaction was shock but also frustration. He was surprised to hear such racist and stereotypical comments from those he considered close friends, but he was also frustrated that the bystanders had laughed at the racist comments Jeff made, only one person complaining, which surely reaffirmed Jeff's racial stereotypes and his belief that it is okay to make such comments. David also found it disheartening that Mimi, who is Asian herself, was brushing off such racist comments as a joke and not standing up for herself.

Treating such comments as a "joke" normalizes racism as a form of humor and enables people to target others if they are even the slightest bit different from themselves. David speculated that perhaps Mimi did not stand up for herself because she was aware of her own reality, that things will not change even if she does say something, and that by laughing along with the group, she can at least belong. But in doing so, she demeans herself. David then asked why it is that Asians are mocked, scrutinized, and discriminated against for an overall false claim that they all eat dogs, while Europeans are glorified and romanticized for eating delicacies like frog legs, snails, and squid. These are only cultural differences.

"It's called the Nutcracker, *not the* Nut-Ni***r*"

This observation was made by a White male student named John, while he was home for Thanksgiving vacation. John drove to see a performance of the *Nutcracker* with his girlfriend Sue, her family, and their friends. Her cousin Ned, who was a couple of years younger and had become a good friend in the three years John and Sue had been dating, was also in the car. As they got near the theater, they saw two young Black women walking along the sidewalk in the direction of the theater.

Ned saw the two Black women out the window and said, "Black people going to watch the *Nutcracker*? It's called the *Nutcracker*, not the *Nut-Ni***r*." Ned then laughed and the other members of Sue's family in the car laughed with him. John couldn't believe what he heard. So he said, "Chill, bro, that's messed up. That's not right to say." Ned then said, "You're right, bro, my fault." John was just glad he did say something, realizing that if he hadn't been taking a class on racism that semester, he probably would have either shrugged the comment off and gone on with his day or laughed along with them. The fact that Ned apologized so quickly is not evidence that he really understood the problematic nature of his comment, but only that he understood that with John he needed to be "PC" and watch what he said. After John left, the family may have had another good laugh about the comment and the fact that John objected to it.

There are several things going on in this observation.

First, a White student who cares about racism suddenly found himself in a situation with people he really likes who were being overtly racist. These are very common situations. What he realized was that only because he was thinking about the importance of racism for class did he actually call out his girlfriend's family on their behavior. Usually everyone just laughs, which tends to confirm that the behavior is okay, and then it happens again, and again, and again.

Second, there is the question of how the girlfriend's family found anything funny about what Ned said in the first place. There is a poetic mirroring of *Nutcracker* and *Nut-Ni***r* that could sound clever. The problem with that explanation is that *in order to even think* of the poetic mirroring in the first place, the cousin had to "see" two Black women going to the theater as such a strange thing that it not only called for explanation, but called the title of the performance itself into question. This in turn raises a number of other questions: How does one see two Black women walking toward a theater, to which one is also going, as a very strange thing?

What kind of racially segregated life does a person have to live to see that as a strange enough thing to comment on? Let alone to make a racist joke about it? How deeply embedded in segregated living do the other people in the car need to be to laugh?

Third, John did something about it that let his girlfriend's family know this behavior is not okay with him. Often in the context of being called out on overtly racist jokes like this, people complain about "political correctness." They will complain about being forced to be PC or made to sound like racists, as if these statements would be funny—and not damaging to the society and its members—if only people would just stop asking them to be politically correct. This is not about political correctness. It is about deeply corrosive ways of seeing, talking, and thinking about one another, which have become embedded in the American way of life.

What it really means is not being able to see Black Americans as people. Two Martians walking toward the theater might have occasioned a similar comment.

"You dirty N-word"

This observation was reported by a White male college student we call John, who was mistaken for a Black student at one a.m. on a Saturday night. Dressed in a hoodie and sweatpants, John was talking on his cell phone while he walked across campus in the dark. As he went past one of the dorm buildings, a White guy on the third floor opened his window and started yelling the N-word at John. The White guy was trying to get John to turn around and acknowledge him. John was stunned at the N-word being yelled that loudly on his own college campus. When John didn't respond or turn around, the White guy in the window kept trying to get his attention, calling out, "Hey, you. Hey, you," and then again yelling, "Hey, you N-word!"

John still didn't look up at him. But the White guy kept yelling at John, "I know you can hear me, N-word!" Then as John walked farther away, the White guy began yelling, "Come on, you dirty N-word! Give me a look." After he said that, John could hear other students inside the room laughing. He realized that the White guy was showing off for his group of friends and thought about how stupid guys can get when they do that. Even though John is a White guy himself, and recognized the behavior as a drunken White guy showing off, he was shocked that showing off would go so far. John wondered what would have happened if he had actually been Black, as the White guys in the room assumed.

As it was, John just kept on walking and talking on the phone—moving away and ignoring the comments, as they kept yelling the N-word at him.

Conclusion

A national conversation in which we all discuss our observations of the racism in our own lives is necessary. Racism is everywhere. Developing an awareness of racism, and of the fact that most White people are not seeing it, is what we mean by *White people developing their own double consciousness about Race*. What this double consciousness can do is help people understand that racism can be so tacit that only some people involved in an encounter are aware of it. White students who are aware of the tacit racism in social interaction will begin to see the racial divide in a way that is similar to how Black and Other people are forced to see it in terms of its omnipresence: they will start seeing it everywhere and *realize that most other White people are not seeing what they see.* This insight will separate them from White Americans who are not aware of the tacit racism around them. *This experience of separation can lead to a form of double consciousness.*

When White students can no longer be in the presence of racism without seeing and hearing it, they may begin to feel compelled to do something about it. In fact, it is hard *not* to do something when you actually see what is going on. It also becomes impossible to pretend that things are fair, and most Americans do believe in fairness—whatever else they believe in.

As we see in the last set of narratives, the kind of overt expressions of racism that trigger campus demonstrations are not that rare. White guys being what John called "stupid" and showing off for their friends are capable of doing a lot of damage. It is also possible that these White guys would have welcomed a fight in order to liven up their Saturday night. Even in this case, however, the racism is not by itself the point of yelling the N-word. The purpose is to impress their friends or start a fight. So we come back to the issue: if White friends would stop laughing at this behavior and make it clear that they would no longer be friends with someone who continues to yell the N-word, it would lose its appeal.

What is happening to Asian, Latinx/Hispanic, and West Indian/African students is also an important revelation. That the Black/White binary works to divide members of these communities, positioning some as insiders and some as outsiders, is confusing and insulting. That many "Black" Latinx/Hispanic, West Indian, and African students self-identify as White in their own communities is something that had not occurred to most Americans. It is not a possibility that the Black/White binary allows. Furthermore, to Black American students, this self-identification appears as a kind of treason against the Black community, and they judge harshly those "Black" students who self-identify as White. For Asians, who are often Americans, the problem is doubly complex. They do belong. They are American. But the binary and its stereotypes define them as permanent outsiders—foreigners—who are so strange that they are not even competent to do ordinary things like talking, walking, and driving, while at the same time they are stereotyped as excelling at other things in ways that Americans who believe these stereotypes resent.

Ultimately, as long as the Black/White binary divides Americans into separate and unequal groups in ways that Americans are not aware of and don't talk about, these things will keep happening. Nothing will get better until White Americans in particular become aware of the racism all around them and realize that they are participating in it every day. We all participate in it. We all do it ourselves. At this point in our history, racism is, unfortunately, as American as apple pie. Developing an awareness of how we participate in racism, and how our actions damage not only Black Americans, but the society itself and the possibility of achieving democracy, is necessary.

Racial inequality is destroying our democracy.

CHAPTER SEVEN

The Interaction Order of a Poor Black American Space

Creating Respect, Recognition, and Value in Response to Collective Punishment

See, we are safe here. We are safe. If I have a problem, then they're going to take care of it, 'cause I'm part of their kingdom. And I'm a big part of their kingdom. You know how safe that makes you feel?   —Mr. Guthrie, an older Black resident

In the popular imagination, urban areas inhabited by impoverished Black Americans and other people of color are pictured as chaotic places where street crime and random violence make daily life dangerous. Black citizens are depicted as being unwilling to work. Black culture is judged inferior and blamed for high rates of what is referred to as "Black" crime. Black drug dealers, in particular, are depicted as dangerous predators, "animals" who need to be exterminated: as if they were ants or cockroaches (while the White CEOs of pharmaceutical companies who created the opioid crisis killing hundreds of thousands of Americans only pay fines). The physical dilapidation of rental housing, vacant storefronts, and the prevalence of empty lots all reinforce this perception of social disorder. It is comforting to White outsiders to believe that if only they would stop hurting each other—"Black-on-Black crime"—clean up the neighborhood, and act more like White people, things would be okay for Black Americans. This is not true. But believing it absolves them of responsibility.

Contrary to such misconceptions, we argue that while they are poor and systematically oppressed by racially biased practices and policies, residents of poor Black communities often manage to create a zone of relative safety for themselves that is grounded in a culture of mutual respect, common cause, and a deep sense of shared injustice. Although outsiders see only chaos, the residents of poor Black neighborhoods are usually much safer in their own neighborhoods than they would be in middle-class White spaces—and they know they are. Whereas some researchers suggest that such feelings of safety are an illusion born of familiarity, we find that the main danger to these poor Black citizens comes from White society and the agents of surveillance and control that it sends into their neighborhoods: not from each other.

In this chapter we introduce the idea of a neighborhood interaction order, which is similar to the idea of an interaction order, but in this case, it is specific to a place and its circumstances. This local order, we argue, works to protect poor Black residents, confirm their identities, and give them respect and control over their lives. We present a series of narratives and personal stories drawn from our field research, introducing the reader to a cast of characters who, in the words of one older resident, represent the "kingdom" to which all residents of the neighborhood are mutually committed and that gives them the value and respect denied by White society.

In our research in a poor Black neighborhood we call Lyford Street, in a city we call Bristol Hill (Rawls and Duck 2012; Duck 2015), we found a neighborhood interaction order—with strong moral commitments at its center—that enables neighborhood residents to survive under desperate circumstances. We found that the residents of this neighborhood are not passive victims of poverty and racism—but rather the active creators of an alternate social order that they control. Among those who recognized elements of this local order, or "code of the street" (Anderson 1994), and tried to explain it to us in the field were defense attorneys, teachers, school administrators, church officials, social workers, patrol officers, and employees of the juvenile justice system. These outsiders were aware of it. But none of them saw its positive value, insisting that residents would be better off without it.

Misunderstanding order for disorder and survival tactics for crimes, the social institutions of American society and their agents of social control have been *collectively punishing* Black citizens in a sustained effort to force them to conform to White American norms—while at the same time making it impossible for them to do so. The distinctness of two different ways of doing things in this country—one Black and one White—which we have documented in this book, keeps those who take the White perspective from understanding what is going on in Black communities. As a consequence of this "twoness," those taking a White perspective make mistakes: they can't tell the law-abiding citizens of a poor Black neighborhood from the lawbreakers; they can't distinguish who is dangerous from who is not. Elderly Black residents tell us that it is the drug dealers who protect them: people for whom society at large has no use.

From a White perspective, it is a mystery why so many Black people "break the law," and racist beliefs about a genetic tendency toward lawbreaking and racist myths about "hypermasculinity" arise as explanations. It is important to see that many laws that are recorded as "broken" at high rates in poor Black neighborhoods—such as driving without a license, defaulting on rent, not paying traffic tickets, not paying fees associated with court cases, as well as dealing drugs—are beyond the control of residents. It is not that they break these laws more often, but rather that that they are *reported for breaking them more often*. Middle-class White Americans routinely break traffic and drug laws. But unless the police write them a ticket or arrest them, there is no report of a crime. Black drivers are ticketed at a much higher rate than White drivers, and the vast majority of drug arrests are of Black citizens, even though White Americans have a higher reported rate of drug use. Most people don't realize that "crime rates" count the number of "crime reports filed" by the police and not the number of crimes committed. Most Americans break at least one law every day. Most of these "crimes," however, do not contribute to "crime rates." Through no merit of their own, White people are not reported for breaking traffic laws and drug laws with high frequency. Consequently, they don't default on tickets they don't get, and there are no court fees to pile up and land them in jail. White Americans also use and deal drugs and get drunk in public. But they rarely go to jail for these crimes.[1]

More importantly, none of these crimes (including drug dealing) are violent in their own right, and none of them are inherently disruptive of the safety of the poor Black neighborhood we studied. It is the police response to them in most cases that leads to violence. The fact that poor Black residents go to jail for crimes like not paying tickets and fees, that poor Black fathers and mothers lose their jobs, that poor Black children lose their parents and parents lose their children, are what disrupt the neighborhood. The power struggles and turf wars among drug dealers that are triggered by police activity also lead to violence. But this is not Black-on-Black crime. It is White-on-Black crime perpetrated by the society at large on Black communities nationwide.

In this chapter, we explore the consequences for all of us—for the American democratic experiment—of not understanding the positive function and value of Black culture in the American context. What has been done to Black communities in the name of "order," in a sustained effort to force conformity to White norms, is not only unconscionable—it has further destabilized a population that was already systematically disadvantaged. Yet we find that Black citizens have responded by taking control of their own lives in creative and democratic ways. Whereas many White Americans still buy into myths of White racial superiority dating from the 1600s, Black Americans have rejected those myths, refusing to emulate rich White Americans. Instead Black Americans have constructed their own egalitarian community behind the "veil" of Race. We maintain that it is within the local order of a Black American community that we find the best existing template for democratic and egalitarian interactions based on fairness, equality, and mutual reciprocity.

Unfortunately, it is this democratic creation by Black Americans that is under siege. In the Lyford Street neighborhood, overlapping surveillance systems aimed at poverty and Race—manned by police, schools, lenders, social workers, public housing officials, landlords, probation and parole officers—impose multiple and contradictory expectations on all residents, such that they are caught up in a constant catch-22 situation. It is impossible to satisfy everyone. In a situation where life is precarious, residents have improvised a set of interactional strategies that protect them. Because these strategies are responsive to poverty, racism, and hyper-surveillance, they invest the local interaction order with characteristics that differ greatly from the White middle-class norm. Black culture is criticized for these differences. But it would not work otherwise—since the point is to offer protection *from* the White middle-class norm.

Black expectations and identities are misunderstood by police and other outsiders, who all too often fail to acknowledge the legitimate identities of residents (viewing them instead as "animals," "thugs," and "scumbags"), thus undermining the security of residents and the very possibility that the police could protect them. By contrast, we argue that the self-preservation strategies of the neighborhood are rational—even necessary—adaptations to otherwise impossible circumstances, and as such have great positive value. Without these strategies, maintaining positive self-identity, self-esteem, and physical survival would not be possible.

Racist beliefs play a powerful role in obscuring the positive value of these neighborhood interaction orders. A belief in the prevalence of Black-on-Black crime, for instance, is a powerful myth. Most people seem not to realize that 95% of all crime is within Race. Since about 70% of *reported* crime is committed by White Americans, even given the underreporting of White crime, that means that about 70% of all *reported* crime is "White-on-White" crime. *Why don't we hear more about that?* The problem is not Black-on-Black crime. It's not even White-on-White crime (since most White people also report feeling safe in their neighborhoods). Rather, the problem is the persistent and sustained collective punishment of Black people as a whole, by social organizations (police, social workers, school zero-tolerance policies, landlords, etc.) that attempt to force an impossible and unwelcome obedience to White norms in ways that disrupt the integrity of Black neighborhoods and their residents. When this is combined with the refusal of White Americans to recognize the legitimate identities and status of Black professionals, or even to admit that there is a Race problem, let alone take responsibility for their daily role in perpetuating tacit racism and the myths that sustain it, the situation has reached a breaking point.

We open with narratives from five neighborhood residents: one is a White Christian missionary living in the neighborhood, the other four are older Black long-term residents. Their narratives emphasize a reliance on drug dealers—not the police—for safety, respect, and self-esteem. Even the missionaries are wary of the police. Following these narratives, we present three incidents that illustrate what happens when law-abiding residents come in contact with the forces of "law and order": Brent, a model Black student, was arrested in school under a zero-tolerance policy; Justin, a Black resident employed as a security guard, was arrested because of a rent problem; and Benita, a Black resident nurse and mother driving without a license, was *not* arrested even though she was involved in a serious accident. The accounts show the pervasiveness of the system of collective punishment in the face of which residents have banded together.

The Perspectives of Law-Abiding Neighborhood Residents

We present the experiences of these neighborhood residents with the police, courts, landlords, and law enforcement more generally, as they were narrated to us in the field, with a particular focus on the value these residents place on elements of the local interaction order. The main point, in our view, is that their local sense-making is organized differently from that of outsiders. Long-term residents—even though they are law-abiding and opposed to drugs—understand what the neighborhood as a whole is up against. Their attitude toward the police and their understanding of what makes them safe—even in the case of the White Christian missionaries—aligns with their neighbors and friends (including drug dealers).

Our analysis starts from a simple fact: Because the neighborhood is poor and Black, it has been heavily policed since at least the 1980s when the War on Drugs began (a response with roots in the strong White resistance to the Civil Rights movement). Before this it was a White neighborhood. Policies directed at Black drug dealing imposed a system of collective punishment on the urban Black population that makes no presumption of the innocence of individuals. In the face of this collective punishment, Black neighborhoods have developed a collective response that we document here. White Americans who advise that Black Americans should act more like White Americans must consider that Black Americans are not treated like White Americans; they are not recognized as individuals and are not considered innocent until proven guilty. Finally, and most importantly, everyone needs a place where their identity and self-worth are confirmed—and where there is sufficient trust and mutual commitment for everyday sense-making and self-making to occur. The neighborhood interaction order provides that.

In our interviews, older African American residents of the neighborhood described the feelings of respect and value they get from the local neighborhood social order, as well as their attitudes toward the police and the "system" more generally. These narratives show that experiences with hyper-surveillance have shaped the entire community's perception of police authority. Whether residents are law-abiding or not, they *fear the police* and place their trust in the neighborhood. Through these narratives, we gain a sense of the underlying tensions that exist between residents and those whose job is *supposed to be* to serve and protect them. Interactions between residents and police are powerfully shaped by an underlying asymmetry: the police treat all citizens in the neighborhood as potential lawbreakers—whom they will ticket and/or arrest if they can—and not as the citizens it is their job to protect.

Stacy, a White Missionary: Only Willing to Report a Brick of Cocaine to a "Legit Officer"

Stacy, one of a group of Christian missionaries who had been living together in a house on or near Lyford Street since the early 1980s, explained how they had aligned with the interaction order of the neighborhood.

Although members of the group had never been the victims of violence themselves, they had learned how long-term residents could stay safe. They knew the neighborhood well enough to avoid places and times where crime and/or violence were likely. This predictability is important. They understood the difference between crimes related to the drug trade—which are highly predictable—and those connected to interpersonal disputes, which are less so. They also learned they could stay safe by avoiding interactions with the police.

Having adopted the general distrust of the police that is characteristic of the neighborhood, Stacy, a White missionary in her mid-twenties, continued to rely exclusively on the neighborhood patrol officer, whom she had gotten to know personally and therefore trusted, even after that officer had been transferred to another area. "I miss her," Stacy told us. Sounding like other long-term residents, she said, "She was the only legit officer." Then Stacey told us the following story:

> One time we found drugs at our house, in the garden. It was a brick of white powder . . . solid, which was worth a fortune. I called the former patrolwoman, who promised to get it taken care of right away. Then another officer called back and said, "Don't go outside. Stay in your house until we get there. Don't come outside." They came in their unmarked cars, undercover. He calls me, like, "Where is it?" I'm like, "Okay, you're parked." He's like, "You're watching me out the window?" I'm like, "Yeah. Heck, yeah, I'm watching this go down!"

Stacy laughed as she told this story. The position she found herself in stood squarely between the two worlds. Her understanding of (and commitment to) the local interaction order had led them to wait a few days to give the owner of the drugs a chance to retrieve their property before calling the police—and then calling the one officer that she knew personally instead of calling 911. In the meantime, she simply left the cocaine in the garden as if she hadn't found it. Being associated with this incident in any way could have dangerous consequences. When the police did come—alerted by the one "legit officer"—they carefully handled the incident as if the missionaries had nothing to do with it.

Stacey's story illustrates the complexities of dealing with the police in a community in which the drug trade is embedded. Her eventual decision to cooperate with the police is significant—many residents would not have called any police officer. But her experience in the neighborhood also led her to act like a neighborhood resident in respecting the ownership rights to the cocaine, and then when she did call the police, she again reflected the neighborhood sentiment that some officers are more legitimate than others.

The assessment of their legitimacy shapes patterns of contact with the police. Stacy's story indicates that even missionaries in the neighborhood recognize the significance of particular forms of *local trust* amid the more general distrust of outsiders. Although Stacy is not only a law-abiding resident but a White religious missionary with special moral commitments, she understands that in a community which depends on drug dealing and where surveillance is hypervigilant, once she is connected with drugs there will be problems. She hoped that whoever owned the cocaine would return for the drugs. When they didn't, she made sure that contact with the police was handled anonymously, adopting the neighborhood practice of trusting only officers whom she personally considers "legit."

Longtime Law-Abiding Residents Say They "Feel Safe" in the Neighborhood

Given the lack of jobs and the prevalence of drug dealing and hypersurveillance by the police, we wondered why law-abiding residents would stay in the community if they could leave. We initially thought they might only be staying because they could not afford to leave. But we found that this is not the case. In fact, many older law-abiding residents told us they stay because they not only feel safe but are highly valued in this community—safer here than anywhere else. Furthermore, they said that the drug dealers make them feel safe because they are not going to let anyone "break in on you" and told us about residents who left and experienced break-ins in the places they moved to. Given that the police and other outsiders enforce a system of racial bias, while the neighborhood social order treats everyone as equals, it makes sense that residents would feel safe and valued within it.

Mrs. Wells, a Long-Term Resident: "I Feel Protected"

When Waverly asked Mrs. Wells, a seventy-eight-year-old African American woman who had lived in the neighborhood all her life, why she stayed, she replied:

> You know what, in a way it sounds crazy, but I feel protected. A lot [of] people who have moved out of the neighborhood have gotten broken in on, robbed.

> Here, I feel protected. As bad as it seems out there with the drugs and things, I feel protected. Because the guys out there with the drugs and things were out there doing their thing. They weren't going to break in on you and they weren't going to let no one else break in on you. Here I feel protected.

Mrs. Wells is repeating a refrain that we heard often: the drug dealers make sure that crimes that would victimize neighborhood residents, like property crimes and robberies, do not occur in their neighborhood: "they weren't going to let no one else break in on you." Although they are themselves committing crimes, those crimes are well organized and do not victimize neighborhood residents. In fact, we found that violence in the drug trade in this neighborhood tended mainly to come after police intrusion. It is in the business interests of the drug dealers to keep the neighborhood crime rate down, to minimize police interference, and keep their business orderly so as not to scare customers away. But, more importantly, the drug dealers live in this neighborhood and want to keep the place where they live safe.

We also got the distinct impression that the drug dealers genuinely like and respect these older residents—who returned those feelings. When we interviewed Mrs. Wells's daughter, a forty-nine-year-old high school English teacher, and asked why she "let" her mother stay in the neighborhood, she told us she had tried to get her mother to leave. But Mrs. Wells told her daughter that they "would have to dynamite her out":

> That's all she knows. And she is not—my two sisters will take her if she wanted to go. She does not; she's fiercely independent and she will not leave. She told me one time we would have to dynamite her out, and told me to get out of her house when we were trying to tell her to leave because of the violence and stuff. And the house I live in, my uncle he would give it to my mother. My mother did not want it. She loves where she stays and that's where she's going to be at. She said "dynamite her out," so.

Mrs. Wells trusts the drug dealers to look out for her. We heard the same thing from other long-term residents. This is their community. They feel safe and valued here and don't want to leave.

Whereas some researchers have suggested that residents like these feel the illusion of safety in familiar places, when they are not really safe, we argue that these residents are actually safer here—where drug dealers and other young members of the neighborhood will look out for them and prevent them from being victimized, and where they are valued and respected and give respect back in return—than they would be as unwanted Black outsiders in White suburbs. This is a local order they know, and they are protected and highly valued within it.

Mr. John, a Long-Term Resident: "If I Fall Down, [They Will] Make Sure I'm Okay"

Mr. John, a sixty-seven-year-old long-term African American resident, is locally regarded as a success story by everyone—including the drug dealers—because he is legitimately employed. He told us that many of the dealers had sought his advice over the years about ways of finding a job in the hope that with legitimate employment they could avoid returning to jail. They deal drugs because they are unemployed and remain unemployed because no one will hire them. Mr. John offered an eloquent, and deadly accurate, account of their predicament:

> You read the paper about these guys out there selling the drugs and all that kind of stuff. And they're not all bad guys. Well, some of them are, but most of them aren't. But when you belong to that world . . . now, like I said, I don't sell drugs, I don't do drugs. But I'm in a world with them, you know. This is their world. If I go down, guys on the corner could be selling drugs. There're a million out there. If I fall down in the middle of the street, that guy is going to come over to me to make sure I'm okay. And that's the hard part. No, I don't want to see 'em selling drugs. No, I definitely don't want to see 'em selling drugs. And if I can get by . . . if there was some kind of magic wand that I could take, I'd take it and none of them would sell drugs. And my magic wand would be to get rid of all people that took drugs, 'cause if you get rid of all people that take drugs, ain't no need for a person to sell drugs.

While he would like to see them stop selling drugs, Mr. John would get rid of the *users*, not the *sellers*. The problem as he sees it is that the "system" is stacked against them:

> But I also see the way the system runs. I've had people get felonies for selling drugs, and then they come over and knock on the door after they get out. I don't know why, but after they get out, they gotta come here and explain to me what happened. "Well, let me tell you, Mr. John, we don't want you mad." It's like, "Hey, it is what it is. Anything I can do." And I tell them the same thing:

"Anything I can do, let me know." They say to me, "Well, do you know anybody hiring?" Then you go out there and look around and try and get them a job. And a lot of these temp places around here tell you, "Well, there is no jobs; he got a felony." Post office, if they got a felony, can't hire them. Then that same guy who just got out of jail two months ago, he has a family. It might not be a wife and the regular family, but he has kids or whatever. He needs a place to stay. What does he do? He goes right back to selling drugs. That hurts. That hurts.

Mr. John likes these young men and knows that they have tried to get jobs, because he has tried to help them find jobs. He also knows why they get turned down, because he gets turned down for the same reasons when he tries to help them. He knows they feel badly about not being able to get jobs, because they come and apologize to him when they go back to dealing drugs again. He understands that they need to work to support their families. But, most importantly, he knows they will look out for him and that he is safe here because of them.

Mr. Thompson, a Long-Term Resident: "You Got to Look at It from Both Ways"

The carrying of weapons by the police is supposed to be primarily symbolic. The trick in police work is not to force people to obey, but to create preconditions for obedience, as Egon Bittner (1970: 98) argued in his classic *The Functions of the Police in Modern Society*. In this neighborhood, however, as in other poor Black neighborhoods, the police regularly resort to using guns in an attempt to force people to obey. This further erodes the preconditions for obedience. If an officer does discharge a weapon, their training emphasizes that they should shoot to kill. This shortcuts obedience and cuts straight to violence. Local citizens and law enforcers alike understand this: whenever a weapon is discharged, it should be discharged with intent to kill (Bittner 1970; Manning 2013). This leads to frequent police shootings.

We conducted one of our interviews with Mr. Thompson, a fifty-year-old resident, just after a police shooting. The victim was a twenty-one-year-old African American man from the neighborhood who had been shot in the back by a White police officer while he was running away from the officer. When Waverly talked with Mr. Thompson after this incident, he was visibly upset. Word of the shooting was spreading quickly. When we mentioned the shooting, he echoed Mr. John, saying:

It hurts, man. I mean, and then they say they're gonna get a cop. If they take a cop out, it's gonna be unbelievable. I understand these kids have guns, but to shoot somebody in the back through the heart, I mean—you got to look at it from both ways, but the guy was running. We don't know—and it almost started a riot yesterday at the hospital. They had to call all kind of units in, okay, but, uh . . .

Unlike most suburbanites, Mr. Thompson maintains that there are two sides to the story. Like many White gun rights advocates, he takes gun possession for granted. Of course the "kids" have guns. However, the police shooting a person in the back while they are running away is murder. Mr. Thompson understands the anger felt by community members. But he also fears that some of the young men will want to target a police officer in retaliation for the shooting. This will make things worse for everyone in the neighborhood: "If they take a cop out, it's gonna be unbelievable." Mr. Thompson values the "peaceful" day-to-day order of the neighborhood and understands that the police "are going to shoot first and ask questions later." He worries about what will happen to the neighborhood and its young Black men in the aftermath of this shooting.

The local interaction order on Lyford Street developed through a complex of interactions between residents, and between residents and police officers and other outsiders. While this order, and its code of conduct, creates stable expectations for meaningful social action and identity within the neighborhood, it does not work well when outsiders disrupt it. When the young men of the neighborhood are murdered, Mr. Thompson fears they will take action that will jeopardize both themselves and the local order he relies on. The situated identities the local order provides for are positively valued within the neighborhood. It is police action that produces dangerous disruptions, resulting in a lack of mutual cooperation, trust, and reciprocity between officers and residents, disrupting the local order at least temporarily.

Because it has been necessary for residents to create their own local order to survive, they are also prepared to defend that order when it is threatened. Outsiders use terms like "thugs" and "rioters" to describe this response. We suggest that there is more to it. Black citizens in poor communities like Lyford Street receive few services—and those they do receive come with a great deal of unwelcome surveillance. Constantly arrested, fined, and jailed, they have nevertheless managed to create a local social order that not only protects them, but adds value and self-esteem to their lives. As Chris Hayes (2017) maintains, outcast from society at large,

Black Americans have been forced into their own "colony within a nation." However, they have made it their own, and not unreasonably it is a space that they are more than willing to defend.

Mr. Guthrie, a Long-Term Resident: "They Make Me Feel Special"

An elegant understanding of this local order is exhibited in the account of a sixty-year-old long-term Black resident named Mr. Guthrie, who described this neighborhood as a "kingdom" with a varied cast of actors who all have a particular role to play. His direct interactions with drug dealers are limited. But he explicitly acknowledges them as his neighbors. This acknowledgment is reciprocated. As a recognized member of this community, he says he is known and protected:

> See, we are safe here. We are safe. If I have a problem, then they're going to take care of it, 'cause I'm part of their kingdom. And I'm a big part of their kingdom. You know how safe that makes you feel? You know how it is to walk out your house and everybody speaks. Everybody speaks. I don't even know their names sometimes. You know, nine out of ten of these girls around here are Baby, Sweetie, Honey. You know, nine out of ten of these guys are Little Bro, Bro, Young Buck, whatever, you know. Don't even know their names. But they make you feel wanted, make you feel special. And you know what, I need them as much as they need me, 'cause they make me feel special. They really do, you know. It's wild. I'll do anything for them.

The poor and racially oppressed have managed to create a context of mutual respect in the neighborhood that they experience nowhere else. In Mr. Guthrie's terms, "I need them as much as they need me, 'cause they make me feel special." These feelings of being wanted and needed—experiences of being valued, respected, and protected, of being special—are so important to him that he says he would "do anything for them."

The popular depiction of drug dealers as predators does not mesh with the experiences of these residents. If law-abiding residents value drug dealers as protectors, they will not welcome police action against them. This is a side of Black neighborhoods that outsiders don't understand. The young men are not "thugs," and protests against police intrusion are not "random violence." Understanding what is going on requires insights from the other side of the veil. Because of the way racism and stereotyping prevent residents from being respected and valued outside of the neighborhood, the local interaction order is very important to them. Until Black residents can get respect and confirmation elsewhere, they will continue to depend on this local order.

When the Forces of Collective Punishment Intrude

The three cases that follow illustrate what happens when neighborhood residents get caught up in the forces of collective punishment from which their neighbors cannot protect them. All three cases involve citizens who are succeeding well beyond neighborhood standards. This should count for something, but in looking at their cases, we can see that it did not.

Brent, a Model Student: Caught in a Zero-Tolerance Policy

Being a model student who stays out of trouble is no protection against the intrusion of the outside world into the neighborhood. While Waverly was volunteering as a tutor in a local church after-school program (doing fieldwork), a ninth-grader named Brent came to our attention. Brent not only participated in the program; he also tutored the younger participants. Brent was especially memorable because he introduced us to a young-adult book series that highlighted the challenges facing urban youth. The books, called the Bluford Series, comprise twenty or so novels set at a fictional high school in Los Angeles named after Dr. Guion Stewart Bluford Jr., the first African American to go into space, in 1983. When he found out that his tutor was from Detroit, Brent pointed out that one of his favorite characters in the series was from Detroit.

Counselors and tutors in the program recognized Brent as a young man with great promise. Brent was a successful student and a talented writer, and his parents kept him constantly busy. He did not hang out on the street. He was doing exactly what society says they want young Black students to do: he was a neighborhood success story. But none of this made any difference when he got caught up in a zero-tolerance policy at his high school four years after we met him.

We rediscovered Brent during his senior year of high school after he had been charged with bringing a "deadly" weapon to school. The incident prompted both a criminal court hearing and a school disciplinary hearing. Just months before his expected graduation, the school district sought to expel him, in spite of the fact that that he was excelling in a college preparatory program (at the high school) that was sponsored by a local church. This project was designed to mentor and monitor students' academic achievement from ninth grade through college, and Brent was a project success story. Fortunately, the director of the program worked diligently to organize teachers, politicians, counselors, and school administrators on Brent's behalf. So, what happened to him, bad as it was, should be seen as a best-case scenario.

Since we already knew Brent from the after-school program and had been impressed by him, we followed his situation closely. We learned that criminal and disciplinary charges had been lodged after he brought a *shuriken* (a Japanese throwing star) to school. But, according to Brent, he had done this as part of a class assignment. Through the project sponsored by the local church, Brent was taking classes in Japanese. He had been given a homework assignment that required students to bring items from home that showed Japanese cultural influence. He had a *shuriken*, probably the only Japanese thing he did own, so he put it in his school bag—making no attempt to hide it—and brought it to school for the assignment. Of course, the *shuriken* was found in his bag as he went through the school's metal detectors. He did not think it would be a problem. Thinking of it as a piece of Japanese culture, he did not think of it as a weapon. Security at Bristol Hill High School, however, is provided by city police officers who can act independently of the school. Working under a policy of zero tolerance for weapons, they arrested him.

The Bristol Hill High School code of conduct stated that the school district has a zero-tolerance policy with regard to the safety of the school and disruptions to the educational experience of other students and teachers. The policy lists a number of offenses that would result in a mandatory hearing, including violence and the possession of weapons and drugs. It did not, however, define what might be considered a "weapon." This blurring of the line between what is and is not permitted makes it difficult for students and their parents to stay within the guidelines.

Brent had no history of violence, yet he faced expulsion. Upon hearing all the details of Brent's case, the high school principal, several of his teachers, counselors from the project, and other mentors agreed that the situation should have been handled differently. They also thought that the decision about how to respond should have been made by the school principal rather than by police officers. However, the high school principal found that he had no authority to change the outcome. According to the guidelines, *anyone who works in the school* could enforce the zero-tolerance policy, which once invoked automatically required an expulsion hearing.

Brent first had to appear before the city court for the charge of possessing a deadly weapon. After testimony from teachers, counselors, his pastor, and people from the community, the court dismissed the charge. While the consensus all along had been that the whole situation was a misunderstanding, proving Brent's innocence required a community effort, countless testimonies, and an account that was verified by everyone "in the know." After being cleared in court, however, he still had to go before the school disciplinary court. His pastor told us that before this court they would need to show not only Brent's innocence, but that violence was improbable and uncharacteristic of him. Even the school principal and superintendent believed in his innocence. But getting him reinstated in school required more than proving his conformity to the rule of law. They needed to prove that he would not be violent in the *future*. Zero-tolerance polices leave little room for negotiation. Once accused of an offense, reversing the original decision is almost impossible.

The director of the college preparatory program spoke to several of the hearing officers, who gave her a grim warning that Brent would most likely be expelled. They admonished her that weapons charges were serious offenses and that if they let Brent go, they would have to treat other cases similarly. To ensure Brent's chances for a successful graduation, she reached out to the superintendent. They strategized to find loopholes in the bureaucratic process. The superintendent was able to schedule Brent's disciplinary hearing for after he received his diploma—a decision that exploited a technicality. Had they not worked around the process, this model student most likely would not have graduated.

Brent's experience reflects the effects of the "youth control complex," which subjects young people of color to collective punishment (Rios 2011). That such collective punishment is wrong has been codified by the international law of war and justice, which states that it is a crime against humanity and a violation of the rule of law to punish a group of people collectively for acts committed by some of them, even if those individual acts are violent and illegal.[2] In Brent's case, treatment by officers, courts, and even school administrators took the actions of others into account in deciding his case—rather than hearing it on its own merits.

The superintendent of schools and the high school principal were both stripped of their authority by the zero-tolerance policy. The policy justifies the actions of whoever invokes it with the claim that they were "just applying the law" and that they could not have done otherwise. This produces the appearance of an impartial "color-blind" decision-making process—which in reality is used to criminalize poor Black youth. The policy put important educational decisions into the hands of police and other disciplinarians who are not educators.

Most of the time when a policy violation leads to an arrest and criminal charges, a student is propelled into the school-to-prison pipeline. They will be denied further education, end up with a record, and will subsequently have difficulty getting a job. If they are male, they will likely become a drug dealer, end up in prison, and be denied the right to vote. Brent's case had a relatively positive outcome because he had numerous powerful advocates. But even then he was still not able to convince the school disciplinary court. His advocates were ultimately able to save him only by bypassing that process entirely.

Justin, a Security Guard: Arrested for Trying to Retrieve His Own ID

Justin, a twenty-six-year-old African American resident, was one of the few young Black men in the neighborhood with legitimate employment. But that didn't help him when he ran afoul of his landlord. Landlords in neighborhoods like Lyford Street have special relationships with the police that give them leeway in skirting around or even breaking the law (Desmond 2016). Like most of the employed men in the neighborhood, Justin worked for a low hourly wage, making nine dollars an hour as a security guard. His credit was poor, and he didn't earn much, so he usually had a roommate to share expenses. But even then his situation was precarious, and he often got behind on his rent. Because of this problem, he had been forced to move at least three times in the previous two years, and as a consequence didn't receive the summons sent to him for a court appearance related to an earlier DUI. His failure to appear in court led to a warrant being issued for his arrest that he did not know about. The summons and warrant were triggered by more than $3,000 in fees that he owed related to court costs for the DUI seven years earlier when he was nineteen. Fees and fines from tickets and court are the most frequent form of debt for residents of this neighborhood and often lead to warrants and jail time.

Shortly before Waverly met him, Justin had been unlawfully evicted from his home. When he met with his landlord to try to retrieve his work ID and other possessions, he was arrested on the outstanding warrant for unpaid court fees and fines. The arrest was instigated by the landlord. Justin had been given two weeks' notice by the landlord to vacate the house he shared with a roommate because they were behind on the rent. But before the two weeks were up, the landlord changed the locks while Justin and his roommate were both out. All of his possessions were locked inside—including his work ID and work clothes.

Justin called the landlord and arranged to meet with him at the house to retrieve his belongings. When Justin arrived to meet with the landlord as arranged, a police officer the landlord had called to the scene ran a background check and arrested him. Justin's property was legally his and the landlord had no legal right to withhold it from him. In fact, the landlord had no legal right to evict him and change the locks without going through a legal process. But the likelihood that Justin (or any other neighborhood resident) would have an outstanding warrant allowed the landlord to make use of the police to withhold Justin's possessions from him. Justin spent several days in jail and was then released.

Because he was only scheduled to work for two of the four days he was in jail, Justin hoped that if he could retrieve his ID and work clothes, he could still keep his job. As soon as he got out, Justin called the landlord and the two agreed to meet at the property again so that Justin could retrieve his things—which he still needed in order to work. Instead of letting him get his things as agreed, however, the landlord met him at the property and told him he could not have his things and then left. Justin decided to just "take" his things and proceeded to do so. The landlord came back and found Jason removing his belongings from the property and called the police again and had him rearrested. Justin explained:

> So I get out, I don't have anything, I don't have a phone, I don't have keys, I only had six dollars on me. . . . So that's the main thing I'm doing all day, trying to figure out how I can get my ID for work and some work clothes so I can at least keep my job because I had been off work for three or four days. Luckily, I was already off on Tuesdays, and Monday was a holiday, but I'm trying to get to work. I speak to the landlord, he tells me he's going to meet me. He doesn't show up until forty-five minutes later, and then he tells me, "No, I can't let you in to get your things." I am furious, so I decide to get my belongings. So basically I waited for him to leave. I go in there, come out, he's waiting outside; mind you, this is three hours later. He just so happens to be pulling up when I was leaving. Next thing I know, I hear police sirens. I'm confused. I'm arrested again, taken to jail again. . . . First they were going to charge me with breaking and entering, but there was no proof of breaking or entering, so then they tried

to charge me with burglary but couldn't because I was taking my own belongings, so they charged me with criminal trespassing.

To be clear: the possessions were Justin's and he had a legal right to them. In the end, the only charge they could make stick was criminal trespassing. In court, Justin can probably get that charge dismissed too. It is Justin, not the landlord, who is in the right here. There are legal procedures for eviction that the landlord did not follow. The willingness of the police to back up the landlord's illegal dealings is one of the main things that makes them possible.

Justin could have called the police right away when he found out he had been unlawfully evicted. He explained that he didn't because he felt they would treat him as a criminal instead of seeing him as the victim in this situation. Justin's mistrust of the police—combined with the willingness of the police to aid and abet landlords in breaking the law in their treatment of tenants—meant that Justin could not turn to the police to protect his rights and get his ID and possessions, resulting in two arrests to add to the neighborhood "crime rate."

Justin's assumption—based on experience—that his identity and concerns will never be acknowledged in situations that involve the police created a problem with trust and legitimacy. The police didn't recognize the legitimacy of Justin's grievance, instead criminalizing him *twice* for trying to retrieve the identification he needed to keep his job. Now one of the few employed men in the neighborhood will be burdened with two more arrests and more court fees and expenses. He may also lose his job. Lack of trust between the parties—which includes the refusal of the police to treat him as a tenant with legal rights—restricted Justin's options.[3]

Unlike their tenants, landlords in a neighborhood like this are given a relatively free hand to operate outside the law. What the landlord did is not only illegal—it threatens the stability of the neighborhood. Justin's attempt to solve his problem without engaging the landlord or law enforcement by trying to enter his apartment after the locks had been changed, when interaction with the landlord failed, illustrates a basic understanding among many residents in precarious positions that, despite being wronged, they have little or no legal recourse in the matter. When landlords rent to tenants like Justin, they know that the tenants' legal situation makes them vulnerable (Desmond 2016). This knowledge factors into the landlord-tenant relationship.

Under such circumstances, disengaging from problematic interactions with outsiders like landlords and the police and taking independent action are essential survival strategies for those who live in neighborhoods like Lyford Street. All interaction has a promissory character. In order to engage with others, it is necessary to take it on faith that the other party is who they claim to be and will keep their word (Goffman 1959: 2–3). When this social contract fails, then further interaction with those parties who have shown themselves to be untrustworthy Others becomes impossible. In this case, the landlord violated the terms of this basic working consensus by lying to Justin, and the police backed him up by arresting Justin for an unrelated matter of court fines. This made it impossible for Justin to continue the interaction with either the landlord or the police. But he still needed his work ID and work clothes, so he took independent action to take his belongings, and the landlord had this law-abiding, working man arrested again.

Benita, a Nurse and Mother of Two: The Perils of Driving without a License

The consequence of hyper-surveillance and the racial profiling of Black drivers is that they are stopped by the police with much greater frequency than their White counterparts. For most less-affluent Black people who drive, this means that they have been stopped so many times that they have lost their licenses because they cannot pay the fines, and then can't register their cars because they cannot afford to pay the increased insurance premiums caused by the tickets. Because jobs tend to be located in White suburban communities that are not served by public transportation, however, those who are employed need to drive through those communities to get to work. Many end up in jail because they were trying to get to their jobs—which further adds to the neighborhood crime rate and is another reason why so many end up in illegal careers.

Benita, a twenty-nine-year-old African American mother of four young children, has managed to remain employed—but only by driving to work illegally. Several years prior to the incident we describe, she had been arrested for unpaid traffic tickets. While most Americans do not accumulate enough traffic tickets and unpaid fines to be arrested, this situation is surprisingly common in Bristol Hill, and indeed for Black Americans nationwide. In an attempt to curb the drug trade, local law enforcement agencies have for years received additional state and federal funding to patrol Bristol Hill and its boundaries. Many traffic stops are a by-product of the extra vigilance, leading to disproportionate contact of Black residents with law enforcement.

As the Justice Department study of Ferguson, Missouri, and other cities made evident, such practices have taken on a life of their own. By 2016 it had been documented that many communities are using the practice of ticketing and fining non-White citizens to fund local government and keep tax rates low. Arrests resulting from this practice are common among the residents of heavily policed Black communities. Arrests for debt resulting from such state-enforced sanctions were a common theme in our interviews and observations: the end result is a new form of debtor's prison for Black Americans.

Law enforcement tends to focus particularly on the borders/boundaries where poor Black neighborhoods transition into White middle-class suburbs—making it difficult for Black Americans to leave segregated areas without getting into trouble. Many jobs in the surrounding suburban areas require low-wage workers who can't afford to live there. In order to access those jobs, workers have to cross those heavily policed Black/White boundaries. Public transportation was available within Bristol Hill. But not between Bristol Hill and the suburbs. There are no legitimate jobs available within the neighborhood. Like other employed members of the community, Benita, a nurse, worked in suburban areas accessible only by car. Because Benita needed to cross that line to get to her job, she had been caught in the net many times.

While driving to and from work, Benita got a lot of tickets: for speeding, driving an uninsured vehicle, failing to wear her seat belt, and improperly displaying her license plate. She explained the ticket for an improperly displayed plate:

> I had the license plate in my window instead of on [the] back of the car. I can't remember why. I just got the plates to put on the car, and I didn't have the screws to screw it in, so I just stuck the plate in the window. And they pulled me over for that [*laughs*]. The city doesn't care about that. So it's like, it's outside the city—suburban areas, mainly, like, when I'm goin' to work, or, you know, goin' to look for a job—where you get a ticket.

Benita could not pay the tickets immediately, and penalties for unpaid fines increased until the amount she owed was $2,200. Then Benita was arrested for failing to pay the tickets, and she served three days in jail and lost her driver's license. After her release, Waverly asked her how she got to work:

Yeah, I drove, because there's . . . how am I gonna get there? I can't lose my job, so now I'm cautious. I have to watch for the police, and when I see them, I turn off and go a whole 'nother route and then get back on track, and then I'm off.

This loss of license is a typical outcome for Black Americans. However, to keep her job and support her family, she needs to continue driving to work.

Then, although Benita was a cautious driver, she got into an accident. One morning on her way home from her night shift, a young White man riding his bike — on his way to work, but running late — rushed into the street in front Benita's car. As she passed through the intersection, her car hit the front wheel of his bike. The impact threw the man off his bike onto her windshield. She stopped to help him. Even though Benita was operating her car without a license or insurance and owed more than $600 in fines, she called 911. An ambulance and the police were dispatched. Meanwhile, she stayed at the scene. She described being so distraught herself that the bicyclist hugged and comforted her while they waited.

When the police arrived on the scene, she recognized both officers from previous traffic stops. She quickly explained that she did not have a license and that she was in the process of paying off the previous fines, but stressed that she had to drive to work every day in order to support her family. Still in her nursing scrubs and obviously distraught, she was then comforted and hugged by one of the officers, who explained that most people in her circumstances would have fled the scene of the accident. Moreover, because she remained until the police got there, the officer told her that he would not give her a citation or place her under arrest. No one was severely injured, and the bicyclist took responsibility for the accident. After the officers left, one of Benita's coworkers picked her up and they drove the bicyclist to work.

In the eyes of the police officers, Benita had exceeded their expectations for someone like her. The expectation is that someone in her circumstances would have fled the scene of the accident. She not only acted contrary to their stereotyped expectations, she over-conformed to the rule of law, hoping to receive a lighter sanction. This kind of over-conformity with expectations was described by Du Bois as "submissive civility" (see chapter 5). In this case, the practice was rewarded. As Goffman (1963) observed, negative social anticipations can be transformed into normative expectations, especially toward stigmatized groups. If the officers expected Benita to leave the scene, then remaining there was abnormal and unexpected, but in a positive way. In addition, she was so upset and remorseful that one of the police officers responded by comforting her. The role of the bicyclist was also crucial, in that he also comforted her and admitted wrongdoing. The situation was resolved to the satisfaction of everyone concerned.

Because recognition of performed identity often depends, as Goffman (1963) put it, on the use of "stereotypes" and "previous experience with individuals roughly similar," inconsistencies between stereotyped expectations and performed identities are important. While they are often barriers to recognition that lead to arrests for tickets and minor infractions, they can also lead to positive outcomes, as in this case, when a person exceeds the expectations of the stereotype in a positive direction: an instance of submissive civility.

This situation also highlights the different functions of law enforcement: issuing tickets and levying fines are very different from writing an accident report. Even though she is driving illegally, the police don't consider Benita a problem in the context of this quite serious accident. Given the circumstances, ticketing her would have been complicated, involving lots of paperwork, and would have been very punitive. However, these are the same police who issued her the tickets in the past that led to her arrest and loss of license. And, in accordance with local practices of racially profiling Black drivers, they will continue to ticket her for minor infractions to such an extent that she will inevitably be arrested again for not paying the tickets/fines.

Conclusion: Navigating a System of Collective Punishment

In theory, the American legal system punishes individuals only when they break the law. In practice, what we find in Bristol Hill and other Black communities is a system of collective punishment in which entire communities are punished and the rights of citizens denied through a whole host of practices—both legal and illegal—through which social institutions (the "system") combine forces to strip Black residents of their rights. Citizens living in poor, racially segregated neighborhoods tend to live out their lives without access to legitimate jobs, let alone jobs that pay a livable wage. They attend failing schools that have been condemned by state boards of education; and, all too often, they find themselves and their relatives imprisoned for petty offenses. Yet within their communities, these Black citizens typically treat one another with equality and mutual respect.

Poor Black neighborhoods are crisscrossed by surveillance systems that negatively impact the daily lives of residents. Patricia Fernández-Kelly (2015) argues that liminal institutions—such as prisons, schools, child protective services, and public housing officials—interfere with the lives of Americans in precarious circumstances, and that we should reconsider the design of those public institutions that perpetuate irregular conditions in American cities. Michelle Alexander (2011) describes a neo-caste system, "the new Jim Crow," created by the criminal justice system via prisons, probation, parole, and the mark of a criminal record. This system exercises punitive control over African Americans, compromising their basic human rights, as well as their access to housing, education, employment, and voting. It should not be surprising that Black Americans share a general sense of the unfairness of the situation.

Victor Rios (2011) developed the concept of the "youth control complex," a system that functions to monitor, stigmatize, criminalize, and collectively punish young people of color. Rios examines how this complex operates in schools, in which local police and school officials provide security, and where even educators in positions of power have little discretion once zero-tolerance policies are invoked. Reuben Miller and Amanda Alexander (2016) coined the concept of "carceral citizenship" to describe the legal and extralegal sanctions imposed on the criminalized poor, their families, and the communities to which they return post-incarceration. This new form of citizenship, produced and sustained by a host of actors with the power to sanction, shapes the everyday lives of the Black and Brown poor—producing legal exclusion and stigmatization. Black citizens, not surprisingly, do not feel protected by this system.

The neighborhood interaction order that developed in response to these exclusions and intrusions gives residents relief, respect, and protection among themselves. Focusing on this interaction order is therefore a useful approach for understanding the complexities involved in relations between poor Black communities and outsiders like police, social workers, and landlords. Attitudes of residents toward outsiders are shaped by the threat they pose to neighborhood stability through constant surveillance and negative sanctions.

The failure of *outsiders* and *intruders* to ratify the identities and normal practices of Black residents, what we called in the second chapter a non-recognition of identity, leads to the employment of an important self-preservation strategy of null-response for these residents. Refusing to recognize the legitimacy of the police and other outsiders protects residents from threats to their identities and feelings of self-worth. However, when residents attempt to ignore the police, citizens and police are left in different social worlds, with differing definitions of the situation and different possible identities. As we saw in chapters 4 and 5, meaningful communication dissolves under such conditions, resulting in the misunderstandings of Black masculinity and the resulting police violence we have become so familiar with through cell phone, dash cam, and police video documentation in recent years.

The police play a huge role in the hyper-surveillance that exists in poor spaces, constantly penalizing small infractions, while remaining unaware of what might be helpful to residents. As such the police have become the focus of controversy. In implementing such strategies, however, the police carry out policies like broken windows policing and other misguided directives they have been told, or convinced, to implement. The police are in a very real sense only doing what they have been asked to do. The police don't have this kind of power in middle-class White neighborhoods.

If the police would treat these communities as they do the White suburbs—in which they overlook many crimes that residents consider normal in an effort to protect the integrity of the neighborhood—poor Black citizens could get some relief. It would be more effective for educators, landlords, and debtors to stop using sanctions and fines, and for schools to distance themselves from zero-tolerance policies. Simply, *recognizing the constitutional rights* of poor Black Americans and treating them as citizens in their own communities would change things dramatically. Implementing intrusive policies that treat Black Americans as if they are less than human rather than American citizens not only damages the neighborhood but the police psyche as well. You can't treat people—any people—as if they are less than human and remain whole yourself. In the end, the police also become victims of these practices.

We advocate a focus on the policies and those who administrate them, and not only on the police, who are themselves relatively powerless and also have been damaged by the role in which society has cast them. In order to improve the situation for people in neighborhoods like Lyford Street, it is essential for policy makers to pay attention to *how* people in the community make sense of their interactions, and to *respect* the strategies they have adopted to cope with the uncertainties and dangers they face. Violating the identities of residents consistently, the police quite simply do not know them.

As William Julius Wilson (1987) and others have argued, the concentrated disadvantage in such communities has been intensified by the War on Drugs, the criminalization of schoolchildren for minor offenses, the elimination of welfare programs, and the loss of jobs. Combine all these with a lack of awareness by most White Americans that such conditions even exist, and it becomes clear that poor Black communities have been left isolated and racially oppressed. Arguing against the tendency to blame residents of such neighborhoods for being poor because their "culture of poverty" is said to be inadequate, Wilson insisted that poverty, not culture, is the primary cause of these conditions. Building on Wilson's insights, we agree that poverty is a major factor. But so is racism. Moreover, we also find that *the culture of this neighborhood is a positive* and not a negative response to the poverty and racism that its residents face.

We argue that far from being inadequate, the local interaction order of this poor Black neighborhood works to *restore to residents the equality and self-worth* that the larger White society has attempted to strip from them. The local interaction order is not an impoverished culture. It is a powerful and creative democratic response to the poverty and divisions of Race and class that seek to isolate and oppress residents of the neighborhood—a response that restores the social supports that residents need in order to flourish as autonomous human beings. We find this culture especially rich in its support for a democratic equality that confers value and respect on citizens who cannot get respect from the society outside the neighborhood, and it cements strong moral commitments between residents.

Conclusion

Digging Out the Lies by Making the Ordinary Strange

> . . . have brought humanity to the edge of oblivion: because they think they are white . . . they do not dare confront the ravage and the lie of their history . . . for there *are* no white people.　　　　　　　—James Baldwin, "On Being 'White' . . . and Other Lies"

In January 2018 police officers in Milwaukee, Wisconsin, dragged Sterling Brown, an NBA guard with the Milwaukee Bucks, to the ground and repeatedly shocked him with a Taser. As he lay there taking ragged breaths, one of the officers stood on his ankle, shifting his full weight on and off in a slow rhythm while other officers watched and joked about the "shit storm" of complaints about "racism" they were going to face. They were right about that. Sterling Brown's crime? Parking in a handicap spot in front of an all-night pharmacy at two in the morning in an otherwise empty parking lot. At the moment he was wrestled to the ground and repeatedly tased, video shows him standing and waiting for an officer to write him a parking ticket. The failure of basic human empathy and reciprocity put on display by the behavior of the police during this incident is the all too common face that White Americans extend to Black Americans.

Racism is a basic failure to recognize the racial Other as a human being like oneself: a failure of empathy and reciprocity. Rocking back and forth while standing on the ankle of a professional basketball player is a shockingly graphic display of such failure. In the United States, it has been a 350-year failure of White Americans to recognize the humanity of Black Americans. Some White Americans are aware of this failure and embrace it: a conscious process of overt racism. More often, however, the process is unconscious, and those White Americans who fail to recognize Black Others as equals believe it is the fault of the Other for not acting in socially acceptable ways that have nothing to do with Race (they were rude, or loud, suspicious, or made them feel fearful, etc.). In this book we have shown that those differences in how people act and expect Others to act *are* related to Race. Forms of tacit unconscious racism have become so deeply embedded in the expectations of ordinary interaction—in what we call interaction orders of Race (Rawls 1987, 2000)—that we interpret the behavior of Others in racist ways constantly without being aware of it. This tacit racism, which has been institutionalized in our daily interactional practices, divides the nation and provides a fertile ground for the political manipulation of issues that the many lies and fantasies about Race have falsely associated with Black Americans.

People cannot make sense of the world, or even extend each other basic human decencies, when they think in terms of a boundary between themselves and the Other. The interaction orders that we use to make sense and self are fragile and require a great deal of care and reciprocity. When we abuse the equality that social interaction requires, basic human cooperation and reciprocity across social boundaries fail. The inability of White Americans, the police, and other authorities to recognize the humanity of Black Americans and "see" them as citizens like themselves undermines the moral character of all Americans and makes our social institutions undemocratic. Without fairness in the application of laws, there can be no democracy based on the "rule of law." There is an urgent need to close the reciprocity gap between Black and White Americans.

It is our position that exposing the tacit racism in everyday life, *digging out the lies*, and teaching people to observe the racism in their own daily lives by making the familiar strange can generate the required empathy and reciprocity. We call this teaching White double consciousness and we have been teaching it this way for two decades. It is difficult for White Americans to remain detached from racism—and to continue believing in the lies—when they start to see the part they are playing in creating racism. It also becomes clearer to Black Americans just how much of what they have been experiencing really is racism. Contrary to what most White people think, we find that Black Americans tend to *underestimate* the racism they face (it is so constant and pervasive that they don't want to call it racism unless they are sure).

We have devised simple strategies for what to do when you think you might be in the middle of a racist happening. Just ask people what they mean or what they are doing. It will not make the racism go way. Usually racism gets even more explicit as the person you asked tries to explain what they meant or what they did (see chapter 6). But that's the aim of the strategy. It is a way of digging out tacit racism and preventing it from masquerading as ordinary talk/action: bringing it out in the open where it can be seen and talked about. If we all did this simple thing every time we saw or heard something that looks or sounds racist, it would make a big difference.

But even asking "What do you mean?" requires being able to see the possibility of tacit racism in action. The need for racial self-awareness is critical. After nearly four centuries of building American society on a foundation of racism, inequalities of Race have become so deeply embedded in the social expectations of American life that White Americans can look at Black Americans and literally not "see" another human being with human thoughts and feelings. An unconscious White "racial framing" (Feagin 2009) of situations, actions, and identity accompanies us everywhere. It is not possible to live in the United States and not be tainted by the deep vein of racism upon which our society is built.

The situation is critical. Divisions between White and Black Americans are being exploited by foreign regimes and wealthy alt-right extremists to push an anti-democratic and explicitly racist agenda that undermines the well-being of the nation and all of its citizens. Our elections and democratic institutions are being attacked. It took skillful manipulation by powerful interests over many decades to encourage the virulent racism needed to provide cover for such efforts (Alexander 2011). Largely unnoticed until recently, powerful interest groups funded by "Dark Money" have been working since the 1950s to amplify lies and fantasies about Race that would enable them to repeal the democratic gains of the twentieth century (Mayer 2016; Maddow 2019). The fear and lack of empathy that many White Americans have been encouraged to feel toward Black Americans have turned them into political pawns in a war of influence with both national and international repercussions (Wylie 2019).

Racism has emerged as our biggest national security threat. It threatens the core institutions essential to democracy: national and international law, voting rights, the free press, individual freedom, the right to asylum, the separation of powers, separation of church and state, and even the principle that the president is not above the law. However, it would not have been possible to use racism to manipulate the American public unless there was a strong undercurrent of racism—and the lies that support it—ready and waiting to be exploited. While many White Americans were celebrating a "post-racial" America after the election of President Obama, others were privately seething because they could not openly express their racism. Their silence is over. We are now facing a moment of truth.

The Importance of Talking about Race and the Legacy of Slavery

It has been popular for decades to insist that we would be better off not talking about or even mentioning Race: an approach known as "color-blind racism" (Bonilla-Silva 2003). Slavery was a long time ago, many White Americans say: "Why can't Black Americans get over it?" The simple answer to that question is that the legacy of slavery is still structuring American lives—including White lives. It will not be possible to put slavery behind us until we finally eliminate the many lies and fantasies about Race that are the consequence of our slave legacy, all of which have become deeply embedded in our daily lives. However, that will not be the end of talking about slavery—it will be the beginning. Because, really, as a nation we have never talked about slavery. In fact, we have never talked as a nation about any of our problems with Race, believing the lie that Race problems belong to the past and are better forgotten. The recent outpouring of overt racism, combined with the many books documenting how deeply embedded racism has become in our lives and how dangerous it is, have hopefully put that belief to rest. Rooting out racism means *never forgetting* the evils done in its service.

Race may not be the *only* thing dividing America. But a close look at the many points of division reveals that, because of the way lies about Race have been used to manipulate the public, these points of division *all* intersect with Race, and not talking about these lies has not only allowed racism to flourish, but policies based on such lies have increased its effects. For instance, while liberal politics has often been driven by the pretense of racial justice, it is also shot through with tacit racism. As a consequence, many liberal policies have actually increased the inequality and intrusion experienced by African Americans, even though they were explicitly designed to decrease it. Such policies include the Clinton "tough on crime" agenda that was intended to help poor Black communities become "crime free," but succeeded only in violating the rights of residents, inflating crime rates, and incarcerating vast swathes of the Black population. Liberal policies that increased racial inequality also include "mandatory sentencing" guidelines, which began in an effort to reduce racism in sentencing but resulted in much higher rates of incarceration and much longer sentences for Black men and women; they include social service efforts to force a middle-class nuclear family model on the poor, which does not meet the needs of Black families (Ladner 1971; Stack 1974), and consequently has resulted in high rates of Black children being removed from their families and placed in foster care (Mosby et al. 1999). They also include efforts to make schools "safer" through zero-tolerance policies that have given rise to a school-to-prison pipeline that imprisons Black children at high rates for normal childhood behavior (Rios 2011).

Attempts to "improve" the lives of Black citizens that proceed in ignorance of how tacit racism impacts the problem the policy targets inevitably increase racism whether they are liberal or conservative. And it's not just liberal *policies* that result in racism: studies also show that in spite of professing a belief in racial tolerance, *liberals themselves* score no better than other Americans on measures of implicit racism. A study by researchers at UCLA in 2015, for instance, found that self-identified liberals who are proud of their racial tolerance nevertheless associate people with Black-sounding names with negative attributes similar to those of uneducated White men with criminal records in test answer after test answer. The lead researcher on the UCLA study, Colin Holbrook, said, "I've never been so disgusted by my own data" (Hewitt 2015). Other studies show that White Americans perceive dark-skinned Black Americans as less intelligent than lighter-skinned Black Americans, are less likely to empathize with Black than with White men, perceive Black children as adults who deserve harsh punishment, are more likely to think that Black men deserve the death penalty, are more likely to describe dark-skinned Black men as criminals with no college education, and so on.

Conservative politics is driven more *explicitly* by Race. The rural conservative movement is a White movement—underwritten by rich White elites—and fueled by feelings of alienation, fear, resentment, and anger that coalesce around Whiteness and are reinforced by false narratives about Race (involving lies about civil rights, welfare, "Obamacare," guns, and crime). The movement in general seeks to preserve a mythical past in which America was alleged to be both White and Christian and where all the cowboy heroes were White. The fact that this past is a fiction—a lie—only seems to strengthen its appeal. The movement is intrinsically anti-government because the alleged destruction of this fictional past is blamed on government intervention in the Civil Rights movement. This makes White discontent useful to rich conservatives, who are also anti-government but for very different reasons. The rich want to do business without constraint: no matter whom it hurts (Mayer 2016). Oil and gas corporations, for example, have consistently supported policies that starve local government to maximize their profits, even when those policies threaten to bankrupt the states those corporations call home (Maddow 2019). Racial myths about the alleged "preferences" and "privileges" that many White Americans mistakenly believe Black Americans receive are used to motivate efforts to increase profits for the rich while dismantling social support programs for working Americans. That the same White citizens who support such efforts are the ones who lose the most when the programs are gone—because they were the ones getting the social services—doesn't stop them: reality does not make a dent in the popularity of the fantasies.

The wish to cling to the past is itself motivated by a belief in a mythical pre–Civil War, pre-industrial era. In this myth, all White people held the same values, no White person was poor, and every White person was safe and Christian. In reality, however, before 1700, America was a class-based society in which a bottom class of very poor *bought and paid-for* English, Irish, Scotch, and African slaves labored *together* for the profit of aristocratic English landowners. Irish and Scotch laborers were sold to colonial plantation owners as a consequence of wars between Catholics and Protestants: being "Christian" was not a point of agreement. In addition, estimates are that over half of the original White population of the American colonies came as convicts serving terms of labor for crimes in England and Ireland—sold into slavery for crimes as small as stealing six cents—while others were sold because they were poor, Irish, Catholic, or prisoners of war.

Rural White Americans who believe the lies about a pure White Christian past complain about the prosperity that urban Americans—both Black and White—enjoy today, believing erroneously that this prosperity has been built on the ashes of a glorious lost White Christian civilization. Fictions about White superiority and the White Christian character of American history sustain these beliefs. Studies tell us that White Americans also vastly overestimate the amount of equality and opportunity in their own lives (Piketty 2014), while a number of recent books (Hochschild 2016; Cramer 2016; Vance 2016) document a growing rural White resentment. It seems that rural White Americans believe not only that urban prosperity dilutes the mythical pure White culture they value; they also express the view that urban prosperity is unfair because they mistakenly believe it siphons off their tax dollars—the fruits of their own hard labor—which they think are then redistributed to urban populations.

While it is true that working poor and rural White Americans are worse off today than at almost any time in the past, it is not because their tax dollars have been funding urban prosperity. To the extent that there has been a wealth transfer in the US, it has gone in the other direction: urban wealth has been supporting impoverished rural areas for generations. In spite of the high value placed on self-reliance, rural America has not been self-supporting since before WWII. Neither has the oil and gas industry, which has been the biggest beneficiary of public assistance in American history (Maddow 2019). This reality, however, does not stop rural White communities from believing that Black Americans have stolen their fair share of the American pie.

Some of the lies about Race have come down to us almost unchanged from those seventeenth-century English landowners who invented Whiteness to encourage their newly freed English and Irish slaves to keep African slaves working and "in their place." Others were the creation of powerful special interests trying to manipulate White resistance to civil rights and unions to the political advantage of corporations and business after the Civil War and again in the 1950s and 1960s (when most monuments to the Civil War enemies of the US were erected). Funded by a small number of conservative billionaires and their think tanks (Mayer 2016), the 1% have contributed more than their share of lies through rumor and myth via the conservative media, manipulation of Facebook, Twitter, and other social media, all unwittingly supported by the allegedly "free" mainstream media, which in an effort to provide "balanced" reporting, repeats many of the lies. Many fictions about Race, slavery, and the early colonies have also been institutionalized in textbooks.

Since they were baptized White in the seventeenth century, the typical White American (particularly men) has identified with the White "Strong Man" ideal and tended to support policies that benefit narcissistic wealthy individuals and corporations that have shown so little regard for the general welfare. Promising resistance movements by White workers that occurred just before the Civil War and during the Depression were short-lived. The current dire situation of poor White America is a direct result of this paradox. As poor White communities experience declining health and wealth, combined with increased violence and drug use, they are doubling down on their support for the very policies that are producing these problems. It is a vicious circularity, kept in motion by the fact that these White Americans still identify with their rich oppressors. Their need to develop an awareness of class oppression and replace their White racial identification with an awareness of status/class is acute.

Much of the White fear of Black Americans is driven by false beliefs about crime and the persistent image of the "criminalblackman" (Russell-Brown 1998), which are the creation of a racially biased criminal justice system. The hyper-surveillance of Black neighborhoods that fills our prisons and has led to an explosion of mass incarceration—making the US by far the most punitive nation in the world—sustains racist perceptions of Black citizens as criminals and their neighborhoods as disorderly. However, as with attempts to eradicate welfare and what is called Obamacare in order to penalize Black people, the criminalization of Black Americans has also had unintended negative consequences for poor White Americans. The criminalizing net has been cast more and more widely, and an increasing number of poor White Americans now also find themselves in prison.

The US prison population was 2.3 million in 2018, by far the largest in the world; with 4.4% of the world's population, the US accounts for 25% of the world's prisoners. The rate of imprisonment rose from 100 per hundred thousand in 1970 to 750 per hundred thousand in 2018. Russia is our closest competitor at around 600 and South Africa is next at 300. The European average is 100 (which was the US rate before we began using prison to negate the civil rights of Black citizens in the 1960s). One of every 32 Americans in 2018 was under some form of criminal justice supervision, and most of these were poor White or Black people. While Black Americans are vastly overrepresented in the criminal justice system, incarceration rates in poor White communities are much higher than in middle-class White communities. In states with the highest rates of imprisonment, poor White Americans are incarcerated at rates closer to those of Black Americans (four times less rather than the middle-class White rate of fifteen times less).

Many current crises in White communities—including the high incarceration rate, high rates of opiate use and drug overdose, high rates of pollution, poor health and nutrition, high unemployment, and rates of violent death that are 50% higher than those for White Americans in more integrated communities (Males 2017)—are the unintended consequence of acting on racist fantasies about Black Americans. Ending racism would directly benefit 99% of White Americans. But this is a truth that the 1% do not want them to know.

The Many Lies at the Foundation of American Culture

Of the many lies, myths, and fantasies about Race that stand at the center of American life, one of the most effective is the powerful reinforcement of the White strong man ideal in the twentieth century by the Hollywood depiction of the myth of the self-reliant White "John Wayne" cowboy. Often cast as a US Marshall or Sheriff, this strong White man was offered as the keeper of social order in a wild and unruly land—dominating through sheer strength of character. As Baraka and Durham (1965) document in their classic *The Black Cowboy*, this fantasy about strong White men has not only been resilient, but the popularity of cowboy movies that feature White cowboy heroes has effectively spread the lie about the racial superiority of strong White male protectors of law and order around the world.

In reality, however, the cowboys of the American "Wild West"—even the most famous—were more often Black, Mexican, Native American, or foreign born than they were American-born White men. Furthermore, in the short era of the cowboy—which lasted only from 1840 to 1890—the law-abiding heroes were much more likely to be Black, Native American, or Mexican than White. The US Attorney in 1888 estimated that of the 20,000 White persons living in the Indian Territory (Oklahoma/Texas) at that time, only one-fifth were law-abiding. In addition, of every eleven men convicted in the federal court in the territory during that period seven were White, while only three were Black and one Indian (Burton 2006: 31). It turns out that Black cowboys were more likely to be the real-life heroes.

This suggests a difference between White and Black/Indian men in the West that is the reverse of the cowboy hero myth on two scores. First, most cowboys were not White, and second because their motivations for going west were very different, White cowboys were much more likely to be outlaws while Black cowboys were more likely to be upstanding law-abiding men. There is a simple explanation for this. Before the Civil War, the primary motivation for going west was to escape from society back east—and Black and White men had very different reasons for wanting to escape. Many early Black cowboys were escaping from slavery and bringing their skills as cowhands, horse breeders/trainers, and blacksmiths to the West. White men, by contrast, were typically escaping from legal problems or social rejection. In the early days, life in the territories was not stable enough to lure those who had other opportunities. Although displaced southern White men did begin to move west in greater numbers after the Civil War, most who were members of society in good standing could still find better opportunities in the East and stayed there. Law-abiding Black men, on the other hand, had few opportunities east of the Mississippi even after the war. For them, the western territories offered coveted opportunities for those with skill and enterprise to carve out successful careers, at least until the 1890s.

Estimates suggest that American-born White men never made up more than a quarter of the cowboy population before 1890. According to Katz ([1971] 2005), author of *The Black West*, Oklahoma—a center of cowboy activity—was once virtually an all-Black territory. (Tulsa retained a vibrant Black business center called "Black Wall Street" until the Tulsa Race riots of 1921, when Black residents were massacred by envious White residents to drive them out—an all too common occurrence in the US.) The same population demographics existed in parts of Texas, and the original Texas state police were a third to half Black. It was only at the end of Reconstruction that they were replaced by the all-White Texas Rangers (Burton 2006: 5).

Census taking at the time was local, sporadic, and inaccurate, so relative estimates of population by Race are necessarily rough. However, taking the several best estimates together, it seems that cowboys in the western territories during the heyday of the cowboy from 1865 to 1885 were roughly one-quarter Black, one-quarter Native American, one-quarter Mexican, one-quarter new European immigrant (mostly from Scandinavian countries), and one-quarter American-born White and mostly male. Most books report the proportions in quarters. The totals then involve five quarters, which is bad math, but also conveys the guesswork involved.

That White cowboys were in the minority, however, did not stop Hollywood filmmakers from creating and marketing the myth of the dominant White self-reliant cowboy. Unbeknownst to their audiences, beloved cowboy characters played by White actors like John Wayne and Clint Eastwood were often based on the exploits of famous Black cowboys, like Bill Pickett and Nat Love. Pickett invented bulldogging (a form of bull wrestling that involved biting the bull on the lip) and appeared in many of the most famous Wild West shows. He was the only Black cowboy from the era to star in cowboy films—appearing in seven—often identifying as Cherokee. In 1905 he appeared with Will Rogers at Madison Square Garden. Unbeknownst to many Rogers was himself a citizen of the Cherokee Nation. Nat Love was a handsome and imposing man, as the many pictures of him to be found on the internet attest. Nat arrived in Dodge City, Kansas, in 1870, at the age of sixteen, a skilled cattle and horseman who was also reputed to be a fast and deadly accurate shot. In 1907 Nat published his autobiography, *The Life and Adventures of Nat Love*, which is the source of much of the details about his life, and his exploits have been portrayed in several films.

Baraka and Durham (1965) speculate that the general replacement of Black cowboys with White heroes was done to provide White Americans with "an American folk hero" with whom they could identify. In other words, because White Americans were too deeply steeped in racism to identify with the real heroes of the West, Black heroes were made over as White men to support the fiction of White male superiority. Black cowboys like Bill Pickett often had to identify exclusively with their Indian ancestry to gain admission to the rodeos in which they competed. Black US Marshals like Bass Reeves, who is legendary for capturing over three thousand outlaws—and came closer than any other actual person to the exploits of the fictional Lone Ranger—and the skilled Black horsemen and gunfighters like Bill Pickett and Nat Love who invented bulldogging and other famous rodeo "tricks" were eliminated from our national story to support the lie of Whiteness. Not only did John Wayne play the roles of Black and Indian cowboys like Bill Pickett while publicly espousing White superiority, he even copied their equipment. Tom Threepersons, a famous Cherokee lawman in El Paso in the 1920s, designed a fast-draw holster that was named for him. This is the holster worn by John Wayne in his later films (Burton 2001: 6).

If you want a sense of the true Wild West, try imagining John Wayne as a strong Black man galloping on a fast horse while shooting accurately at White "bad guys."

Puerto Rico and Plymouth as First Colony Myth

Another powerful myth about the Pilgrims and Plymouth Colony is closely intertwined with the neglect of 3.5 million American citizens in Puerto Rico in the years after Hurricane Maria and the mistreatment of refugees and asylum seekers at the southern border between Mexico and the US (who are widely referred to as "Mexican" but are actually from other South American countries and turn out to be a high proportion of Mayan/ Indigenous ancestry). This mistreatment is an example of how categories of Race and Otherness from the deep colonial past, and the moral coding they embed in the daily lives of Americans, effect not only current American practice but also international relations. The White/Black binary categorization system is not just a racial category system—it is also an "Anglo" category system. And while tensions between England and Spain in the sixteenth and seventeenth centuries have not been a focus of this book, it is important to note the lingering effects of colonial anti-Spanish feeling on our national culture in the context of current immigration "policy." Puerto Rican citizens and immigrants from Mexico and South America tend to be people of color, who are also culturally Spanish, Latinx, Hispanic, or Mayan/Indigenous. This puts them in direct conflict with deeply embedded fictions about the free White and English character of the American colonies.

After Hurricane Maria devastated Puerto Rico in September 2017, the United States shamelessly left more than 3.5 million American citizens to languish in the dark without clean water or medicine for years. The problem has been referred to as genocide. Deaths from the hurricane were vastly underreported, and government services were woefully inadequate. In addition, Trump repeatedly talked about Puerto Rico as if its population were not American citizens, and reports have come in from around the United States of Puerto Ricans being denied services (at motels, liquor stores, state motor vehicle registries, and voter registration offices) because their Puerto Rican IDs are not being accepted as "American." Many apologies to customers have ensued.

The irony is that not only are Puerto Ricans American citizens—but *Puerto Rico was the first American colony*, dating back to 1508. Every year we celebrate a first colony Thanksgiving myth that memorializes the false narrative of happy feasting between Puritan settlers and Massachusetts Bay Wampanoag Indians at the Plymouth Plantation—calling it a celebration of the First Thanksgiving in the first American colony. There are several problems with this story. Colonized in 1620, Plymouth was not the first colony, and in the late 1600s, days of thanksgiving were called to celebrate *the massacre of Indians* not happy feasting with them (Lepore 2009). Over the past decade, knowledge of American history has improved somewhat, and some Americans now realize that the colony founded at Jamestown, Virginia, in 1607—which was based on slavery—was earlier than Plymouth. The recent "1619 project" (Hannah-Jones 2019) is helping to increase awareness of this issue.

However, that's still as far as it goes. What about the four Spanish colonies in America that were founded before Plymouth? Caparra, Puerto Rico, in 1508; Saint Augustine, Florida, in 1565; Santa Fe, New Mexico, in 1609; and Taos, New Mexico, in 1615.[1] These are all important locations in the United States today and all were colonized before Plymouth.

Why are none of them accorded the status of first colony? Race and the Anglo bias of the colonial conception of Whiteness also determine this. We are comfortable counting only the English colonies in a country that was colonized first by the Spanish, and also by the French and Dutch (not to mention our Scandinavian cowboys and the Wampanoag, Crow, Cherokee, Sioux, and other Indigenous people whose land it was). We are comfortable treating descendants of the original Spanish colonists—who were the first colonists—as second-class citizens. And we are happy to extend that bias to descendants of the Spanish colonizers of Mexico and Latin America: refusing to let them immigrate to this country or even seek asylum here. The fact that Texas, New Mexico, Arizona, California, Nevada, and Oregon used to be part of Mexico, or the earlier Spanish colony of Santa Fe, and that many ancestors of those trying to gain entry into the US today had their property stolen and were thrown out of the country violently and illegally after our conquest of Mexico, only makes our refusal to recognize their humanity worse.

Every year we celebrate Columbus Day as a national holiday. But when Columbus "discovered America" in 1492, the only place he actually located that is currently part of the United States is Puerto Rico, and it was one of the men who accompanied Columbus on the original expedition, Juan Ponce de León, who returned to found the first colony there on August 8, 1508. Yet we celebrate Columbus Day every year without acknowledging the special status of Puerto Rico as our first colony. We even managed to officially recognize the national historical status of Caparra in 1994 without acknowledging that it was the first colony. Americans treat Puerto Rico as if its people are not American citizens—let alone our first citizens.

A closer look at US history suggests that the Plymouth first colony myth has been so resilient because it has played an important role in deflecting attention from the class-based English and Irish slavery on which America was founded, helping to solidify the myth of pure White English Christian origins. The focus of the myth on the quest for religious freedom by free White people makes a lot of Americans feel good. But the problems with it go way beyond the fact that Thanksgiving in the 1600s typically celebrated the massacre of Indians, and not sharing food with them (Lepore 2009). In fact, the Pilgrims even outlawed Thanksgiving several times because of the excesses associated with it.

The Plymouth first colony myth is problematic even if we agree to count only English colonies. The first English colony was founded at Jamestown, Virginia, on May 14, 1607, not at Plymouth in 1620, and the myth that Jamestown failed, and therefore can't be counted as the first English colony, is another fantasy. The richest colonists in Jamestown did board two ships, preparing to leave during a famine in 1623 when the British supply ships did not arrive on time. But before anyone left, the ships were spotted on the horizon (Allen 1994). The tens of thousands of slaves—all but a handful of them English and Irish—never boarded ship. And in the end, the colony was not abandoned. It has been convenient to use this *ship boarding* by the wealthiest slave owners as a justification for saying that the Jamestown colony was abandoned.

What would the problem have been with embracing an origin myth built around a colony settled by slave owners rather than religious pilgrims? It would give America an origin myth based on the horrors of slavery rather than on a myth of religious freedom; not that the religion aspect of the Plymouth story is true, either—the Pilgrims were sponsored by businessmen who hoped they would stabilize the colony for business purposes (Bailyn 1979).

The problem with a Jamestown origin myth is twofold: not only would it emphasize southern slaveholders rather than the pursuit of religious freedom; more importantly, it would challenge the myth of White superiority. In the early days of the Jamestown colony, from 1607 to 1670, the vast majority of unfree laborers were English, Scotch, and Irish peasants and convicts. These White slaves suffered enormously, laboring on tobacco plantations to produce profit for their English owners. An origin myth focused on Jamestown would be a celebration not only of slavery, but of *the enslavement of English and Irish workers by their fellow countrymen for profit*. It would undermine the myth of White superiority and expose status inequalities that the wealthy want hidden. It is not surprising that this has not been the preferred myth.

Moreover, the institutionalization of the Thanksgiving first colony origin myth as a federal holiday had a purpose that was related to both Race and slavery. It was Abraham Lincoln who elevated the Thanksgiving myth to the status of a national holiday in 1863, during the Civil War, by presidential proclamation. Lincoln enshrined the myth in an effort to solidify a nation that had been torn apart by a war over slavery. He hoped that giving White Americans a national origin myth that obscured the slave origins of the country would unite them whether they were in the North or South.

It is easy to see how the elevation of the myth was meant to work. Lincoln was preparing the ground for reuniting the country after the Civil

War. A national holiday—Thanksgiving—that located the origin of the country in the quest for religious freedom of White English colonists would deflect attention from the slave origins of the South and give the country a better chance of healing the wounds of a war over slavery. At this point we need to admit not only that *it did not work*, but that it further solidified the fantasy of White Anglo superiority that not only led to the Civil War in the first place but encouraged a general silence about the legacy of slavery ever since. Forgetting our nation was founded on slavery is the problem not a solution.

Developing White Double Consciousness

In exploring how all of this factors into the contemporary crisis in America, we refer again to Du Bois's conception of double consciousness. Double consciousness explains why the Black American experience is unlike any other colonial (or master/slave) experience. It also explains why poor White Americans, an oppressed group that did not develop double consciousness, often do not realize what is in their own best interests, while even the poorest and least educated Black Americans usually recognize the politics of wealth and exclusion. Because of the strong White/Black binary that developed as a caste system in the United States, many features of colonialism—including the aspiration to be like the White colonizer, which scholars such as Fanon (1952) have argued leads to self-hatred and low self-esteem—are largely missing from the Black American experience. Their exclusion from Whiteness was so complete that Black Americans were able to create an alternate community of their own that they control. Because Black Americans have experience in both the Black and White worlds, they understand that White Americans are orienting toward different interactional expectations and can try to understand those differences. This awareness or "second sight" about Race is part of the experience of double consciousness.

White Americans, by contrast, live in only one social world—the White one. Generally unaware that Black social life follows its own organizing principles, which are based on different values and expectations, they cannot take this into account. Not realizing that they have traded social class for Race, they cannot take that into account either. Thus, when White Americans look at themselves, they vastly overestimate their potential to move up the social class ladder and become rich, and hence confuse their own interests with those of the rich (Stiglitz 2012; Piketty 2014).

When White Americans look at Black Americans, they look through a White lens that shows them deviance and disorder. They do not see the order and legitimacy that is there. All deviations from the White ideal are judged as flawed, lesser, inferior. There is a tendency to treat Black social action as chaotic and irrational: "Why do Black people act like that? Why can't they act more like White people?" White Americans tend to experience differences as "deviance" from their own norms that should be *stamped out*, punished, and eliminated in an attempt to force assimilation and restore *order*.

This is why the *mandate for order* that motivates much current social policy is so inherently racist. The focus is on White order, treating Black forms of order as if they do not exist. Ironically, this racialized lens not only penalizes Black Americans—it also penalizes poor White Americans, who in many ways share common cause with African Americans and thus are often hurt by the same policies that penalize Black Americans. Working-class White Americans often do not realize this because in emulating those who oppress them, they have lost sight of their own self-interest. But suffering from the colonial mentality that has them emulating the rich, voting politically as if they were the 1% they pretend to be does not change the facts: working-class White Americans have given themselves no way of escaping from the gap between who they are and who they aspire to be.

Developing a double consciousness of their own might offer White Americans a means of escape. Ironically, to overcome their own inequality, White people—who believe they are superior—must learn something important from Black people. For Black Americans there has not been much choice about double consciousness, which has been a positive outcome because it offers some protection from the envy and alienation experienced by many White Americans. The racial binary in the US is so rigid that Black Americans could not assimilate even if they want to. Racial discrimination is still so inflexible that uneducated White men with felony records are twice as likely as Black men with college degrees and no records to get a job interview (Wise 2010). But this fact does not stop White people from believing that affirmative action gives Black people preferential access to jobs or easier admission into colleges, and it does not stop them from stereotyping Black people as lazy criminals, while in the same breath complaining that they took all the jobs.

For White Americans to develop their own experience of double consciousness would require the ability to see themselves through the eyes of Black Americans. It would also mean acknowledging the differences between themselves and rich White elites. Double consciousness, as Du Bois pointed out, is an experience of seeing oneself as different and less than in the eyes of the Other. It is not a comfortable experience. The way White Others see Black citizens is not the way they would like to be seen. White eyes often do not recognize competence, identity, or success (Du Bois [1940] 2017). The way Black Others see White citizens will not be the way those White citizens want to be seen, either. Experiencing how rich White elites view working White people will also be unwelcome. The experience should and will be uncomfortable. It is easy to understand why White Americans get defensive when the topics of Race and class come up. If they stick with the discussion, they are likely to be confronted by facts that challenge their fictions with unwelcome images of themselves as they are seen by Black Americans and by the White 1% (who view them as gullible "sheep" or "marks").

Currently, White Americans do not seem to recognize that Black Americans are dealing on a daily basis with a racial boundary line that severely limits their life possibilities. In spite of affirmative action programs that White people complain endlessly about, White students are still twice as likely as Black students to get a scholarship (Wise 2010). Most White Americans assume the reverse. Our research on college campuses (chapter 6) shows that when White students see Black students on campus, they often assume that those Black students are less qualified than themselves—in their words, "stupid." They are so confident about this—and about its "factual" status—that many of them are comfortable stating these beliefs loud enough to be overheard by other students. However, these same students will deny that they are racist and claim they are just stating facts. Ironically, because it is still harder for Black students to get into college, in many cases Black students are smarter and better qualified than the White students who are making fun of them. Such false and racist assumptions lead to a high and constant level of racism on college campuses that we call Race pollution.

In this context, the interaction order that has developed in the Black community, which allows for self-definition rather than letting the White community define Black self-worth, has been crucial to the survival, success, and social health of Black Americans. It has shaped the expectations and obligations of members of the Black community in ways that explain why the details of interactional expectations between Black and White Americans differ the way they do. White students, by contrast, are not able to escape from the racism of the White people who surround them.

Developing racial self-awareness would be a solution. It will not be a comfortable process. Most Americans will find that actions they were proud of have deep components of racial entitlement. But if a person can't see themselves as Others do, then they are fundamentally incomplete—only a partial self (Mead 1913, 1934). Without a full understanding of how we are all making racism real every day, America will continue to be a country founded on racism and *populated by incomplete beings*.

Changing the National Perception of Black Americans

Achieving democracy in the US will require changing the way we view African Americans. The tendency to equate Black Americans with disorder is one of the most damaging misperceptions. Outsiders looking at the poor Black neighborhood on Lyford Street, where we did extensive fieldwork from 2005 to 2017 (chapter 7), see disorder everywhere they look (Rawls and Duck 2012; Duck 2015). For insiders, however, the neighborhood has an orderly character, knowledge of which can keep them safe, and they count on that order. It is when this local order is disrupted—as it constantly is by the police and other outsiders—that neighborhood lives are put in jeopardy.

Because Black men are routinely denied jobs, many neighborhood men deal drugs for a living, and, as in other poor Black neighborhoods, the drug dealers are well organized. In spite of the large labor pool, this is the only local economy: let's underscore that. Because of racial exclusion in this city, even though they live in the richest nation on earth, drug dealing is the only local economy. Drug dealing is work. For anyone who knows what to look for, several features stand out as identifying the activities of drug-dealing spots. For the most part, these markers are intentional: people need to know *where* they are and *which* set of interaction order expectations are in force in that place. As one enters a drug-dealing area, they might see memorial murals to those killed in the War on Drugs, gym shoes hanging suspended from electrical wires (usually at points of entry and exit), broken streetlamps, and strategically placed small piles of trash (used to hide drugs and guns).

It has become popular to treat such features of poor urban Black neighborhoods as evidence of disorder, of the failure of collective efficacy, and as invitations to further lawlessness (Sampson, Raudenbush, and Earls 1997). Memorial murals are described as graffiti and treated as vandalism.

Dangling gym shoes and piles of trash are seen as uncollected litter and treated as evidence of disorder and neglect. The argument by Kelling and Wilson (1982) that such "disorder" leads to further deterioration of the physical and social aspects of an area and opens it up to "predators" has been used to justify the adoption nationally of a punitive "broken windows" form of policing as a way of enforcing "order" in Black neighborhoods. This is an inherently racist and classist form of policing. In most middle-class White neighborhoods, by contrast, the emphasis is on safety.

On Lyford Street we find that each of these markers—targeted as disorder—has an orderliness embedded in its execution, and while the "broken windows" thesis treats them as evidence of neglect that needs to be forcibly corrected, we found that these markers were meaningful and intentional: part of the local order that residents count on for safety. When these markers are forcibly removed, residents almost immediately put them back as they were. They do this not because they are engaging in vandalism, but to restore the local order they rely on. Constant efforts to eradicate this neighborhood order in favor of a White middle-class conception of order that will not work under the conditions of inequality in this place make everyone in the neighborhood less safe. Broken windows is an approach to policing that puts Black lives in danger.

While outsiders perceive the drug dealers here as predators, they belong to the neighborhood, and, as we show in chapter 7, they play an important role in keeping people safe. By contrast, the police are seen as dangerous predators. In addition to their investment in the safety of the community in which they reside, drug dealers need to keep crime out of the neighborhood to minimize police presence and protect their customers. Toward this end, they prevent outsiders from hurting law-abiding residents and are valued by older community members for the respect and dignity—the affirmation of self—these older Black citizens get from interacting with them. The local order practices, along with the drug-dealing spots they mark and help organize, are certainly evidence of poverty and unemployment. But they are also positive expressions of drug-dealing practices and the local order and money they bring to the neighborhood. Memorial murals that are considered "graffiti" by outsiders are highly valued expressions of broadly shared community sentiment (and the artists are paid): neighborhood residents mourn the young men they have lost to the drug wars—fathers, brothers, cousins, friends, husbands, and sons.

What Black communities need is not order. They have their own order. *They need jobs.* Until Black men and women have jobs, they will put food on their tables any way they can. It is a matter of life and death. The social contract that society has extended to White Americans has been withheld from such communities. What their residents need is the respect and acceptance as equal human beings that would allow them access to employment, education, and housing: basic human needs. They need to be treated as equal partners in the quest for the American dream.

There is a parallel to consider. As Chris Hayes (2017) reminds us, in our fledgling nation the primary occupation was smuggling, and for much the same reason that Black men deal drugs today. It was smuggling that so incensed the British, whose taxes on the imports of colonial merchants had motivated the smuggling in the first place, that they started taking action against the colonists. Those "police" actions enraged the colonists, who banded together to engage in "illegal activities" and eventually threw off British rule. Some of our greatest heroes and signers of the Declaration of Independence were smugglers: John Hancock, for instance, remembered as an American hero, whose namesake tower now dominates the Boston skyline. Was he a criminal, as the British said, who should be locked up, or an American hero who stood by his community and provided money and jobs for those who shared his predicament? The residents of Lyford Street talk about the neighborhood drug dealers much the same way the colonists talked about John Hancock, valuing his protection and helping to protect him from British "police" action.

Toward a Sociological Approach to Justice

The chapters in this book expose the many ways in which the tacit racism hidden in our daily lives damages people, relationships, and society at large without conscious intent or awareness. They also offer empirical demonstrations of what it means to say that inequality impairs the ability to cooperate in the social practices of a diverse modern society whose meaning and effectiveness depend on mutual orientation toward, and full reciprocity in, shared expectations about those practices, and not on the authority of beliefs and values that ground sense-making in more homogenous societies. It is not possible in a diverse and highly specialized society to force everyone to believe the same thing. The argument that equality and justice are necessary conditions for the use of "constitutive practices" in a society with a specialized modern division of labor was first made in 1893 by Emile Durkheim, who maintained that progress and stability in diverse modern societies is damaged by inequality (Rawls 2019, 2020). Du Bois made the same point in 1890 in the context of his argument that the practice of submission to the good of the whole, which he called a Black American ideal, is a necessary counterbalance to the inequalities created by the individualism and narcissism of the White American strong man ideal (chapters 4 and 5).

The insight that inequality is destructive was also taken up in the 1940s by Harold Garfinkel, who argued that reciprocity and equality—what he called "Trust Conditions"—are necessary for constitutive practices to succeed, and that when they fail in a modern context that is not grounded in traditional loyalties and symbolism, then self and sense-making also fail (Turowetz and Rawls 2019). The point with regard to self was then elaborated by Goffman in the 1950s (Rawls 1996a, 1996b, 1987, 2017), and with regard to sense-making by Sacks in the 1960s (Rawls 1990). Because modern science, professions, and public life depend increasingly on a form of practice that Durkheim called "constitutive" (in which voluntary cooperation in the use of tacit constitutive practices is necessary to create meaningful social facts), modern culture can free itself from authority structures and transcend tradition. This is the turning point that makes the development of modern democracy and its sciences and occupations possible. Instead of depending on an authoritative foundation of fixed symbolic meanings and beliefs that people bring with them into interaction, meaning and self in modern social contexts come more and more to depend on the in situ coordination of interaction order resources within actual situations of interaction. But this can only work insofar as these situations and their practices are open equally and with full reciprocity to all competent parties who may want or need to participate.

It is the development of diverse societies—like the US—in which beliefs are not shared that makes a reliance on these new forms of situated practices necessary and the development of science and modern occupations possible. When this happens and meaning-making processes come to depend on a displayed orientation toward the turn-by-turn details of constitutive practices in interaction, it is important to note that the process requires sufficient equality to support reciprocity between participants. Durkheim called this "justice requirement" an "implicit condition" of contract in modern society; Garfinkel called it the "Trust Conditions," and Goffman referred to it in terms of "involvement obligations" and "working consensus."

Because a commitment to using the same practices, with the same expectations, in the same way, and doing so competently, is a condition for making sense in any social context based on constitutive interaction order practices, divisions and inequalities between people that prevent them from being able to fully commit to the required reciprocities of practice (or that prevent Others from recognizing their commitment and competence) make it impossible to make sense and self together. It is possible to learn the practices on the spot, but only in a context of inclusion and cooperation.

Our research on Race documents the fractured interactions and reciprocity failures that occur when these implicit conditions of justice—of social contract—are not met and opposing interaction orders develop. The social cost is not just to those who are discriminated against. We argue that such inequalities fracture society and *undermine the common good*. To the extent that social cohesion and understanding in a society depend on the ability to reciprocate in the coordination of shared practices and their expectations, inequalities like Race that are so serious that they produce survival responses that change those expectations and prevent reciprocity undermine the basic ability to achieve self and mutual understanding across lines of inequality. This, in turn, reinforces the original inequality, allowing a seventeenth-century Race distinction to hold contemporary social life captive to a distant pre-democratic past.

New empirically driven work in economics documents the negative effects of inequality on price and growth (Stiglitz 2012; Piketty 2014; Krugman 2012). We make the corresponding sociological argument that the social cohesion necessary to sustain any cooperative exchange that depends on constitutive practices—and most do—is undermined by inequality.

The problem of fractured reflection that we identify in chapter 2 illustrates Durkheim's (1893) argument that unfairness in the distribution of opportunities disrupts the very fabric of mutuality, cohesion, and mutual intelligibility in modernity (Rawls 2012, 2019, 2020). That argument is echoed by Goffman and Garfinkel in their emphasis on social contract and trust conditions. Some have objected that the actual unfairness that is so obvious in modern life proves that justice cannot be a constitutive necessity in interaction. But those who say this *have not been looking at interaction*. In interaction, justice—in the form of equality and reciprocity conditions and expectations that match—*is* a basic requirement, and when it fails, interaction fails. As we show in the case of fractured reflections, the fragile processes of interaction literally fail to produce mutually intelligible sense and self when there is not sufficient equality to meet trust conditions. In the interactions we examine, the unfairness built into definitions of the situation and the framings of identity they incorporate—durable structures with deep histories—make face-to-face self and sense-making impossible, just as Durkheim and Garfinkel said it would.

Tacit racism is a matter of life and death. But people who are not aware of the racism embedded in the interactional processes of their own daily lives *cannot change* what they are not aware of, and people who believe that their identification with Whiteness makes them superior to Others *will not* change it. The purpose of this book is to make this hidden racism visible, exposing the lies and the ways those lies and their consequences have been coded into our daily lives. The big problem is not racists—although overt racial prejudice is certainly a problem—the big problem is the deeply embedded tacit racism that we don't see and therefore don't believe we are acting on. Anyone living in a society whose social practices embed assumptions about Race will do and say racist things constantly without knowing or intending it. The authors include themselves. This means not only that racism is constantly being enacted unintentionally, but that this interactional process keeps prejudices about Race alive for those who *do* intend and *want* to exploit them, explaining how racism can pop up again, as it periodically does, with such virulence after seeming to disappear. It was never gone. We are all doing racist things—tacitly creating it—all the time while congratulating ourselves that we are not.

This is what we need to talk about.

Acknowledgments

Most scholars hope to have students who become valued colleagues and collaborators. Waverly Duck is such a student. Not only has our collaboration helped to solidify my own work, but his profound insights have developed the work in new directions distinctly his own that add immeasurably to the value of the overall project. It has been a pleasure to watch Waverly become a scholar of stature and gravitas. This book is the culmination of over two decades of our collaborative work to develop an interactional approach to Race and justice.

My quest to discover *interaction orders of Race* began in 1986 while interviewing for a position at the University of Chicago. In describing my career objectives, I explained that I had started college as an African and Black studies major in 1971 because I was committed to racial justice, and then had turned to social theory on realizing that existing academic theories did not afford a way of addressing that issue. Not only were existing theories ethnocentric in ways that excluded important issues involving Race; they embedded assumptions about psychology and social order that made it impossible to see either the social order or the need for equality in modernity. Social contract aspects of the positions of Harold Garfinkel and Erving Goffman suggested to me a way of regrounding social theory on empirical documentation of underlying practices and their prerequisites in ways that would accommodate Race. My job talk at Chicago outlined the argument about interaction orders that was published the next year. But there was no mention of Race in my talk.

William Julius Wilson and Gerald Suttles took me aside after the talk and issued a challenge. If I was serious in arguing that all social facts are produced in and through social interaction, and also serious that my reason for becoming an academic was to study racial injustice, then I needed to start explaining how racial inequality was being produced in social interaction. If I was right, they said, it must be possible. I spent the next six years trying to figure out how to locate racism in the interaction orders that organize social interaction, finally discovering the "nosey" argument in 1992. The difficulties involved in meeting this challenge were enormous, and I have always felt grateful to Wilson and Suttles for setting me to the task in such a way that I felt I could not give up. The argument has been over thirty years in the making. I hope Bill is not too displeased by the result.

The journey had begun fifteen years earlier when, having been raised to believe in justice and equality, I discovered that when I actually tried to treat everyone as equals, White people were not amused. In fact, they were often exceedingly cruel. It was my realization that I didn't have the facts needed to fight back against this racism that sent me to college to focus on African and Black studies in 1971. Fortunately, the Lowell family had endowed Harvard University with support for an extension program that is open to members of the community and often taught by Harvard faculty. Taking advantage of this opportunity, I was able to take courses with the brilliant Ephraim Isaac (now at Princeton), who taught African religions and philosophy, and with Martin Kilson, Harvard's first African American professor of government, who taught the history of Black politics in the US. I also connected with Hollis Lynch, then director of the Institute of African Studies at Columbia University, giving me access to Lynch and his students.

Two years later Frances Waksler introduced me to sociology and the work of Goffman and Garfinkel, which suggested how questions of Race and justice could be approached by an interactionist sociology, leading me to Boston University in the fall of 1974 to study with George Psathas, Jeff Coulter, and then in 1975 with Harold Garfinkel (and Emanuel Schegloff). Harvey Sacks and Anita Pomerantz also taught at BU. Pursuing degrees in both philosophy and sociology, I also studied with Alasdair MacIntyre, Tom McCarthy, Bernard Elevitch, Erazim Kohák, John Findley, Kurt Wolff, Gila Hayim, and Dieter Henrich. Yearly conferences in ethnomethodology brought students and colleagues from around the world to BU (including Wes Sharrock, John Heritage, Rod Watson, Christian Heath, Doug Maynard, Alene Terasaki, Mike Lynch, John O'Neil, and Lindsey Churchill), greatly enriching my experience there and eventually leading to a collaborative relationship with Garfinkel.

The connections between a sociological/philosophical approach to how people organize meaning in interaction dovetailed nicely with my training in African and Black studies—a fruitful combination that eventually

ACKNOWLEDGMENTS

enabled the sociological approach to questions of Race and justice presented in this book.

Many colleagues and students have been supportive over the years at Wayne State University and later at Bentley University, including a number of key scholars who took action to support my work at critical points, including Randall Collins, Norbert Wiley, and Bill Wilson. Those who studied Race and social theory with me and/or collaborated in the research, deserve particular thanks, including Waverly Duck, Gary David, Lynetta Mosby, Derek Coates, Ramona Coates, Bonnie Wright, Perry Hall, Cathy Pettinari, and Kelley Taylor. I also owe a large debt to my fellow board members on the Southern Oakland County NAACP, especially Frank and Ola Taylor, who tolerated my naïveté and taught me a great deal.

As the project expanded globally after 2000, many new friends and colleagues gave valuable support; these include Lorenza Mondada, Albert Ogien, Bruno Karsenti, Sandra Laugier, Louis Quéré, Carole Gayet-Viaud, Giolo Fele, Cyril Lemieux, Alain Caillé, Philippe Chanial, Francesco Callegaro, Frederic Vandenberghe, Michel de Fornel, Gary David, Jason Turowetz, Mike Lynch, and Charles Lemert, many of whom translated, reviewed, published, and in other ways helped to bring my work into print. I want to give a particular call-out to Charles Lemert, who is one of the few to comprehend the overall project, and to Dean Birkenkamp, who worked with Charles to publish many of the volumes. John O'Neil, Bryan Turner, and Simon Susen at the *Journal of Classical Sociology* have also been very supportive.

I owe a huge debt to Tristan Thielmann and Erhard Schüttpelz, who started a center in Siegen, Germany (Media of Cooperation), funded by the German government to support work on the Garfinkel Archive. The support brings interested scholars to the center, including Clemens Eisenmann, Martin Zillinger, Christian Meyer, Elliott Hoey, and Jason Turowetz. Jason (who did his PhD with Doug Maynard) has become a valued collaborator working tirelessly with me on the archive materials, editing Garfinkel's work, and joining in the efforts of Waverly and myself to bring the theoretical issues to bear on questions of Race and justice. Jason's work on Garfinkel's early PhD proposals and their connection to Race is of particular importance. Special thanks are also due to Gary David, a former PhD student from Wayne State, not only for his continued collaboration with me on research on Race and inequality, but for doing the heavy lifting as department chair for the past decade, which has eased the stresses of what has become for me a very complicated academic career.

Peter K. Manning has for many years been an invaluable soundboard, one of the handful of scholars able to follow the range of issues I have been trying to weave together—and more often than not, he was actually present when important things happened that we need to know about! Over and over again, Jason and I find that Peter can answer questions we had given up on. ("I wonder whether Harvey Sacks actually gave that paper in 1967 with Garfinkel?" Manning: "Yes, I saw them give the paper and Sacks was there.") Jason calls him "the oracle."

And lastly, thanks are due to my father for showing me what it means to pursue Justice.

Anne Rawls

This book expounds a sociological theory of justice situated in the work of Emile Durkheim, W. E. B. Du Bois, Erving Goffman, Harold Garfinkel, and Anne Warfield Rawls. George Davis Herron once wrote, "It is idle to talk of good will until there is first justice." *Tacit Racism* is about equity and justice in everyday interactions. An ethnographic, ethnomethodological, and conversational analytic study of Race in the everyday world, it is also steeped in the Black American intellectual traditions of the visual and performing arts, music, poetry, plays, and fact-based fiction.

My journey in the study of Race and interaction began in 1996 when, as a freshman at Connecticut College, I took a senior seminar called Race and Ethic Relations, taught by Robert Gay. Although I was not yet a senior, Robert allowed me into the course after I repeatedly showed up during his office hours and pleaded with him to make an exception for me. I desperately wanted to take the course not only because I was interested in the content, but also because several of the authors we'd be reading would be guest speakers over the semester. It was in that course that I met such scholars as Tricia Rose, Howard Winant, Pagent Henry, and Stephen Steinberg. I challenged Robert on everything, and he made time to engage my curiosity. In the process, I became a sociologist, and I will be forever grateful to him.

Financial circumstances beyond my control led me from Connecticut College to Wayne State University. When I arrived, I asked the graduate student teaching assistants for the first courses I took which faculty members would best prepare me for the rigors of graduate school. The consensus was Anne Rawls, and she did not disappoint. It is difficult to describe a scholar as multitalented as Anne: she is a brilliant theorist, but she is also a committed activist who has been fighting for social justice her entire life. Her guidance and her body of work have helped me to navigate a world fraught with anti-blackness, elitism, and a peculiar underestimation of people of color, and to develop into the scholar I am today. She prepared me for an academic world that is often hostile to my very existence.

No intellectual endeavor is possible without the support of friends, family, colleagues, and academic institutions. I would like to acknowledge Scott Brooks, Jean Beaman, Karida Brown, Raymond Gunn, Juho Härkönen, Nikki Jones, Grey Osterud, and the late Reverend Bernice Warren for their intellectual support and friendship. I am in awe of your intellect, effortless kindness, and friendship.

Whenever I tire from the emotional labor of doing the "work," or the sense of isolation that comes with inhabiting spaces that feel lonely, I think of Joyce Ladner, Elijah Anderson, Robin D. G. Kelley, Larry Davis, Patricia Hill Collins, the late Anthony Lemelle, Joe Feagin, Jennifer Hamer, Marcus Hunter, Zandria Robinson, Gary Alan Fine, Doug Maynard, Patricia Fernández-Kelly, Charles Lemert, John Wallace, the late Werner Troesken, and the late John Hope Franklin. All of these scholars were generous enough to give me the time of day, first as a graduate student and later as an assistant professor, and their example helped me to cultivate a way of being and flourishing in the academy and the world. Elijah Anderson in particular gave me a home at the University of Pennsylvania and then later at Yale. I hope this book lives up to the grand lessons I've learned from all of you.

Although I never met Walter Allen, his experience of exclusion in particular prepared me for an academic life in ways that I never thought imaginable. I would also like to acknowledge those who shared their love, friendship, and support over the last several years. Joyce Bell is a friend and former colleague whose insights and scholarship continually remind me that we all have a role to play not only in the academy, but in our families and the wider community. I would literally be miserable without the camaraderie, intellectual support, and brotherhood provided by Raymond Gunn, Noah Lemert, Jerry Flores, Victor Rios, Ty Rawls, John Eason, Reuben Miller, Jason Turowetz, and Michael Walker, all of whom are kind, humble, and unconditionally loving.

I am grateful to have received support from Joe Trotter, director and founder of Carnegie Mellon's Center for Africanamerican Urban Studies and the Economy (CAUSE), who provided financial and academic support to finish this manuscript. Joe is a revelation whose perseverance and encouragement made this book possible.

I owe special thanks to the late Doug Mitchell, who believed in this project from the beginning. His support was unwavering and his friendship invaluable. Equally, Elizabeth Branch Dyson has been entirely supportive in seeing this project to fruition.

I dedicate this book to all the students at the University of Pittsburgh, Community College of Philadelphia, the Cheshire Twenty, and those at the Mission House in Haiti who constantly gave me the strength and inspiration to achieve what I believe is my calling: to teach and learn. A student once commented on a teaching evaluation that I was "militantly happy." I speculate that I am this way because I believe in them and their ability to create a future that is more equitable and just than the world they are inheriting.

Finally, I want to thank my mother, Georgia Duck. Five years ago she began to notice early signs of what would come to be diagnosed as Alzheimer's disease. She sat me down and explained to me not only the love and admiration she had for me, but for all of her eight children and over twenty-three grandchildren and great-grandchildren. Growing up, I often watched her struggle, especially during periods of poverty when we barely had enough to eat, but even under those circumstances, she was unfailingly kind and giving. I will never forget the time when I was five years old and my mom took in our elderly neighbor Mrs. Mae after she lost her husband. Gestures like this left an indelible mark on me, and let me know that people will always be more than things.

Waverly Duck

Notes

Epigraph

1. There is a similarity to the Bible passage Amos 5:24: "But let justice roll on like a river, righteousness like a never-failing stream!"

Introduction

1. Robert Mueller's investigation uncovered the extensive efforts by several Russian government-backed internet research agencies to effect the outcome of the 2016 American presidential election. Their efforts focused on fanning the flames of racial division in the US through the creation of false internet personas who would post false stories about issues associated with Race. They also directly sponsored both White supremacist/White nationalist events and Black activist events through such false online personas. In addition, they drove many false stories about Democratic candidates that were seen many millions of times on the internet. The agencies involved were indicted, but intelligence reports confirm that they are still very active on social media and that little is being done about it. Connections between these efforts and the special interests of oil and gas corporations in particular have also been documented (Wylie 2019; Maddow 2019).

2. Harvard University has an online implicit bias test that anyone can take. Called Project Implicit, it can be found at https://implicit.harvard.edu/implicit/. The project website invites people to take an implicit bias test. It also warns that if they do not want to discover they have implicit bias, they should stop and not take the test. Studies (Greenwald and Krieger 2006) find that only 18% of people taking these tests have so little implicit bias as to qualify as neutral.

3. The Black/White binary remains the primary classification scheme for Race in America. Other ethnic, cultural, religious, and social class categories have been secondary to Race in this country since the invention of Whiteness after 1670 in

Virginia (Allen 1994). For that reason, we use the binary categories White/Black almost exclusively in discussing Race and racism in America and position other categories (Asian/Asian American, Latinx/Hispanic, and West Indian/African) against that binary. The exceptions are an "Anglo" vs. Spanish bias and an anti-Indigenous bias, also dating from the 1600s, which we reference in the conclusion in discussing current attitudes toward Mexican and Indigenous Mayan immigrants, the willingness to destroy Spanish-speaking families and children, and the shameful genocidal treatment of Puerto Rican citizens of the United States. While the idea of Whiteness has been exported to other countries, in most cases the application of the categories—that is, who is White or Black and how it matters—is very different in other countries. Most countries have more than two categories, with Brazil having as many as twenty-three, because as a social convention, ideas about Race develop in ways that match the significance of various Race distinctions to the history of a country.

4. Hostilities between Spain and England had been ongoing since at least 1568 as the English tried to break the monopoly of Spain on the Atlantic trade. What is referred to as the Anglo-Spanish War, an undeclared war lasting from 1585 to 1604, was initiated by Spain in an effort to defeat Protestant rule in England under Queen Elizabeth and restore the Catholic faith. Because the Spanish crown ruled over parts of the Netherlands, Spain was positioned as a direct threat to the English coast. Spain launched its most famous attack on England in 1588. As the Spanish Armada—a seven-mile long line of 130 ships—advanced, English heavy guns drove them back to Calais. The ensuing battle was decisive with Spain losing half its ships. In three other large battles in 1589, 1596, and 1597, they failed to conquer England. In 1602 the Dutch East India Company was founded with English support to assist in the Dutch war of independence from Spain and protect Dutch trade in the Indian Ocean. This was recent history when the Virginia colony was founded. But it is rather shocking that so much animosity toward Spain persists to this day.

5. During Reconstruction in the 1870s, southern White men began to recognize that if they banded together with freed slaves they could achieve a democratic populism in the South. The fully integrated Populist Party gained momentum and began winning elections. The planter class was forced to make a deal with the KKK to terrorize members of the party in order to stay in power (Woodward 1955). Something similar has been reported among White farmers today. Jim Pat Wilson (2019) reports that southern farmers are being pressured by bankers and landowners into supporting the policies that are destroying their farms: "Caught in the Republican Party's political crosshairs, farmers are stuck in an environment that has cultivated fear for anyone who dares to speak against the mighty GOP. . . . Why aren't we hearing more concern? Because the current administration has made it impossible for farmers to criticize without retaliation from Republican landowners. A farmer who wrote an opinion piece early last year in response to farmers' incomes dropping more than 50% since 2013 that highlighted the increase

in farmer suicides due to status-quo policies, lost 300 acres of sharecropped land because word got out that he was a Democrat."

6. While Cornel West ([1982] 2002: 70) initially categorized Du Bois as a proponent of what he called "exceptionalism"—the idea that African Americans and their culture are inherently superior—and Du Bois may or may not have believed something like that, our interest is in Du Bois's sociological argument. That argument does not rest on any inherent qualities of Black Americans or their culture, but rather outlines a dynamic sociological process of response and self-reflection unique to the American experience of racial oppression that is transformative and from which current African American culture is generated through collective acts of positive self-affirmation and principled adoption of equality—which have become institutionalized in the American Black interaction order. It is this dynamic and transformative character of the Black American experience that makes it something White Americans can look to for strategies with which to transform their own understandings of Race and justice.

7. The "Take a Knee" protest that was initiated by Colin Kaepernick on August 14, 2016, initially had little impact. He was protesting the fact that so many unarmed young Black men are being shot by the police without consequence. As the American national anthem played during a preseason game that August, he refused to stand for the first time. No questions were asked, no objections were raised. In fact, playing the anthem itself is a post-WWII innovation that became even more militaristic after 9/11, and not all Americans approved of the increasing militarism. But when Trump criticized Kaepernick, his protest suddenly became a racially divisive issue, and Kaepernick, who had quarterbacked his team to a Super Bowl win, found himself without a job. A similar thing had happened on October 16, 1968, when the Black American Olympic sprinters Tommie Smith and John Carlos, who won the gold and bronze medals in the 200-meter dash, had their medals taken away for silently making the Black Power sign (a raised closed fist) during the playing of the national anthem. Smith and Carlos had also taken off their shoes to symbolize poverty and wore scarves and beads to represent the lynching of Black men. (Peter Norman, the White Australian sprinter who won the silver medal, also wore symbols of protest. His medal was not taken away, but he was treated as an outcast by his country.) Their point was to call attention to the hypocrisy of pretending to be a democratic country when Black Americans are still being treated as if they are not citizens.

8. Karl Marx wrote an article in October 1861 during the Civil War explaining that the Southern attempt to expand the slave system was not just about expanding the system of Black slavery, but rather legitimating unfree labor for both Black and White workers. Getting White workers to support the spread of that system threatened to reduce all White workers to slavery as well. He used the term "helotry" in this regard. "The slave system," Marx (1861) wrote, "would infect the whole Union. In the Northern states, where Negro slavery is in practice unworkable, the

white working class would gradually be forced down to the level of helotry. This would fully accord with the loudly proclaimed principle that only certain races are capable of freedom, and as the actual labour is the lot of the Negro in the South, so in the North it is the lot of the German and the Irishman, or their direct descendants." It could be argued that the end of Reconstruction marked the failure of the North to win the war against the Southern labor system, and brought into being the expanded system of labor oppression that Marx was warning about.

9. In the spring of 2019, Trump began using the term "patriot" with reference to the problems that his trade war with China was inflicting on American farmers, in an effort to keep those farmers aligned with him. Senator Tom Cotton (R-AR) even suggested that farmers were literally like troops in battle suffering casualties for the country. As the trade war worsened and a record number of farms began going bankrupt in May 2019, farmers began speaking out. NowThis News tweeted a short video on May 20, 2019, of farmers who had voted for Trump responding that they would not vote for him again. One interview with a farmer from Ohio, Christopher Gibbs, taken from a CNN clip, speaks directly to the way farmers are being manipulated into supporting policies that are not in their best interest. The clip shows him responding directly to being called a patriot. Gibbs said to the interviewer: "A minute ago you, the president, you played a clip that he said that we were patriots. Well, I'll tell you what. To me, that's just a design to make me continue to be quiet and I am not gonna be quiet."

10. The way Race is handled in the US has had a fragmenting effect on the Latinx/Hispanic community. Beginning with Bonilla-Silva (2003), who worried that those in the community who could pass for White would abandon the rest in the US, the conversation has progressed to explicitly embracing the idea of Afro-Latinx—and the saying that there is no Latinx without Black is becoming popular. Amara La Negra is a popular hip-hop artist who has been pushing this message. What seems to be happening parallels the "Black Is Beautiful" movement among Black Americans in the 1960s and 1970s.

11. Native Americans are the original inhabitants of the US. But even more than other groups, they have been treated as strangers—often as less than human. Think about how collections of Indian bones have been kept in various museums for both display and research purposes, as if they were prehistoric "cave men." When it became a state, Oklahoma (which had formerly been Indian Territory) voted for a Jim Crow "two color" Black/White Race system that classified Indians as White. As a consequence, many Indians in Oklahoma disappeared into the White population. Other states, like New Mexico, did not classify Indians as White, with the consequence that Indians were still not able to vote until the Snyder Act of 1924 admitted Native Americans born in the United States to full US citizenship—last after Black Americans and women had both achieved full citizenship. Because of various state barriers to suffrage in some states, many Indians were still not able to vote until after WWII.

12. "Definition of the situation" is a foundational theoretical idea of social interactionism. Originating with W. I. Thomas, it was picked up by Garfinkel in the 1940s and then by Goffman in the 1950s. Additionally, Goffman did an extended analysis of the relevance of frames and framing to sense-making in *Frame Analysis* (1974).

13. There is an effect on women that is more complicated. Because Whiteness as a political cause seeks to reinstate an older form of society in which White men dominated and women did not vote, the rise of White power politics is inevitably accompanied by legislation, such as anti-abortion laws, that aims to restrict the autonomy and equality of women. It has also been suggested that in the panic to make sure that White people remain in the majority, preventing the abortion of White babies has become a priority.

14. Constitutive criteria are the necessary and defining criteria of an action, meaning, or object. The conception first appears in Kant in the context of both constitutive criteria and social contract. A similar conception appears in Durkheim. For Garfinkel, the three constitutive "Trust Conditions" are (1) that participants/players orient a set of basic constitutive rules that they expect to use regardless of personal preference; (2) the participants/players expect that the same set of constitutive expectations are binding on the other participants/players as are binding on themselves; (3) the participant expects that as they expect conditions 1 and 2 of the other participants/players, the others expect 1 and 2 of them (1963: 190).

15. Black West Indians do not orient toward a Black American interaction order. In the Islands and in Africa, the racial hierarchy is much more complex and flexible. Because there was never a binary category system for Race there, it was always possible to move "up" to the next highest category. In this context, it is normal for people in lower categories to aspire to become like the people in higher categories. The general aspiration is to avoid getting darker and to try hard to become lighter through marriage and behavior. There, the terms White and Black have very different meanings than they do in the US. There is no White/Black binary. It is reasonable, for instance, for a fairly dark-skinned Dominican to aspire to being seen as White. The category is not racial but social, and if they adopt a high-status manner and lifestyle and marry well (i.e., up), they may succeed in being known as White. Because of this, Black people from the West Indies and Africa often do not understand African Americans and are likely to blame them for their problems—not seeing that in the context of the inflexible American racial binary, there is no possibility of aspiring to be White. More importantly, they fail to appreciate the great social achievement that the creation of a democratic and transcendent sense of Blackness is. This problem is exacerbated by the fact that a high proportion of "Black" college students in the US are from the West Indies and Africa, and consequently do not share a sense of Blackness with Black American college students (Coates 2004; Rawls, Taylor, and Coates 2019).

16. Those who are identified by the Black/White binary as Black but who

identify as White—even if they are very dark or of African descent—are not orienting to the interaction order of the Black American community. Only those who have the experience of *doubleness* will have the protections and insight that it gives about the White power structure.

17. While this book was in press, Nicole Hannah-Jones spearheaded "The 1619 Project" at the *New York Times*, which has brought a great deal of public attention to the continuing impact of slavery on both racism in the US and on the sustained efforts of Black Americans to make the American claim a democratic reality. Although there is resistance to the idea, response to the series has started a discussion about essential curriculum changes in US classrooms and to the understanding of the history of Race in the US more generally.

18. When Australia became a prison colony in the early 1800s, it also relied on White labor. But that was two centuries after Jamestown, and there was no later transition to Black labor. The social control issues were never the same.

19. Native Americans on both continents have obviously been discriminated against more than any others. However, they are also a special case. First of all, they are not immigrants, and it would not be appropriate to consider their categorization alongside that of immigrants. The colonizers have periodically allowed some individual American Indians to become White if they totally abandon their ancestry. Some have done this. However, where Indian populations have had significant color, or "looked like" Indians, this has not worked. When Indians have chosen to maintain their culture, they are still actively discriminated against and resented, especially by conservative White Americans.

20. This did not change until a slave system developed in the 1700s in which slave status was determined by the status of the mother, and slavery had become an entirely Black system that meant all White mothers were free.

21. The tacit racial differences we document have little to do with class or gender, but vary instead by racial self-identification. What we mean is that Black and White Americans typically embrace the interaction order corresponding to their racial identification regardless of their social class.

22. In chapter 1, we identify two distinct interaction orders that we argue correspond with the particular racial Black/White binary that developed in colonial America and persists today. While it has become popular to deal with Race in terms of a variety of ethnic, cultural, racial, and religious identities, we argue that while these may all be associated with experiences of discrimination and inequality, they have not resulted in a distinct and incompatible set of interaction order expectations. The rigidity of the American Black/White racial binary has produced a unique phenomenon—and it is this on which we focus. The position of Asians relative to this this binary is particularly problematic. Not seen as White, they are also not seen as Black. There is a strong tendency for Americans to see Asians as foreigners that we attribute to the rigidity of the binary that has no room for them (see Chou and Feagin 2014).

Chapter One

Parts of this chapter appeared in Rawls 2000.

1. At this point we would like to thank William Julius Wilson for issuing a direct challenge to Anne Rawls in 1987 to formulate an interactional theory of Race that would build on her 1987 publication on interaction orders.

2. Waverly Duck, one of the coauthors, who was an undergraduate at the time, joined the team and began taking part in the research and discussions in 1996.

3. Conversational Analysis is an offshoot of Ethnomethodology pioneered by Harvey Sacks working with Harold Garfinkel, Gail Jefferson, and Emanuel Schegloff. The Jefferson Transcription System, or Jeffersonian, is widely used in Conversation Analysis, which was devised by Gail Jefferson in the 1960s. Explanations can be found online (e.g., universitytranscriptions.co.uk/Jefferson-transcription-system-a-guide-to-the-symbols/). Several universities have websites. See Jefferson (2004) and Hepburn and Bolden (2013).

4. "Preference" and "dispreferred" are technical terms in conversation analysis. The idea is that there are basic constitutive rules or expectations (see introduction, note 10) and preferred variations on how they are used. Variations against those preferences convey meaning about interaction. So, for instance, if someone asks you a question, the preferred response is an answer. Not answering, however, also conveys important information about how the question was heard. For instance, a woman asked the question "How old are you?" who does not answer is letting the questioner know something about the rudeness of the question. The idea is not that rules need to be "followed," but rather that they comprise a background or framework against which inferences about what actions mean can be reliably drawn. Obviously, it only works if both/all parties are orienting toward the same constitutive expectancies and preferences.

5. Signifying has other meanings in Black culture as well. See Labov (1972) and Hannerz (1969) for the classic discussion of communication games by this name.

Chapter Two

An earlier version of this chapter was published as "'Fractured Reflections' of High-Status Black Male Presentations of Self: Nonrecognition of Identity as a 'Tacit' Form of Institutional Racism," Sociological Focus 50 (1) (Rawls and Duck 2017). That paper received the 2018 Article of the Year Award from the North Central Sociological Association.

1. In cases where non-recognition is occasioned by gender or stigma the effects can be similar. But the problem would be definitions of the situation involving gender and stigma, and the recipient will belong to a different community of shared

narrative about the event, which will have adopted its own type of response. See Goffman (1963) for an extended discussion with reference to stigma.

2. This likely also happens with gender. The men we talked with made the analogy to gender themselves. But while one of the authors is female and has experienced gender bias, the descriptions these men give of how they understand the problem are not familiar to me, and even though I might agree that I sometimes give a null-response, I would not have described either the response or the problem in quite the same way. One reviewer suggested that the difference might have something to do with color-blindness. It might. As a woman, I am free to dismiss the responses of others that I believe are sexist. It can also be openly said. The men we talked with were not dismissing the non-responses to their self-presentations as racist. They were even reluctant to mention Race. So, yes, the color-blind taboo character of Race was likely hampering their efforts to sustain self in the face of non-recognition. They could not name the problem. I can. Earlier generations of Black men likely could as well—but they would probably not have been in high-status positions in the first place.

3. All names have been changed to protect the identities of informants.

4. Conversation analysis documents a set of conversational resources that are used across many situations and cultures. For a good summary discussion, see Suchman (2006), chap. 5. See Rawls (2015) for an application to designing digital information systems.

5. Such fractured reflections constitute a natural occurrence of the violation of trust conditions—and the ensuing meaninglessness—that Garfinkel (1963) tried to produce experimentally for his trust papers beginning in 1947. No trust—no shared meaning—means no resources for resolving problems. We have argued that as a Jewish American in the 1940s, Garfinkel was experiencing something similar (Turowetz and Rawls 2019; Duck and Rawls 2019).

6. It was Victor Rios who first suggested to us that null-responses might be playing a role in interactions between Black men and the police. Having viewed some of that data, it seems that the police often begin by being nonresponsive to Black men: ignoring whatever they say. But then, yes, null-response to non-recognition would describe much of what comes next.

Chapter Three

1. It has been reported to Anne that Jehovah's Witnesses, who also try to maintain a strong boundary around the group and do so through a focus on the idea that the group is stigmatized, share a similar notion of honesty.

2. For White Americans, referencing facts or causal accounts is how accounts are given that excuse behavior. If referencing facts is not recognizable as making excuses for Black Americans, then it must be done another way. We hazard a guess that while White Americans prefer to avoid having to make an explicit excuse/

apology—and avoid having to do so by naming facts and causes in accounts and justifications—Black Americans will be doing the opposite: preferring to express an explicit excuse/apology.

3. In the narratives we have collected, there are many instances in which Black employees complained about being given instructions that were too vague to follow. They interpret this as intentional and don't trust people who do this. There are number of possibilities here. White employees may be trying to give "hints" that they are doing something wrong—observing the White taboo against being too obviously critical and confusing Black Americans, who would simply never hint about a thing like that: they would be direct. But it may also be that the problems White people are having with their work are getting caught up in stereotypes, making it impossible for White people to be direct in their criticisms without naming those stereotypes—so this "vagueness" could be another Race problem.

4. It has been argued that women are more often given roles that require not only a complete suppression of the personal self, but which also abuse their emotions. For instance, Arlie Hochschild (1983) argued in *The Managed Heart* that airline stewardesses are expected to respond personally even when customers are extremely rude to them. She argues that this sort of abuse of the person, making emotions part of role performance, is something that is happening increasingly with the development of the service economy. However, there are examples of more traditional roles, such as the English butler, where the control of emotions was always considered to be an essential part of the performance of the role. To be a "true" English butler required the complete suppression of reactions. The idea that the truth requires the expression of internal feelings from moment to moment could not be in greater conflict with the ideal performance of this role, wherein internal feelings do not exist. This idea was very persuasively explored in Kazuo Ishiguro's novel *The Remains of the Day*. It is interesting that the author is a Japanese writer who had studied at Oxford. Presumably he had found the desire of the categorical self to become one with its role performance intriguing.

Chapter Four

1. In poor areas, the distinction is often made between "aboveground" and "under-the-table" employment. It is not just a simple distinction between legal and illegal employment, however. In poor neighborhoods, most under-the-table jobs are legal, but the way employers are paying workers is not legal. Because the people are poor, employers who are willing to break the law can find employees they can hire without giving them any benefits. These workers will not be able to pay taxes legally or qualify for social security on the basis of such jobs.

2. We suspect that many Black men still classify AIDS as incurable, even though it can now be managed effectively, and consequently avoid diagnosis and treatment.

Chapter Five

1. This may be hard for some people to get their heads around, because in the context of the "Strong Man" ideal, being submissive is considered "feminine," a popular way that men taunt each other when they show weakness. But considering submission as negative because it is associated with women reproduces gender stereotypes that are sexist while preventing the expression of a full range of natural emotions. This, in turn, leads to an unhealthy state of repression and lack of fulfillment. Women are not weaker than men, weak men are not like women, and emotion is not bad; however, these ideas are popular ways of thinking that most Americans subscribe to.

2. Interestingly, the media have started referring to Trump as a "Strong Man" (see, for instance, Ecarma 2018) and to the religious Right that supports him as "Strong Man Religion." According to Tony Schwartz, the ghostwriter of Trump's book *The Art of the Deal*, "People are not people to him, they are instruments of his ego. And when they serve his ego, they survive, and when they don't, they pass into the night."

3. The incident at the Waffle House in April 2018 and another with a former NFL player in Georgia that also took place in April 2018, both of which went viral on YouTube, illustrate how the police do not respond to questions from the Black citizens they are manhandling and arresting, nor do they explain why they are arresting them.

4. In a recent video of a Black man detained and questioned outside of a restaurant in Royal Oak, Michigan, this is made crystal-clear by the police themselves. There had been a citizen call reporting to the police that a Black man had looked "suspiciously" at a White woman while walking past her car in a parking lot. When the police arrived, the Black man was in a restaurant ordering food. Witnesses at the scene, including the restaurant manager, explained on video that nothing had happened. The driver who had called the police was parked across the street and witnesses kept pointing to her. But the police did not question her. The police asked the Black man to leave the restaurant, and the White manager and another White customer (who made the video) came out with them. Looking at someone is not a crime. Nevertheless, more police kept arriving on the scene and asking the Black man questions (the video is fourteen minutes long). The Black man remains civil during this long interrogation. The restaurant manager and the woman shooting the video keep asking the officers why they are questioning this man who has not done anything wrong, asking why they don't question the driver who made the call. The officer in charge explains that the fact of the citizen call in and of itself requires them to question the restaurant patron in order to do their job (which is not actually true). That the questioning is excessive does not seem to occur to them: fourteen minutes is a long time (https://www.rawstory.com/2019/08/watch-michigan-police-stop-black-man-for-looking-suspiciously-at-white-woman/).

5. According to a *Huffington Post* survey (Edwards-Levy 2018), 48% of White Americans said the incident at Starbucks was an isolated incident, a third said that

it was emblematic of a broader pattern of how society as a whole treats Black people, and 6% said that it was a reflection of a broader pattern in the way Starbucks treats Black people. A 57% majority of Black Americans, by contrast, saw the controversy as rooted in broader societal problems, with 19% considering it primarily an indictment of Starbucks, and just a tenth believing it was an isolated incident.

6. Talcott Parsons (Parsons and Bales 1955) pointed out a similar contradiction about American ideals of manhood and equality in his work on the American family. Since he wrote about it in the 1950s, the problem for many traditionally oriented White Americans has been getting worse.

7. As we noted in chapter 4, this has led to frequent misidentification of Black men as feminine. They are not feminine. What they are is more egalitarian than White men.

8. A note on why wearing body cameras didn't change police behavior in this instance: In the video the police seem confident in their assessment of the citizen. It seems not to occur to them that he may be legitimate. This, of course, is in itself racist. But they are not aware of that. They act as if it is appropriate to treat him this way—even though they have verified his legal identity. We suspect that body camera video will be important not for changing police behavior—they have no reason to change behavior that they believe is not problematic—but to document how racism has become both overtly and tacitly embedded in police practice.

9. There was an earlier incident involving Officer Cole and two Black men that went viral on video in August 2014 for which he had been suspended (see Tribune Media Wire 2016).

10. That he has been in prison adds to their suspicions. But because of mass incarceration, on any given day, one in ten Black men in their thirties are in prison or jail (https://www.sentencingproject.org/issues/racial-disparity/) and there is a 52% chance that a low-income Black man has been behind bars (https://www.motherjones.com/crime-justice/2018/02/the-race-gap-in-u-s-prisons-is-glaring-and-poverty-is-making-it-worse/). So, this Black citizen's prison experience is typical.

11. The typical White viewer of the video may use tacit racism in the same way that the police do, drawing the same conclusions about the citizen's identity and motives as the police. The same tacit racism and enforcement of White interaction order expectations is at work in the society at large. The difference is that the police have the ability to enforce tacit racism with direct legal sanctions. The tacit racism of the average White citizen does sometimes factor into police work—for instance, via citizen calls to the police and jury decisions—but they do not have the authority to determine the outcome of police incidents like this one.

Chapter Seven

1. Very poor White Americans are an exception here. The frenzy to incarcerate Black Americans that was fueled by the War on Drugs has begun to collect a

substantial number of poor White Americans as well. The US now has the distinction of having one-quarter of the world's imprisoned population. Not a positive distinction for a country claiming to be democratic.

2. This charge was adjudicated by the International Criminal Court in The Hague and was most recently lodged against the State of Israel for its deliberate and avoidable bombardment of civilians during the war in Gaza.

3. Unlike poor White voters who often seem not to be able to distinguish their own interests from those of the rich White people they admire and seek to emulate, Justin and other poor Black Americans are quite clear about what is going on. Private prisons in the US only make a profit if there are prisoners. Increasing arrest rates are seen in relation to the demand for more of what Justin calls "consumers."

Conclusion

1. Although the French claimed land on the North American continent before either the English or the Spanish, reaching Montreal in 1535, their colonies in what became the United States were founded much later. After the French explorer René-Robert Cavelier de La Salle named the region Louisiana in 1682, the first permanent settlement, Fort Maurepas, was established in 1699 by Pierre Le Moyne d'Iberville, near Biloxi, Mississippi. The colony failed because the monarchy tried to run it as a monopoly without sufficient investment of manpower and money. As a consequence, there was no incentive to maintain the colony for the profit of the colonists, and the colony contributed little to the king's coffers. In 1762 the French first ceded the western part of the territory to Spain, which tried unsuccessfully to run it the same way, and then got it back from Spain in 1803 and ceded the whole territory to the United States later that year.

Bibliography

Alexander, Michelle. 2011. *The New Jim Crow: Mass Incarceration in the Age of Colorblindness*. New York: New Press.
Allen, Theodore. 1994. *The Invention of the White Race: Racial Oppression and Social Control*. Vol. 1. New York: Norton.
Allen, Theodore. 1997. *The Invention of the White Race: The Origin of Racial Oppression in Anglo-America*. Vol. 2. New York: Norton.
Anderson, Elijah. 1990. *Streetwise: Race, Class, and Change in an Urban Community*. Chicago: University of Chicago.
Anderson, Elijah. 1994. "The Code of the Streets." *Atlantic Monthly* 273 (5): 81–94.
Anderson, Elijah. 1996. "Introduction to the 1996 Edition of *The Philadelphia Negro*." In *The Philadelphia Negro: A Social Study*. Philadelphia: University of Pennsylvania Press.
Anderson, Elijah. 1998. "The Police and the Black Male." In *Constructions of Deviance: Social Power, Context, and Interaction*, edited by Patricia A. Adler and Peter Adler, 122–33. Belmont, CA: Wadsworth.
Anderson, Elijah. 2009. "Urban Ethnography: Its Traditions and Its Future." *Ethnography* 10 (1): 371–74.
Anderson, Elijah. 2011. *The Cosmopolitan Canopy: Race and Civility in Everyday Life*. New York: Norton.
Arendt, Hannah. 1958. *The Human Condition*. Chicago: University of Chicago Press.
Bailyn, Bernard. 1979. *The New England Merchants in the Seventeenth Century*. Cambridge, MA: Harvard University Press.
Bagentsos, S. 2007. "Implicit Bias, 'Science,' and Anti-Discrimination Law." *Harvard Law and Policy Review* 1: 477.
Baldwin, James. 1984. "On Being 'White' . . . and Other Lies." *Essence* 14 (12): 90–92.
Baraka, Amiri, and Philip Durham. 1965. *The Black Cowboy*. Lincoln: University of Nebraska Press.
Barber, William, III. 2016. *The Third Reconstruction: How a Moral Movement is Overcoming the Politics of Division and Fear*. Boston: Beacon Press.

Bejan, V., M. Hickman, W. S. Parkin, and V. F. Pozo. 2018. "Primed for Death: Law Enforcement–Citizen Homicides, Social Media, and Retaliatory Violence." *PloS One* 13 (1): e0190571.

Bell, Derek. 1973. *Race, Racism and American Law*. Boston: Little, Brown & Co.

Bell, Derrick. 1980. "*Brown v Board of Education* and the Interest-Convergence Dilemma." *Harvard Law Review* 93: 518–23.

Bell, Joyce M., and Douglas Hartmann. 2007. "Diversity in Everyday Discourse: The Cultural Ambiguities and Consequences of 'Happy Talk.'" *American Sociological Review* 72 (6): 895–914.

Bem, S. L. 1976. "Beyond Androgyny: Some Presumptuous Prescriptions for a Liberated Sexual Identity." In *Psychology of Women: Future Directions of Research*, edited by J. A. Sherman and F. L. Denmark. New York: Psychological Dimensions.

Bem, S. L. 1985. "Androgyny and Gender Schema Theory: A Conceptual and Empirical Integration." *Nebraska Symposium on Motivation: Psychology and Gender*. Lincoln: University of Nebraska Press.

Bennett, M. 2010. "Unraveling the Gordian Knot of Implicit Bias in Jury Selection: The Problems of Judge-Dominated Voir Dire, the Failed Promise of *Batson*, and Proposed Solutions." *Harvard Law and Policy Review* 4: 1207–30.

Bittner, E. 1967. "The Police on Skid-Row: A Study of Peace Keeping." *American Sociological Review* 32 (5): 699–715.

Bittner, E. 1970. *The Functions of the Police in Modern Society*. Chevy Chase, MD: National Institute of Mental Health, Center for Studies of Crime and Delinquency.

Blow, Charles M. 2018. "The Lowest White Man." *New York Times*, January 11. https://www.nytimes.com/2018/01/11/opinion/trump-immigration-white-supremacy.html.

Bolden, Galina, and Jeffrey Robinson. 2011. "Soliciting Accounts with Why-Interrogatives in Conversation." *Journal of Communication* 61 (1): 94–119.

Bonilla-Silva, Eduardo. 2003. *Racism without Racists: Color-Blind Racism and the Persistence of Racial Inequality in the United States*. Lanham, MD: Rowman and Littlefield.

Brehm, J. O., and S. Gates. 1999. *Working, Shirking, and Sabotage: Bureaucratic Response to a Democratic Public*. Ann Arbor: University of Michigan Press.

Brodkin, Karen. 1998. *How Jews Became White Folks and What That Says about Race in America*. New Brunswick, NJ: Rutgers University Press.

Bruce, Toni. 2004. "Marking the Boundaries of the 'Normal' in Televised Sports: The Play-by-Play of Race." *Media, Culture & Society* 26 (6): 861–79.

Burton, Art. 2006. *Black Gun, Silver Star: The Life and Legend of Frontier Marshal Bass Reeves*. Lincoln: University of Nebraska Press.

Cheatham, Cessaly T., Debra J. Barksdale, and Shielda G. Rodgers. 2008. "Barriers to Health Care and Health-Seeking Behaviors Faced by Black Men." *Journal of the American Association of Nurse Practitioners* 20 (11): 555–62.

Chevigny, Paul. 1969. *Police Power: Police Abuses in New York City*. New York: Vintage Books.
Chou, Rosalind S., and Joe R. Feagin. 2014. *Myth of the Model Minority: Asian Americans Facing Racism*. Boulder, CO: Paradigm.
Clift, Rebecca. 2001. "Meaning in Interaction: The Case of Actually." *Language* 77 (2): 245–91.
Coates, R. I. R. 2004. "Hey, Purritty Gurrl! Black Stereotyping: Social Interactions among African-American and West Indian College Students in Metropolitan New York." PhD diss., Wayne State University.
Collins, Patricia Hill. 2004. *Black Sexual Politics: African Americans, Gender, and the New Racism*. New York: Routledge.
Connell, R. W. 1995. *Masculinities*. Berkeley: University of California Press.
Connell, R. W. 1998. "Masculinities and Globalization." *Men and Masculinities* 1 (1): 3–23.
Connell, R. W. 2002. *Gender and Power*. Cambridge: Polity.
Connell, R. W. 2005 *Masculinities*. 2nd ed. Berkeley: University of California Press.
Cooley, Charles Horton. 1902. *Human Nature and the Social Order*. New York: Scribner's.
Cramer, Katherine J. 2016. *The Politics of Resentment: Rural Consciousness in Wisconsin and the Rise of Scott Walker*. Chicago: University of Chicago Press.
Delgado, Richard, and Jean Stefancic. 2001. *Critical Race Theory: An Introduction*. New York: New York University Press.
Desmond, Matthew. 2016. *Evicted: Poverty and Profit in the American City*. New York: Broadway Books.
DiAngelo, Robin. 2018. *White Fragility: Why It's So Hard for White People to Talk about Racism*. Boston: Beacon Press.
Dixon, Travis L., and Keith B. Maddox. 2005. "Skin Tone, Crime News, and Social Reality Judgments: Priming the Stereotype of the Dark and Dangerous Black Criminal 1." *Journal of Applied Social Psychology* 35 (8): 1555–70.
Douglass, Frederick. 1955. "What Negroes Want." In *The Life and Writings of Frederick Douglass*. Vol. 4. Edited by Philip S. Foner. New York: International.
Drew, Paul. 1997. "'Open' Class Repair Initiators in Response to Sequential Sources of Troubles in Conversation." *Journal of Pragmatics* 28 (1): 69–101.
Du Bois, W. E. B. 1890. "Jefferson Davis as a Representative of Civilization." Baccalaureate speech at Harvard University. The Du Bois Archive. http://credo.library.umass.edu/view/full/mums312-b196-i029.
Du Bois, W. E. B. 1903. *The Souls of Black Folk*. London: Longmans, Green & Co.
Du Bois, W. E. B. (1940) 2017. *Dusk of Dawn: An Essay toward an Autobiography of Race Concept*. New York: Routledge.
Duck, Waverly. 2001. "An Examination of the Correlation between Health Seeking and Health Promoting Behaviors with Masculinity." MA thesis, Wayne State University.
Duck, Waverly. 2005. "Blocked Hegemonic Aspirations: A Study of African American

Men's Beliefs about Masculinity and the Impact of These Beliefs on Health." PhD diss., Wayne State University.

Duck, Waverly. 2009. "Black Male Sexual Politics: Avoidance of HIV/AIDS Testing as a Masculine Health Practice." *Journal of African American Studies* 13 (3): 283–306.

Duck, Waverly. 2015. *No Way Out: Precarious Living in the Shadow of Poverty and Drug Dealing*. Chicago: University of Chicago Press.

Duck, Waverly. 2019. "When a Local Interaction Order Clashes with Gentrification: A Community Study of a Food Oasis in the East End of Pittsburgh." Unpublished manuscript.

Duck, Waverly, and Anne Warfield Rawls. 2012. "Interaction Orders of Drug Dealing Spaces: Local Orders of Sensemaking in a Poor Black American Place." *Crime, Law and Social Change* 57(1): 33–75.

Durkheim, Emile. 1893. *Le Division du travail social*. Paris: Alcan.

Durkheim, Emile. (1893) 1933. *The Division of Labor in Society*. Translated by George Simpson. New York: Free Press.

Eberhardt, Janet, ed. 2016. *Strategies for Change: Research Initiatives and Recommendations to Improve Police Community Relations in Oakland, Calif*. Stanford University, SPARQ: Social Psychological Answers to Real-World Questions.

Eberhardt, J. L., P. A. Goff, V. J. Purdie, and P. G. Davies. 2004. "Seeing Black: Race, Crime, and Visual Processing." *Journal of Personality and Social Psychology* 87 (6): 876–93.

Ecarma, Caleb. 2018. "Trump Slammed on Twitter for Proposed Military Parade: 'Repulsive Tinpot Strongman Bullsh*t.'" *Mediaite*, February 6. https://www.mediaite.com/online/trump-slammed-on-twitter-for-proposed-military-parade-repulsive-tinpot-strongman-bullsht/.

Edwards, Derek. 2006. "Facts, Norms and Dispositions: Practical Uses of the Modal Verb *Would* in Police Interrogations." *Discourse Studies* 8 (4): 475–501.

Edwards-Levy, Ariel. 2018. "White Americans Say the Starbucks Arrests Were an Isolated Incident. Black Americans Say They Were Part of a Pattern." *Huffington Post*, April 23. https://www.huffingtonpost.com/entry/white-black-americans-starbucks-survey_us_5addf928e4b0b2e81131de51.

Eisler, Richard M. 1998. "Male Reference Group Identity Dependence: Another Concept of Masculine Identity to Understand Men?" *Counseling Psychologist* 26 (3): 422–26.

Elias, Norbert. 1939. *Über den Prozeß der Zivilisation: Soziogenetische und psychogenetische Untersuchungen*. Basel: Haus Zum Falken.

Elias, Norbert. (1939) 1978. *The Civilizing Process: Sociogenetic and Psychogenetic Investigations*. Translated by Edmund Jephcott. Oxford: Blackwell.

Ellison, Ralph. 1952. *The Invisible Man*. New York: Random House.

Ellison, Ralph. 1970. "What America Would Be Like without Blacks." *Time*, April 6, 1970.

Fanon, Frantz. 1952. *Black Skin, White Masks*. Paris: Seuil.

Fassin, D. 2013. *Enforcing Order: An Ethnography of Urban Policing*. New York: Polity.

Feagin, Joe R. 2009. *The White Racial Frame: Centuries of Racial Framing and Counter-Framing*. New York: Routledge.

Feagin, Joe R., and Melvin P. Sikes. 1994. *Living with Racism: The Black Middle-Class Experience*. Boston: Beacon Press.

Fernández-Kelly, Patricia. 2015. *The Hero's Fight: African Americans in West Baltimore and the Shadow of the State*. Princeton, NJ: Princeton University Press.

Fox, Justin. 2009. *The Myth of the Rational Market: A History of Risk, Reward, and Delusion on Wall Street*. New York: Harper.

Garfinkel, Harold. (1943) 2019. *The History of Gulfport Field 1942*. Vol. 2, *The Aircraft Mechanics School*, ed. A. W. Rawls. Siegen, Germany: University of Siegen.

Garfinkel, Harold. 1946. "Some Reflections on Action Theory and the Theory of Social Systems." Unpublished manuscript. Harold Garfinkel Archive, Newburyport, MA.

Garfinkel, Harold. (1948) 2006. *Seeing Sociologically*. Edited by A. W. Rawls Boulder, CO: Paradigm.

Garfinkel, Harold. 1952. "The Perception of the Other: A Study in Social Order." PhD diss., Harvard University.

Garfinkel, Harold. 1963. "A Conception of and Experiments with 'Trust' as a Condition of Stable Concerted Actions." In *Motivation and Social Interaction: Cognitive Determinants*, edited by O. J. Harvey, 187–238. New York: Ronald Press.

Garfinkel, Harold. 1967. *Studies in Ethnomethodology*. Englewood Cliffs, NJ: Prentice Hall.

Garfinkel, Harold. 2002. *Ethnomethodology's Program: Working out Durkheim's Aphorism*. Lanham, MD: Rowman & Littlefield.

Glenn, Phillip. 2003. *Laughter in Interaction*. Cambridge: Cambridge University Press.

Goffman, Erving. 1959. *The Presentation of Self in Everyday Life*. Chicago: Free Press.

Goffman, Erving. 1963. *Stigma: Notes on the Management of Spoiled Identity*. Chicago: Free Press.

Goffman, Erving. 1974. *Frame Analysis: An Essay on the Organization of Experience*. New York: HarperCollins.

Goffman, Erving. 1979. "Footing." *Semiotica* 25 (1–2): 1–30.

Goffman, Erving. 1983. "The Interaction Order." *American Sociological Review* 48 (1): 1–17.

Goodwin, James S., Yong-Fang Kuo, David Brown, David Juurlink, and Mukaila Raji. 2018. "Association of Chronic Opioid Use with Presidential Voting Patterns in US Counties in 2016." *JAMA Network Open* 1 (2). https://jamanetwork.com/journals/jamanetworkopen/fullarticle/2685627.

Gramsci, Antonio. *1971. Selections from the Prison Notebooks*. Edited and translated by Q. Hoare and G. Nowell Smith. London: Lawrence & Wishar.

Green, A., D. Carney, D. Palin, L. Ngo, K. Raymond, L. Iezzoni, and M. Banaji. 2007. "Implicit Bias among Physicians and Its Prediction of Thrombolysis Decisions for Black and White Patients." *Journal of General Internal Medicine* 22 (9): 1231–38.

Greenwald, A., and L. Krieger. 2006. "Implicit Bias: Scientific Foundations." *California Law Review* 94 (4): 945–68.

Guynn, Jessica. 2018. "BBQ Becky, Permit Patty and Why the Internet Is Shaming White People Who Police People 'Simply for Being Black.'" *USA Today*, July 18.

Hamer, Jennifer. 2001. *What It Means to Be Daddy: Fatherhood for Black Men Living Away from Their Children*. New York: Columbia University Press.

Hannah-Jones, Nicole. 2019. "The 1619 Project." *New York Times Magazine*, August 14.

Hannerz, Ulf. 1969. *Soulside: Inquiries into Ghetto Culture and Community*. New York: Columbia University Press.

Hayes, Chris. 2017. *A Colony in a Nation*. New York: Norton.

Hepburn, A., and G. B. Bolden. 2013. "Transcription." In *Blackwell Handbook of Conversational Analysis*, edited by J. Sidnell and T. Stivers, 57–76. Oxford: Blackwell.

Heritage, John. 1984. "A Change-of-State Token and Aspects of Its Sequential Placement." In *Structures of Social Action: Studies in Conversation Analysis*, edited by J. Maxwell Atkinson and John Heritage, 299–354. Cambridge: Cambridge University Press.

Hewitt, Alison. 2015. "A 'Black'-Sounding Name Makes People Imagine a Larger, More Dangerous Person, UCLA Study Shows." *UCLA Newsroom*, October 7. http://newsroom.ucla.edu/releases/a-black-sounding-name-makes-people-imagine-a-larger-more-dangerous-person-ucla-study-shows.

Hilton, James [Glen Trevor, pseud.]. 1931. *Murder at School*. London: Ernest Benn. Reissued in the United States in 1932 as *Was It Murder?* New York: Harper and Brothers.

Hochschild, A. R. 1983. *The Managed Heart*. Berkeley: University of California Press.

Hochschild, Arlie. 2016. *Strangers in Their Own Land: Anger and Mourning on the American Right*. New York: New Press.

Holbrook, Colin, Daniel M. T. Fessler, and Carlos David Navarrete. 2016. "Looming Large in Others' Eyes: Racial Stereotypes Illuminate Dual Adaptations for Representing Threat versus Prestige as Physical Size." *Evolution and Human Behavior* 37 (1): 67–78.

Holmes, M. D., M. A. Painter II, and B. W. Smith. 2018. "Race, Place, and Police-Caused Homicide in US Municipalities." *Justice Quarterly* 36 (5): 751–86. https://doi.org/10.1080/07418825.2018.1427782.

Hughes, Everett. 1945. "Dilemmas and Contradictions of Status." *American Journal of Sociology* 50 (5): 353–59.

Intons-Peterson, M. J., and Arlene K. Samuels. 1978. "The Cultural Halo Effect: Black and White Women Rate Black and White Men." *Bulletin of the Psychonomic Society* 11 (5): 309–12.

Jefferson, Gail. 1979. "A Technique for Inviting Laughter and Subsequent Acceptance/Declination." In *Everyday Language: Studies in Ethnomethodology*, edited by George Psathas, 79–96. New York: Irvington.

Jefferson, Gail. 1984. "On the Organization of Laughter in Talk about Troubles." In *Structures of Social Action: Studies in Conversation Analysis*, edited by J. Maxwell Atkinson and John Heritage, 346–69. Cambridge: Cambridge University Press.

Jefferson, Gail. 2004. "Glossary of Transcript Symbols with an Introduction." In *Conversational Analysis: Studies from the First Generation*, edited by G. H. Lerner, 13–31. Amsterdam: John Benjamins.

JoanMar [pseud.]. 2018. "Calling the Police on Black People without a Cause Is an Act of Aggression." *Daily Kos*, April 27. https://www.dailykos.com/stories/2018/4/27/1759173/-Calling-the-police-on-black-people-without-cause-is-an-act-of-aggression-StopBrutalizingOurPeople.

Jones, Nikki. 2018. *The Chosen Ones: Black Men and the Politics of Redemption*. Berkeley: University of California Press.

Jost, J., L. Rudman, I. Blair, D. Carney, N. Dasgupta, and C. Hardin. 2009. "The Existence of Implicit Bias Is Beyond a Reasonable Doubt: A Refutation of Ideological and Methodological Objections and an Executive Summary of Ten Studies That No Manager Should Ignore." *Research in Organizational Behavior* 29: 39–69.

Katz, William Loren. (1971) 2005. *The Black West: A Documentary and Pictorial History of the African American Role in Westward Expansion in the United States*. New York: Harlem Moon.

Kelling, George L., and James Q. Wilson. 1982. "Broken Windows." *Atlantic Monthly* 249 (3): 29–38.

Kochman, Thomas. 1981. *Black and White: Styles in Conflict*. Chicago: Free Press.

Kochman, Thomas, and Jean Mavrelis. 2009. *Corporate Tribalism: White Men/White Women and Cultural Diversity at Work*. Chicago: University of Chicago Press.

Krugman, P. 2012. *End This Depression Now!* New York: Norton.

Labov, William. 1972. *Language in the Inner City: Studies in the Black English Vernacular*. Philadelphia: University of Pennsylvania Press.

Ladner, Joyce A. 1971. *Tomorrow's Tomorrow: The Black Woman*. Garden City, NY: Doubleday.

Laguna, L., A. Linn, K. Ward, and R. Rupslaukyte. 2010. "An Examination of Authoritarian Personality Traits among Police Officers: The Role of Experience." *Journal of Police and Criminal Psychology* 25 (2): 99–104.

Lepore, J. 2009. *The Name of War: King Philip's War and the Origins of American Identity*. New York: Vintage.
Lemelle, Anthony J. 1995. *Black Male Deviance*. New York: Praeger.
Lemert, Charles. 1994. "A Classic from the Other Side of the Veil." *Sociological Quarterly* 35 (3): 383–96.
Loader, I., and N. Walker. 2007. *Civilizing Security*. Cambridge: Cambridge University Press.
López, Ian Haney. 2013. *Dog Whistle Politics: How Coded Racial Appeals Have Reinvented Racism and Wrecked the Middle Class*. Oxford: Oxford University Press.
López, Ian Haney. 2019. *Merge Left: Fusing Race with Class, Winning Elections, and Saving America*. New York: New Press.
Maddow, Rachel. 2019. *Blowout: Corrupted Democracy, Rogue State Russia, and the Richest, Most Destructive Industry on Earth*. New York: Crown.
Maghbouleh, Neda. 2017. *The Limits of Whiteness: Iranian Americans and the Everyday Politics of Race*. Stanford, CA: Stanford University Press.
Maines, David. 1993. "Narratives Moment and Sociological Phenomena: Toward a Narrative Sociology." *Sociological Quarterly* 34 (1): 17–38.
Males, Michael. 2017. "White People Should Be More Afraid of Other Whites than They Are of People of Color." *Los Angeles Times*, August 3. http://www.latimes.com/opinion/op-ed/la-oe-males-white-americans-violence-sanctuary-cities-20170803-story.html.
Manning, Peter K. 2010. *Democratic Policing in a Changing World*. London: Routledge.
Manning, Peter. 2013. "The Work of Egon Bittner." *Ethnographic Studies* 13: 51–66.
Marx, Karl. (1861) 1964. "The Civil War in the United States." In *Marx/Engels Collected Works*. Vol. 19. Moscow: Progress Publishers. https://marxists.catbull.com/archive/marx/works/1861/11/07.htm.
Massey, Douglas S. "A Brief History of Human Society: The Origin and Role of Emotion in Social Life." *American Sociological Review* 67 (1): 1–29.
Mastrofski, S. D., J. B. Snipes, R. B. Parks, and C. D. Maxwell. 2000. "The Helping Hand of the Law: Police Control of Citizens on Request." *Criminology* 38 (2): 307–42.
Mayer, Jane. 2016. *Dark Money: The Hidden History of the Billionaires Behind the Rise of the Radical Right*. New York: Anchor.
Maynard, Douglas. 2013. "Defensive Mechanisms: I-Mean-Prefaced Utterances in Complaint and Other Conversational Sequences." In *Conversational Repair and Human Understanding*, edited by Makoto Hayashi, Geoffrey Raymond, and Jack Sidnell, 198–233. Cambridge: Cambridge University Press.
Maynard, Douglas, and Don Zimmerman. 1984. "Topical Talk Ritual and the Social Organization of Relationships." *Social Psychology Quarterly* 47 (4): 301–16.
Mead, George Herbert. 1913. "The Social Self." *Journal of Philosophy, Psychology and Scientific Methods* 10: 374–80.

Mead, George Herbert. 1934. *Mind, Self, and Society*. Chicago: University of Chicago Press.

Meehan, Albert. 1986. "Record-Keeping Practices in the Policing of Juveniles." *Urban Life* 15 (1): 70–102.

Meehan, Albert. 2000. "The Organizational Career of Gang Statistics: The Politics of Policing Gangs." *Sociological Quarterly* 41 (3): 337–70.

Merritt, Keri Leigh. 2017. *Masterless Men: Poor Whites and Slavery in the Antebellum South*. Cambridge: Cambridge University Press.

Metzl, Jonathan M. 2019. *Dying of Whiteness: How the Politics of Racial Resentment Is Killing America's Heartland*. New York: Basic Books.

Miller, Reuben, and Amanda Alexander. 2016. "The Price of Carceral Citizenship: Punishment, Surveillance, and Social Welfare Policy in an Age of Carceral Expansion." *Michigan Journal of Race and Law* 21: 291–311.

Miller, Steven V., and Nicholas T. Davis. 2018. "White Outgroup Intolerance and Declining Support for American Democracy." Working paper. http://svmiller.com/research/white-outgroup-intolerance-democratic-support/.

Moore, Wendy Leo. 2007. *Reproducing Racism: White Space, Elite Law Schools, and Racial Inequality*. Lanham, MD: Rowman & Littlefield.

Morin, Rich, and Renee Stepler. 2016. "The Racial Confidence Gap in Police Performance." Pew Research Center. http://www.pewsocialtrends.org/2016/09/29/the-racial-confidence-gap-in-police-performance/.

Mosby, Lynetta, Anne Warfield Rawls, Albert J. Meehan, Catherine Pettinari, and Edward Mays. 1999. "Troubles in Interracial Talk about Discipline: Discipline Narratives of African American Seniors." *Journal of Comparative Family Studies* 30 (3): 489–521.

Mosher, Chad M. 2001. "The Social Implications of Sexual Identity Formation and the Coming-Out Process: A Review of the Theoretical and Empirical Literature." *Family Journal* 9 (2): 164–73.

Mosher, Donald L., and Silvan S. Tomkins. 1988. "Scripting the Macho Man: Hypermasculine Socialization and Enculturation." *Journal of Sex Research* 25 (1): 60–84.

Mummolo, J. 2018. "Modern Police Tactics, Police-Citizen Interactions, and the Prospects for Reform." *Journal of Politics* 80 (1): 1–15.

Omi, Michael, and Howard Winant. 1986. *Racial Formation in the United States*. New York: Routledge.

Pager, Devah. 2003. "The Mark of a Criminal Record." *American Journal of Sociology* 108 (5): 937–75.

Pager, Devah. 2008. *Marked: Race, Crime, and Finding Work in an Era of Mass Incarceration*. Chicago: University of Chicago Press.

Parsons, Talcott. 1951. *The Social System*. London: Routledge & Kegan Paul.

Parsons, Talcott, and Robert F. Bales. 1955. *Family, Socialization and Interaction Process*. New York: Free Press.

Picca, Leslie Houts, and Joe R. Feagin. 2007. *Two-Faced Racism: Whites in the Backstage and Frontstage.* New York: Routledge.

Piketty, Thomas. 2014. *Capital in the Twenty-First Century.* Translated by Arthur Goldhammer. Cambridge, MA: Belknap Press of Harvard University Press.

Pitts, Leonard. 2019. "Republican Lawmakers in Alabama Are Partying Like Its 1859." *Miami Herald,* May 17. https://www.miamiherald.com/opinion/opn-columns-blogs/leonard-pitts-jr/article230537974.html.

Pleck, Joseph H. 1981. *The Myth of Masculinity.* Cambridge, MA: MIT Press.

Pomerantz, Anita. 1986. "Extreme Case Formulations: A Way of Legitimizing Claims." *Human Studies* 9 (2–3): 219–29.

Ramsey, Donovan X. 2017. "White America's Unshakeable Confidence in the Police." The Marshall Project, July 19. https://www.themarshallproject.org/2017/07/19/white-america-s-unshakeable-confidence-in-the-police.

Rawls, Anne. 1983. "Constitutive Justice: An Interactionist Contribution to the Understanding of Social Order and Human Value." PhD diss., Boston University.

Rawls, Anne. 1987. "The Interaction Order Sui Generis: Goffman's Contribution to Social Theory." *Sociological Theory* 5 (2): 136–49.

Rawls, Anne. 1989. "Language, Self, and Social Order: a Re-evaluation of Goffman and Sacks." *Human Studies* 12 (1): 147–72.

Rawls, Anne. 1990. "Emergent Sociality: A Dialectic of Commitment and Order." *Symbolic Interaction* 13 (1): 63–82.

Rawls, Anne. 1996a. "Durkheim's Epistemology: The Initial Critique 1915–1924." *Sociological Quarterly* 38 (1): 111–45.

Rawls, Anne. 1996b. "Durkheim's Epistemology: The Neglected Argument." *American Journal of Sociology* 102 (2): 430–82.

Rawls, Anne. 2000. "'Race' as an Interaction Order Phenomena: W. E. B. Du Bois's 'Double Consciousness' Thesis Revisited." *Sociological Theory* 18 (2): 239–72.

Rawls, Anne Warfield. 2009. *Epistemology and Practice: Durkheim's "The Elementary Forms of Religious Life."* Cambridge: Cambridge University Press.

Rawls, Anne. 2012. "Durkheim's Theory of Modernity: Self-Regulating Practices as Constitutive Orders of Social and Moral Facts." *Journal of Classical Social Theory* 12 (3–4): 351–62.

Rawls, Anne. 2015. "Getting Information Systems to Interact: The Social Fact Character of 'Object' Clarity as a Factor in Designing Information Systems." *Information Society* 31 (2): 175–92.

Rawls, Anne. 2017. "An Essay on the Intrinsic Relationship between Social Facts and Moral Questions." *Canadian Journal of Sociology* 54 (4): 392–404.

Rawls, Anne. 2019. *La Division du Travail Revisited: Vers une Théorie Sociologique de la Justice.* Translated by Francesco Callegaro and Philip Chanial. Paris: Le Bord de l'Eau.

Rawls, Anne. 2020. *Toward a Sociological Theory of Justice.* New York: Routledge.

Rawls, Anne. Forthcoming. "Harold Garfinkel's Focus on Racism, Inequality and Social Justice: The Early Years 1939–1952." In *Ethnomethodology: A Retro-*

spective, ed. John Heritage and Doug Maynard. Cambridge: Cambridge University Press.

Rawls, Anne, and Gary David. 2006. "Accountably Other: Trust, Reciprocity and Exclusion in a Context of Situated Practice." *Human Studies* 28 (4): 469–97.

Rawls, Anne, and Waverly Duck. 2017. "'Fractured Reflections' of High-Status Black Male Presentations of Self: Nonrecognition of Identity as a 'Tacit' Form of Institutional Racism." *Sociological Focus* 50 (1): 36–51.

Rawls, Anne, and Waverly Duck. 2019. "Developing a White 'Double Consciousness' of Race and Marginality: Implications of Du Bois and Garfinkel for the Scientific Awareness of Interaction Orders." Unpublished manuscript.

Rawls, Anne, Waverly Duck, and Jason Turowetz. 2018. "Problems Establishing Identity/Residency in a City Neighborhood during a Black/White Police/Citizen Encounter: Revisiting Du Bois' Conception of 'The Submissive Man.'" *City and Community* 17 (4): 1015–50.

Rawls, A., K. Taylor, and R. Coates. 2019. "The Clashing Racial Identifications of Black Americans and West Indian College Students." Unpublished manuscript.

Rawls, Anne, and Jason Turowetz. 2019. "'Discovering culture' in Interaction: Solving Problems in Cultural Sociology by Recovering the Interactional Side of Parsons' Conception of Culture." *American Journal of Cultural Sociology*, 1–28.

Raymond, Geoffrey. 2003. "Grammar and Social Organization: Yes/No Interrogatives and the Structure of Responding." *American Sociological Review* 68 (6): 939–67.

Rios, Victor, Jr. 2011. *Punished: Policing the Lives of Black and Latino Boys*. New York: New York University Press.

Roediger, David R. 2007. *The Wages of Whiteness: Race and the Making of the American Working Class*. Rev. ed. New York: Verso.

Russell-Brown, Katheryn. 1998. *The Color of Crime: Racial Hoaxes, White Fear, Black Protectionism, and Other Macroaggressions*. 1st ed. New York: New York University Press.

Russell-Brown, Katheryn. 2009. *The Color of Crime*. 2nd ed. New York: New York University Press.

Sabo, Don, and Sue C. Jansen. 1992. "Images of Men in Sport Media: The Social Reproduction of Masculinity." In *Men, Masculinity, and the Media*, edited by Steve Craig, 169–84. Thousand Oaks, CA: Sage.

Sacks, Harvey. 1992. *Lectures on Conversation*. Vol. 1. Edited by Gail Jefferson. Oxford: Blackwell.

Sacks, H., E. Schegloff, and G. Jefferson. 1974. "A Simplest Systematics for the Organization of Turn-Taking in Conversation." *Language* 50 (4): 696–735.

Saez, Emmanuel, and Gabriel Zucman. 2019. *The Triumph of Injustice: How the Rich Dodge Taxes and How to Make Them Pay*. New York: Norton.

Sampson, Robert J., Stephen W. Raudenbush, and Felton Earls. 1997. "Neighborhoods and Violent Crime: A Multilevel Study of Collective Efficacy." *Science* 277 (5328): 918–24.

Schegloff, Emanuel. 1972. "Notes on a Conversational Practice: Formulating

Place." In *Studies in Social Interaction*, edited by David Sudnow, 75–119. New York: Free Press.

Schegloff, Emanuel. 1996. "Turn Organization: One Intersection of Grammar and Interaction." In *Interaction and Grammar*, edited by Elinor Ochs, Emanuel A. Schegloff, and Sandra A. Thompson, 52–133. Cambridge: Cambridge University Press.

Schegloff, Emanuel. 2007. *Sequence Organization in Interaction*. Cambridge: Cambridge University Press.

Schegloff, Emanuel, and Harvey Sacks. 1973. "Opening Up Closings." *Semiotica* 8 (4): 289–327.

Segal, Lynne. 1993. "Changing Men: Masculinities in Context." *Theory and Society* 22 (5): 625–41.

Skocpol, Theda, and Vanessa Williamson. 2011. *The Tea Party and the Remaking of Republican Conservatism*. Oxford: Oxford University Press.

Skogan, W. G. 2006. "Asymmetry in the Impact of Encounters with Police." *Policing & Society* 16 (2): 99–126.

Skolnick, J. 1977. "A Sketch of the Policeman's 'Working Personality.'" In *The Dysfunctional Alliance: Emotion and Reason in Justice Administration*, edited by D. B. Kennedy. Cincinnati, OH: Anderson.

Smith, W. A. 2004. "Black Faculty Coping with Racial Battle Fatigue: The Campus Racial Climate in a Post–Civil Rights Era." In *A Long Way to Go: Conversations about Race by African American Faculty and Graduate Students*, edited by Darrell Cleveland, 171–90. New York: Peter Lang.

Smith, W. A. 2014. *Racial Battle Fatigue in Higher Education: Exposing the Myth of Post-Racial America*. Lanham, MD: Rowman & Littlefield.

Smith, William A., Walter R. Allen, and Lynette L. Danley. 2007. "'Assume the Position . . . You Fit the description': Psychosocial Experiences and Racial Battle Fatigue among African American Male College Students." *American Behavioral Scientist* 51 (4): 551–78.

Smith, William A., Man Hung, and Jeremy D. Franklin. 2011. "Racial Battle Fatigue and the Miseducation of Black Men: Racial Microaggressions, Societal Problems, and Environmental Stress." *Journal of Negro Education* 80 (1): 63–82.

SouthernLeveller [pseud.]. 2018. "Strong Man Religion: The Reason White 'Evangelicals' Support Trump So Strongly." *Daily Kos*, April 10. https://www.daily kos.com/stories/2018/4/10/1756027/-Strong-Man-Religion-The-Reason-White -Evangelicals-Support-Trump-So-Strongly.

Stack, Carol. 1974. *All Our Kin: Strategies for Survival in a Black Community*. New York: Basic Books.

Steele, Claude M., and Joshua Aronson. 1995. "Stereotype Threat and the Intellectual Test Performance of African Americans." *Journal of Personality and Social Psychology* 69 (5): 797.

Stiglitz, Joseph. 2012. *The Price of Inequality: How Today's Divided Society Endangers Our Future*. New York: Norton.

Stivers, Tanya. 2004. "'No No No' and Other Types of Multiple Sayings in Social Interaction." *Human Communication Research* 30 (2): 260–93.
Suchman, Lucy. 2006. *Human Machine Reconfigurations: Plans and Situated Actions*. 2nd ed. Cambridge: Cambridge University Press.
Terrill, W., E. A. Paoline, and Peter K. Manning. 2003. "Police Culture and Coercion." *Criminology* 41 (4): 1003–34.
Tribune Media Wire. 2016. "City Releases 'Disturbing' Body Camera Video of Greensboro, North Carolina Arrest." *WREG News Memphis*, September 26. http://wreg.com/2016/09/26/city-releases-disturbing-body-camera-video-of-greensboro-north-carolina-arrest/.
Ture, Kwame, and Charles Hamilton. 1967. *Black Power: The Politics of Liberation*. New York: Vintage.
Turowetz, Jason, and Anne Rawls. 2019. "The Development of Garfinkel's 'Trust' Argument from 1947 to 1967: Demonstrating How Inequality Disrupts Sense and Self-Making." *Journal of Classical Sociology*.
US News & World Report. 2019. "Best States Rankings." *US News & World Report*. https://www.usnews.com/news/best-states/rankings.
Vance, J. D. 2016. *Hillbilly Elegy: A Memoir of a Family and Culture in Crisis*. New York: HarperCollins.
Voigt, Rob, Nicholas P. Camp, Vinodkumar Prabhakaran, William L. Hamilton, Rebecca C. Hetey, Camilla M. Griffiths, David Jurgens, Dan Jurafsky, and Jennifer L. Eberhardt. 2017. "Language from Police Body Camera Footage Shows Racial Disparities in Officer Respect." *PNAS* 114 (25): 6521–26. http://www.pnas.org/content/early/2017/05/30/1702413114.
Warikoo, Natasha K. 2016. *The Diversity Bargain: And Other Dilemmas of Race, Admissions, and Meritocracy at Elite Universities*. Chicago: University of Chicago Press.
West, Cornel. (1982) 2002. *Prophesy Deliverance! An Afro-American Revolutionary Christianity*. Louisville, KY: Westminster John Knox Press.
Williams, David R., and Chiquita Collins. 1995. "US Socioeconomic and Racial Differences in Health: Patterns and Explanations." *Annual Review of Sociology* 21 (1): 349–86.
Wilson, Jim Pat. 2019. "Kentucky Farmers Hurt by Trump's Trade Wars Won't Speak Up—They Fear GOP Backlash." *Courier Journal*, May 24.
Wilson, William Julius. 1987. *The Truly Disadvantaged: The Inner City, the Underclass, and Public Policy*. Chicago: University of Chicago Press.
Wise, Tim. 2010. *Colorblind: The Rise of Post-Racial Politics and the Retreat from Racial Equity*. San Francisco: City Lights Books.
Wittgenstein, Ludwig. 1953. *Philosophical Investigations*. Oxford: Blackwell.
Woodward, C. Vann. 1955. *The Strange Career of Jim Crow*. Oxford: Oxford University Press.
Wylie, Christopher. 2019. *Mindf*ck: Cambridge Analytica and the Plot to Break America*. New York: Random House.

Index

abolitionist movement, 26
affirmative action, 169–71, 241
Africa, 16, 162–63, 167, 259n15
Alexander, Amanda, 223
Alexander, Michelle, 223
Allen, Theodore, 2
American colonies: Anglo-White character of, as fiction, 237–38; class in, 25–26, 231; labor control, 11; racism, development of, 26; and slavery, 11, 231; Whiteness, invention of, 24–25
American dream, 245; individualism of, 130
American Revolution, 25
Anderson, Elijah: cosmo approach, 79
Anglo-Spanish War, 256n4
apprenticeship, 90
Arizona, 238
Asia, 5
Asian Americans, 2, 5–6, 24–25, 138, 143, 162, 167, 181, 189, 191, 194–95, 198–99, 255–56n3, 260n22; as Model Minorities, 173; and Otherness, 174; as outsiders, 173–79; stereotypes about, 174
Asian and Asian American racism, 2, 5–7, 162, 167, 173–79, 181, 189, 191, 194–95, 198–99, 255–56n3, 260n22. *See also* racism; retail racism; tacit racism; unconscious racism
assimilation, 241
Australia, 260n18

Bahamas, 6
Baldwin, James, 10, 226
Banerjee, Abhijit, 19
Baraka, Amiri, 234, 236

Barber, Mike, 137
Barber, William J., III, 14
Bell, Joyce, 10
Bittner, Egon, 210
Black Americans, 4, 7, 32, 226–28, 231, 233; aboveground and under-the-table employment, distinction between, 264n1; acting White, in class, 47–49; affirmative action, 241; and AIDS, 263n2; authority, challenging of, 74; authority figures, interaction with, 82; Black criminality, myth of, 3, 19–20; "Black Is Beautiful" movement, 258n10; Black-on-Black crime, 200, 202–4; categorization, avoiding of, 35, 42, 44; class variation, 95; coded contrasting interactional expectations, 12; collective identity, importance of, 104; collectivism of, 10–11, 31; colonial mentality, 3, 28, 107; colony within a nation, 211–12; confrontational style, perception of, 86–87, 99–100; conversation, as misunderstood, 18; culture of poverty, 225; democratic character of, 12–13, 22, 30, 100, 116–17; diplomacy, attitudes toward, 100–103; and disorder, 243–44; double consciousness of, 12–14, 16, 21–22, 27–28, 30, 37, 48, 109, 126, 139, 240–42; drug dealing, 204–10, 212, 243–45; as egalitarian, 109, 126, 133, 203, 265n7; enemies, and trust, 72–73; and equality, 27, 82; and exclusion, 28; excuse/apology, expression of, 262n2; and fairness, 10; false narratives about, 8; fractured reflections, 8, 78; gender, double consciousness about, 109; health

Black Americans (*cont.*)
talk, avoidance of among, 125, 127; high-status occupational identities, 57, 59–77; honesty, conceptions of, 9, 81–84, 94–98, 100–104; hypermasculinity of, 125; hyper-surveillance, by police, 205, 207, 224; immediate setting, focus on, 49–53; implicit bias among, 10; introductory sequences of, 38, 40–53; introductory talk, and maintaining privacy, 33, 35–37; law-abiding neighborhood residents, perspectives of, 204–13; mass incarceration, 120, 127; memorial murals, 243–44; mirror-opposite interactional preference, 97; mutual respect, 200–201, 212; mutual responsibility, 82, 126, 129; not trusting, as defensive strategy, 67–68; null-response, 79; N-word, 17; "plastic" behavior, 81, 86, 88, 103; and policing, 131, 157–58; and pretense, 100–101; racial fatigue, 79; racialized lens, as seen through, 241; as "rude," White American experience of, 8, 34–35, 54–55; school-to-prison pipeline, 127, 230; second-guessing, 66; "seeing it through," 98–100; self-preservation strategies, 203; sexism, insight into, 109; signifying, use of, 44–45; and stereotypes, 21, 76–77, 106; submissive civility, 84, 131–33; surveillance of, 223; 2016 election, effect of on, 29; and twoness, 201–2; uniqueness of, 30; white workplace, conception of honesty, 85–94, 104; workplace, tacit racism toward, 8–9; zero-tolerance policies, effect on, 230. *See also* Black masculinity

Black interaction order practices, 127, 131, 158, 160; democratic practices of civility, elevation of, 133; fractured reflections, 132; health talk, taboo against, 110–12; submissive civility, 15, 129; volunteering information, 132

Black masculinity, 9; adaptations of, 105–7, 110; aspirations of, 105; Black interaction order, 107–8, 110–12; blocked aspirations, as alternative to, 127–28; as conflicted, 128; egalitarian civility, character of, 128; equality, emphasis on, 105; feminine characteristics, 109–10; flexibility of, 126, 128; and health, 105–6; health talk, taboos against, 110–25; HIV/AIDs, 112, 122–23; hypermasculinity, 110, 128, 202; marriage, focus on, 114–15; misunderstanding of, 224; poor White men, similarity to, 107; popular misconceptions of, 107; as positive adaptation to racism, 107–8; preventive care, as unmanly, 123–25; racism, as reasonable response to, 128; sexuality, emphasis on, 110, 113, 127; sexual promiscuity, 117–20; social responsibility, acceptance of, 115–16; STDs, 111–12, 114, 121–23; vs. White American hegemonic ideal, comparison to, 105, 110, 116. *See also* hegemonic masculinity; hypermasculinity; masculinity

Black neighborhoods, 3, 18, 201; "broken" laws, 202; collective response of, 205; drug dealers, 212; police response in, 210; survival strategies in, 218–19; White norms, 204; White Others, 18

Blackness: as democratic conception, 22; false narrative about, 26; inclusion of, 22

Black Other, 54–55; and Black self, 61

Black Power movement, 257n7

Black/West Indian intersectionality, 5–7, 16, 25, 162–63, 167, 189, 198–99, 255–56n3, 259n15

Black/White binary, 2, 5, 7, 16–17, 23–25, 27, 31, 129, 162, 198–99, 236–37, 240, 255–56n3, 259n15, 259–60n16, 260n22; Race, structured by, 6

Black/White citizen/police encounters: enhancement complaints, 135–36; Greensboro incident, 130, 132, 134, 137–58; Starbucks incident, 130–32, 134–38, 160; White interactional preferences, enforcement of, 134

Black/White honesty: clashing conceptions of, 9, 81–89, 91, 94–95, 98, 100, 101, 103, 132, 141, 157, 159

Bluford, Guion Stewart, Jr., 213
Bluford Series, 213
Bonilla-Silva, Eduardo, 7–8, 30, 258n10
Boston, 245
Brazil, 255–56n3
Brown, Sterling, 226

California, 238
Caparra, Puerto Rico, 237–38
carceral citizenship, 223

Carlos, John, 257n7
Carson, Ben, 172, 173
categorial self, 11, 55, 83, 92, 100, 102–3. *See also* egalitarian self; looking glass self; presentation of self; self
Chicago, 120
China, 5, 174, 181, 258n9
Chou, Rosalind S., 173
citizen caller, 130, 134, 137, 141, 150
Civil Rights Act (1866), 14
Civil Rights Act (1964), 14
Civil Rights movement, 205, 230
Civil War, 4, 29, 116–17, 232, 234–35, 239–40, 257–58n8
clashing expectations, 11, 54, 78, 81
Clemons, Chikesia, 130, 135
Clinton, Bill: tough on crime agenda, 229
cohesion, 247
collective punishment, 201, 217–22; school-to-prison pipeline, 216; youth control complex, 215; zero-tolerance policy, 213–15
collectivism, 10
Collins, Patricia Hill, 126–27
colonialism, 240
colonial mentality, 4, 21; of Black Americans, 3, 28, 107; self-hatred, 187
Columbus Day, 238
common good, 247
community: competitive strategic individuals vs. egalitarian solidarity community, 55–56
Confederacy, 13
Connell, R. W., 107
constitutive interaction, 15–16, 37
constitutive practices, 56, 245; and equality, 246; and inequality, 247; meaning-making processes, 246; and reciprocity, 246–47
conversation analysis (CA), 137–56, 261n3; double bind, 159; mutuality, 159; ordinary reasonableness, 158; pretext, 158–59; racial profiling, 159; reciprocity, failure of, 158; submissive civility, 159; tacit racism, 157–59. *See also* Greensboro incident; Starbucks incident
Cooley, Charles Horton, 60; looking glass self, 78
Cotton, Tom, 258n9
cowboys: heyday of, 235; myth of, 234–36; Whiteness, lies of, 236

criminalblackman stereotype, 8, 71, 233
criminal justice system, 20, 127; new Jim Crow, 223
Critical Race theory, 10, 31
cross-race interaction, 9, 86, 97, 159–60, 169, 187

Dark Money: and Race, 228; racial resentment, fanning of, 11
Davis, Jefferson, 13, 130
definition of the situation, 11, 23, 31, 41, 58, 60–61, 63
democracy, 56, 128, 199, 243, 246; and civility, 19; and racism, 4; strong man ideal, 132; submissive civility, 132; tacit racism, 133
DiAngelo, Robin, 7
d'Iberville, Pierre Le Moyne, 266n1
diplomacy, 27, 83, 99–100, 202–3; as class sensitive, 101; and competition, 102; as pretense, 101; secrecy, origins in, 100; as skilled social practice, 102
discretion, 84
Dominican Republic, 183, 187
double consciousness, 21, 23, 28, 30, 37, 48, 58, 126, 139, 241–42; and doubleness, 259–60n16; on gender, 109; second sight, 27, 240; self-awareness, 32; separation, experience of, 198; slave experience, direct effect of, 22
drug dealers, 120, 210; local economy, 243; police, hyper-surveillance by, 205–7; power struggles, 202; as protectors, 202, 205, 244; as work, 243
Du Bois, W. E. B., 3, 7, 12, 37, 65, 116, 246; democracy, importance of submitting to, 128; double consciousness, 21–23, 30, 58, 126, 240, 242; exceptionalism, proponent of, 257n6; second sight, 27, 55; submissive civility, 221; submissive civility, as strength, 132–33, 160; Submissive Man, 9, 13, 129–30
Duflo, Esther, 19
Durham, Philip, 234, 236
Durkheim, Emile, 56, 247–48, 259n14; constitutive practices, 245–46; implicit condition, 246
Dutch East India Company, 256n4

Eastwood, Clint, 235
Eberhardt, J. L., 147

egalitarian self, 31, 55–56, 83, 85, 92.
    See also categorial self; looking glass
    self; presentation of self; self
Elizabeth I, 256n4
Ellison, Ralph, 75
England, 24–25, 231, 237, 256n4
English, 2, 24–28, 231, 237, 238–39, 240,
    256n4; butler, control of emotions,
    263n4; Whiteness, invention of, 12, 232
equality, 8, 16, 27, 55, 76, 132–33, 246; markets, growth of, 20; as necessary, 7; and reciprocity, 18
Europe, 28, 100–101
exaggerated compliance, 147

face: as aspect of self, 102–3; saving of, 102–3
face-to-face challenges, 42, 69–70, 82, 248; and face-saving, 102; seeing it through, 98–100
Fanon, Frantz, 3, 21, 240; colonial mentality, 107
Feagin, Joe, 1–2, 169, 173
Ferguson, MO, 220
Fernandez-Kelly, Patricia, 223
Fort Maurepas, 266n1
fractured reflections, 58, 61–62, 75, 106, 109, 132, 171, 193; Black Americans, 8, 78; empirical contours of, 64–65; null-response, 63; trust conditions, 247–48
fracturing, 60–61; as non-recognition, 78; as racialized experience, 65
French colonies, 266n1
friend talk, 33, 47–48, 51–53, 92, 98, 164–65, 169, 172–73, 177–78, 187, 194–95, 197–98

Garfinkel, Harold, 15, 77, 108, 247–48, 259n12; coat hanger method, 46, 61–62; trust conditions, 59–60, 143, 246, 259n14, 262n5
Gaza, 266n2
genocide, 237
gentrification, 136
Gibbs, Christopher, 258n9
Goffman, Erving, 60, 78, 108, 221–22, 247; definition of situation, 41, 259n12; and face, 103; identity, role of, 41; involvement obligations, 246; presentation of self, 58, 100–101; and reflexivity, 77; working consensus, 143, 246

Great Depression, 232
Greensboro incident, 130, 158; conversation analysis (CA) of, 137–57; disfluency in, 153–54; extreme-case formulation, 142; honesty, 141; null-response, 147; submissive civility, adoption of, 132, 134; tacit racism of, 137–38; volunteering, 141
greeting sequences, 35–36, 38, 41, 49–50, 98

Haiti, 6
Hancock, John, 245
Harvard University: Black students in, 170–71; Project Implicit, 255n2
Hayes, Chris, 22, 211–12, 245
health, 9, 29, 50, 83, 95, 126, 232–33, 242; in Black community, 112; Black masculinity, 106, 112–14, 121, 123–24, 127–28; Black vs. White, differences between, 110–11, 113; and masculinity, 105
health care system: racial exclusion and segregation of, 125
health talk: Black vs. White, differences between, 110–11, 113; taboo against, 125, 127
hegemonic masculinity, 107, 108, 125; White ideal of, 109–10, 114, 116, 126–27. *See also* Black masculinity; hypermasculinity; masculinity
High Status Black Men, 3, 8, 28, 57–65, 75–76, 78–79, 99, 106, 109, 261–62n2
hippie countercultural movement, 23
HIV/AIDS, 112, 122–23, 263n2
Hochschild, Arlie, 263n4
Holbrook, Colin, 230
Hughes, Everett, 31, 61
Hurricane Maria, 236–37
hypermasculinity, 110, 126, 128, 202; Black Americans, 125. *See also* Black masculinity; masculinity

identity, 7, 80; face-to-face challenges to, 70–71; non-recognition of, 57, 223–24; presentation of self, 59–60; and Race, 59; and stereotypes, 78
indentured servants, 26–27
India, 5–6
Indian Territory, 234. *See also* Oklahoma; Texas
individualism: American dream, 130; submissive civility, as counterbalance, 133;

INDEX

White Americans, priority of, 10–13, 21, 31–32, 116, 126, 129, 133
industrial revolution, 25
inequality, 11, 16, 18, 23, 55–56, 132, 199, 245–46; common good, undermining of, 247; as institutionalized, 59; tacit racism, 19–21
institutional racism, 1, 5, 8, 10–11, 30–31, 55–59, 65, 105, 110, 227. *See also* Asian and Asian American racism; Latinx/Hispanic racism; racism; retail racism; tacit racism; unconscious racism
interactional expectations, 23; broken interactional process, 67; clashing of, 53; as constitutive, 34, 37–38, 52; interactional obligations, trust conditions, 12; interactional preference orders, 36, 38; interactional reciprocity, conception of self, 76; interactionism, 60; miscommunication, and stereotypes, 53–54; narratives, miscommunication of, 53–54; of other Race, 47; as preferred, 34, 52
interactional repair, 32, 58, 67, 76
interaction order, 9, 30–31, 205, 225, 227, 242, 247–48; discretion, requiring of, 84; inequality, tolerance of, 56; self and sense-making, 59; tacit racism, 49, 57
Interaction Orders of Race, 1
International Criminal Court (ICC), 266n2
invention of Whiteness, 2, 17, 27–28, 255–56n3; American colonies, 24–25
Invisible Man, The (Ellison), non-recognition in, 75
Ireland, 231
Irish, 2, 24–28, 231–32, 238–39, 257–58n8
Ishiguro, Kazuo, 263n4
Israel, 266n2

Jamaica, 182
Jamestown, VA, 1–2, 25, 260n18; first slaves in, as White, 26; origin myth, 238–39; slavery, based on, 237–39
Japan, 5
Jefferson, Gail, 261n3
Jehovah's Witnesses, 262n1
Jews: as non-White, 25
Jim Crow, new, 223
Johnson, Kevin, 135
Johnson, Lyndon B., 1
John Wayne cowboy: myth of, 234

Kaepernick, Colin: "Take a Knee" protest, 257n7
Kansas, 19
Kant, Immanuel: constitutive criteria, 259n14
Katz, William Loren, 235
Kelling, George L., 244
King, Alex, 109
Kochman, Thomas, 33, 44, 86
Korea, 5
Kremer, Michael, 19
Krugman, Paul, 20
Ku Klux Klan (KKK), 256–57n5

labor movements, 28–29; labor unions, 23
La Negra, Amara, 258n10
La Salle, René-Robert Cavelier de, 266n1
Latin America, 238
Latinx/Hispanic community, 2, 5–7, 16–17, 25, 29, 150, 162–63, 167, 183, 187, 198–99, 237, 255–56n3, 258n10
Latinx/Hispanic racism, 2, 5–6, 17, 25, 29, 162–63, 167, 187, 198, 255–56n3. *See also* Asian and Asian American racism; institutional racism; racism; retail racism; tacit racism; unconscious racism
Lincoln, Abraham, 21, 239
local order, 209, 243–44; local interaction order, 9, 37, 201, 203–4, 206, 211–13, 225
local trust, 207
looking glass self, 78. *See also* categorial self; egalitarian self; presentation of self; self
Louisiana, 266n1
Love, Nat, 235–36

Males, Michael, 3, 19
March for Our Lives, 109
Marx, Karl, 257–58n8
Maryland, 26–27
masculinity: American society, as outgrowth of, 126–27; and health, 105; hegemonic masculinity, 107–9, 116, 127. *See also* Black masculinity; hegemonic masculinity; hypermasculinity
mass incarceration, 30, 106, 120, 127, 233, 265n10
Mayan refugees, 236, 260n18
Maynard, Douglas, 41–42, 45
McDade, D'Angelo, 109–10
Mead, George Herbert, 60, 158
Merritt, Kerri, 4, 29

Metzl, Jonathan, 2, 19, 29
Mexico, 180–81, 236–38
Middle East, 5
Miller, Reuben, 223
misunderstanding, 9, 48, 55, 104, 147, 201; of Black masculinity, 224; consequences of, 53–54 ; in workplaces, 84, 88
Montreal, 266n1
Mueller, Robert, 255n1
mutual intelligibility, 20, 34, 37, 53, 56, 75, 80, 247
mutuality, 159, 247
mutual responsibility, 82, 94, 129, 133
myth of model minority, 173

Native Americans, 6, 260n19; as strangers, treated as, 258n11
neighborhood interaction order, 201, 223
Nelson, Rashon, 131, 135–37
Netherlands, 256n4
Nevada, 238
New Mexico, 238, 258n11
non-recognition, 58, 61, 63, 66–69, 75, 79, 261n1; as fracturing, 78; of identity, 57, 223–24
Norman, Peter, 257n7
North America, 5, 266n1
null-response, 57, 71–72, 81, 86, 107, 147, 160, 223, 262n6; Black interaction order, development of, 59; defensive strategies of, 59; as protection, from fractured reflections, 63, 79; racial fatigue, 79

Obama, Barack, 15; backlash against, 8; post-racial society, 8, 229
Obamacare, 230, 233
Oklahoma, 174–75, 234–35, 258n11
opioid epidemic, 19, 200
Oregon, 238
Others, 3, 58–60, 75–78, 162–63, 227, 243, 248; and Otherness, 174, 236; as racialized, 2, 23, 226; and White, 18, 35, 79

Parsons, Talcott, 265n6
Philadelphia, 130, 134–37
Picca, Leslie Houts, 169
Pickett, Bill, 235–36
Piketty, Thomas, 20
Pilgrims, 236, 238
Pitts, Leonard, 4

Plymouth Colony, 236; myth of, 238–39
Plymouth Plantation, 237
poetic mirroring, 196
Poland, 25
policing: body cameras, 265n8; broken windows form of, 224, 244; citizen racism, abetting of, 161; tacit racism, 265n11; White interaction order practices, enforcing of, 161
political correctness, 8, 30, 186, 196–97
Pomerantz, Anita, 142
Ponce de León, Juan, 238
Populist Party, 256–57n5
poverty, 19, 203, 225
presentation of self, 8, 55, 58–60, 75, 77–78, 100, 102, 106, 261–62n2. *See also* categorial self; egalitarian self; looking glass self; self
Princeton University, 170
prison, 18, 20, 47, 125, 127, 216, 220, 223, 230, 260n18, 265n10, 265–66n3; population of, in US, 233
public spaces, 12, 27, 58, 77; civility of, 133–34; tacit racism, 133–34; White resentment, toward Black Americans, 131
Puerto Rico, 17, 236, 238; as first American colony, 237

Race, 5, 7–8, 12, 14, 21, 30, 32, 49, 55, 78–79, 130, 162, 165, 168, 183, 190, 225, 227, 236, 240, 247–48, 255n1; Black/White binary, structured by, 6; conservative policies, 230–31; and crime, 203; Dark Money, 228; divisions, as danger to democracy, 1; double standard, 73–75; and identity, 59; implicit bias, 1–2; as institutionalized, 58–59; interaction orders, 15–18, 27; invention of, 24; Latinx/Hispanic community, 258n10; liberal policies, 229–30; mutual intelligibility, 80; raced speech, 10; racial fatigue, 65; racial injustice, 137; racial Other, 23, 226; racial profiling, 138, 159; racial profiling, of Black drivers, 219–22; racialized stigma, 107–8; self-identification, 16; self-presentation, 58–59; situated identities, 131; as social convention, 2; social interaction, 36; in social research, 41; tacit interaction orders, 54; vagueness, problem of, 263n3

INDEX

Race pollution, 9, 164–65, 167, 242
racism, 2, 4, 12, 20–21, 25, 28, 55, 109, 162, 203, 225, 233, 242–43, 248; in American colonies, 26; Black masculinity, as reasonable response to, 128; Black/White binary, structured by, 6; circular racist thinking, 164–65, 170, 172; in college classrooms, 187–93; color-blind, 30, 38, 229, 261–62n2; color-blind, dangers of, 7–8, 32; confronting strategies of, 227–28; as constant, 1, 163–64; and democracy, 4; detachment from, 227; as divisive, 1; empathy and reciprocity, failure of, 226; as everyday, 199; as everywhere, 198; the exception, 165; and exclusion, 5–7, 27; explicit, 166–67; hiding in plain sight, 14; implicit bias, 10, 31; as institutionalized, 56, 105; joking about, 194–95; liberal policies, effect on, 229–30; as national problem, 14; as national security threat, 228; N-word, 197; N-word, use of, by Whites, 166, 198; as overt, 15, 166, 193–98, 226, 229; police, authority of, 131; post-racial, 229; as present danger, 15; race pollution, 9, 164–65, 167; racial boomerang, 164, 180, 186, 194; racial rudeness, 179–84; racist assumptions, 188–89; as self-destructive, 19; shopping while Black, 135; in social research, 41; and stereotyping, 212–13; and stigma, 105–6; as structural, 15; submissive, Black American response to, 130; as unconscious, 10, 31, 166–67; understanding of, and interactional details, 35; underestimating of, 163. *See also* Asian and Asian American racism; institutional racism; Latinx/Hispanic racism; retail racism; tacit racism; unconscious racism
Rawls, Anne, 11, 261n1
Reagan, Ronald, 8
reciprocity, 4, 22, 42, 75, 79, 99–100, 134, 145, 211, 245; as constitutive, 59; and empathy, 226–27; and equality, 18, 246–47; failures of, 137–38, 157–59; as interactional, 59, 63, 71, 76; as mutual, 58, 80, 143, 203
Reconstruction, 235, 256–57n5, 257–58n8
Reeves, Bass, 236
repair sequence, 58, 67

Republican Party, 19, 256–57n5; appeal of, 4
retail racism, 135
Rios, Victor, 223, 262n6
risky behavior, 107, 110–12, 124–25
Robinson, Donte, 135–37
rodeo, bulldogging, 236
Rogers, Will, 235
Royal Oak, MI, 264n4
Russell-Brown, Katheryn, 60
Russia, 1, 5

Sacks, Harvey, 83, 246
Saint Augustine, FL, 237
Sanders, Bernie, 173
Santa Fe (colony of New Mexico), 37
Saraland, AL, 130
school-to-prison pipeline, 18, 127, 230; collective punishment, 216
Schwartz, Tony, 264n2
Scots, 1–2, 28, 231, 239
self, 10, 31, 75, 158, 261–62n2; affirmation of, 244, 257n6; Black self, 34–35, 57, 61, 78, 104, 127, 129, 242; as categorial, 55–56, 83, 92, 100, 102–3; and community, 81; damage to, 63, 76; as egalitarian, 55–56, 85, 92; and face, 102–3; and identity, 58–60, 205; meaning, as fragile, 79, 227; presentation of, 59–60, 90, 106; as presented, 60; racist assessment of, 59; recognition of, 75; self-awareness, 30, 32, 108, 132, 166, 228, 243; self-condemnation, 108; self-hatred, 21, 28, 187, 240; self-hood, 107; self-identification, 11–12, 16, 28, 109, 162, 173, 199, 203, 260n21; self-interest, 4, 13, 105, 114, 116, 126, 129–30, 133, 241; self-presentation, 77; self-preservation, 203, 223; self-worth, 205, 223–25, 242; and sense-making, 59, 246–48; as social accomplishment, 60; as stigmatized, 106; White self, 11, 103–4, 129. *See also* categorial self; egalitarian self; looking glass self; presentation of self
self-esteem, 3, 21, 67, 75, 79, 203–4, 211, 240
self-reliance, 105, 114, 133, 232
sequences, 137–38, 145; Black greeting, 50; greeting, 98, interactional, 134; introductory, 34–36, 38, 49, 52, 98; White greeting, 41, 50
sequential order, 36

shared knowledge, 11, 16–17, 20, 37, 41–42, 54, 56, 58, 61, 64, 77–79, 245, 247
signifying, 44–45, 261n5
situated identities, 131
situated practices, 246
1619 Project, 237, 260n17
slavery, 5, 22–26, 231, 237–39, 256–57n5, 257–58n8, 260n20; legacy of, 229, 240; tacit racism, 11
Smith, Tommie, 257n7
smuggling, 245
Snyder Act, 258n11
social contract, 247
social facts, 24, 31, 36, 58, 61, 246
social safety net, 8; dismantling of, 29
South America, 5, 237
Spain, 2, 237, 256n4, 266n1
Spanish Armada, 256n4
Spanish colony, 238, 266n1
Starbucks incident, 130–31, 136–38; enhancement of complaint, 135; as retail racism, 135; "shopping while Black," 135; submissive civility, adoption of, 132, 134–35; tacit racism, 160; unconscious racial bias training, 135; White American vs. Black American response, 264n5
Steele, Claude, 10
Stiglitz, Joseph, 20
Strong Man, 9, 13, 18, 84, 116, 126, 128–30, 161, 232, 236, 246, 264n1, 264n2; contradictions of, 132–33; democracy, undermining of, 132; reinforcement of, 234
submissive civility, 9, 84, 116, 128–29, 134–35, 160–61, 221–22; Black/White citizen/police encounters, 130; conversation analysis (CA), 159; and democracy, 132; as misunderstood, 133
Submissive Man, 9, 13

tacit racism, 1, 4, 7, 15, 23, 30, 32, 55, 84, 89, 104, 131, 138, 160–60, 162, 165, 167, 191, 198, 230, 245, 248; on academic life, 9; commonplace expressions of, 168–73; confronting of, 228; constancy of, 76; conversation analysis (CA), 157–59; democracy, undermining of, 133; inequality, sustaining of, 19–21; as institutionalized, 5, 8, 11–12, 227; interaction order expectations, differences in, 33, 49; interaction orders, 49; learning the ropes, 93–94; police interaction, 157–58; in public spaces, 133–34; and slavery, 11; tacit expectations, institutionalization of, 57–58; White interaction order expectations, enforcement of, 134, 265n11; in workplace, 8–9. *See also* Asian and Asian American racism; institutional racism; Latinx/Hispanic racism; racism; retail racism; unconscious racism
talk: friend, 33, 47–48, 51–53, 92, 98, 164–65, 169, 172–73, 177–78, 187, 194–95, 197–98; health, 110–11, 113, 125, 127
Taos, NM, 237
Tea Party, 8
Texas, 234–35, 238
Texas Rangers, 235
Thanksgiving: institutionalization of, 239; myth of, 237–39
Thomas, W. I., 259n12
Thoreau, Henry David, 116
Threepersons, Tom, 236
Trump, Donald, 13, 15, 17, 19, 28, 101, 130, 172, 237, 257n7, 258n9; as Strong Man, 264n2
trust, 68, 76, 79, 81, 98, 186–87, 205; drug dealers, 208; failure of, 125, 218–19, 262n5; local, 207; mutual, 20; not trusting, importance of, 65–67, 72–73, 82; and police, 158, 206–7, 211, 218; trust conditions, 12, 59–60, 63, 77–78, 143, 145, 246–48, 259n14
trust, and reciprocity, 80, 118, 211
Tulsa, OK: as Black Wall Street, 235; race riots, 235
Tuskegee experiment, 125

unconscious racism, 1, 6, 10–11, 14–16, 31, 34, 36, 55, 135, 166–67, 226–28. *See also* Asian and Asian American racism; institutional racism; Latinx/Hispanic racism; racism; retail racism
United States, 22, 125, 133, 173–74, 226, 228–29, 238, 243, 246, 266n1; Black/White binary in, 2, 5–7, 16–17, 23–25, 27, 31, 236–37, 240, 255–56n3, 260n22; as class-based, 231; labor movements, little traction in, 28–29; occupational advancement, and Race, 57–58; prison population of, 233, 265n1, 265–66n3; and racism, 1